# OF DISCOURSE

ALSO BY GILES GOODLAND

Littoral (Oversteps, 1997)

Overlay (Odyssey, 1998)

A Spy in the House of Years (Leviathan, 2001)

Capital (Salt, 2006)

What the Things Sang (Shearsman, 2009)

The Dumb Messengers (Salt, 2012)

Gloss (KFS, 2012)

The Masses (Shearsman, 2018)

Civil Twilight (Parlor Press, 2022)

# OF DISCOURSE

GILES GOODLAND

grand
IOTA

Published by
grandIOTA

2 Shoreline, St Margaret's Rd, St Leonards TN37 6FB
&
37 Downsway, North Woodingdean, Brighton BN2 6BD

www.grandiota.co.uk

First edition 2023

Typesetting & book design by Reality Street

A catalogue record for this book is available from the British Library

ISBN: 978-1-874400-87-5

ACKNOWLEDGEMENTS

I would like to thank all of the magazine, anthology and website editors who have published sections of this book, often in different forms, over the last few years.

I would also like to thank my many colleagues and associates in the fields of lexicography and linguistics, who have enlarged my sense of language: *what it has done, can and will do*. Errors: *any are all mine.*

# Contents

## One. Of That Which Exists

**Of discourse.** Of arms and the manifold, armaments and monuments, of the undefined rhythm of odd lines, of the arranged and of the spirit of the arranged, of the suave bush of remarkable properties, of embodiments of prayers, of saw of self, of lifting of the top of the head from anaemia of the brain, of the mouths of babes, of small hands, of light fingers, of the formation of foam on pilot-digesters, of the falling off of the hair of the head, of susceptibility of the head to take cold, of a group of large rocks that causes fear of wild beasts, of a Vandyck dress of rich chocolate crimson with slashed sleeves, of the wall of Babylon and the joyful forest of nowhere, the "of" of signal of simile in contemporary poetry, as the egg of a skull, the loss of the capacity to pronounce alphabets, of the smooth surface of lateral moraines, of the tenth moon of the year keng-shench of Hung Wucc, of the complexity in management of increase of materials-flow, of drowners of hope, of the turning house of tidings, of the magnetic induction of crystals, of fluctuations of accent and turning of syntax, entrancing strains of lyre and notes of song and cross-products of return innovations, of the swarm-intelligence of trading decisions, of congestion of blood to the head; of difficulty of swallowing food, of the lustre of atomic clouds, the long experienced finger of the Gulf Stream, of the crowds we are, of flow of the ocean, of the trampling of hoofs of a hundred centuries, the path of a foraging animal, the meditations of the Shangqing scriptures, the notion of a community of spirits, the bones of the ghosts of the victims, of an input parameter of child data-type or of parent data-type, of the acoustic translation of solid particles of waterlike density, of the surface of her crocus-yellow silken lap, of bodies of elephants and cavalry, of the enhancement of erosion-resistance of the seabed sediment alternating thin beds of sand and mud, of the cocking of the snapper claw, of lateral jerks of the pelvis of considerable violence, of the correction of the first of the three errors of experience, the colours of a remote prospect of trees, meadows and streams: of reflections of clouds as the angles of the shadows, of the modification of a route-request's sequence number, of the scribing of a heavy dot or unattached line on the sheet of assertion, of the existence of a single object in the universe of discourse, of the absence of a rear bulkhead, and most of the time, of a roof, of the fall of the house of us/her, of the rise of the hoax of Sokal, of the endless nest of the sentence, of successive sets of future N-time slot segments, of channel-hopping patterns, the scar faces of the preform of the coast, of an anthill, of the roots of the *Tulasi* plant, of shoot of tamarisk, seed of tamarisk, of the twin evils of self and body, of the great graves of the undead, of terror of large rocks, of vomiting of bilious masses, of the expulsion of our adversary with a bow made of the wood of the tree of Grandfather Fire, the disquieting uproar of the obvious, of the players of the *Iklik* and *Barbud*; the players of the Tanbur of an unpleasant nature, of the formation of associative connections, of thousands of blazing arrows, razor-edged discs, the eventual regeneration and restoration of the creature world, of the magical qualities of rowan, of the Horizontal White Crane system, of lack of sorrow over the desolation of Nara, the City-Royal, of other organisms far past the knowledge of external senses, knees and ribs of vessels, of the Lords of the Three Extremities, the Emperors of the Five Directions, the suit of Four Breaths of the Four Seasons, of flushes of heat in the face, a sheet, a cloud, a robe of billowy mist, the tools (paper, pen, cards) of defunct social arts, of a family of bounded repulsive interaction potentials, of plethora of the head, of required elements in the netlist, of visitations of pestilence upon the Director of Human Resources, of Human Destiny, of a line of cranes seen through the interstices of the bracket-arms of a Missouri Rogers single toggle jaw-crusher, of a complete line of fully immersible electric cooking appliances, of cementing of the eyelids of *Honan*, who rose to the highest of offices, of a person chanting a number of meaningless sounds to a sort of tune of friend, or foe, or neutral; of withstanding the fierce pressure of the swelling ice and road material, of people that are called Olaf, of private feeling, of retribution for misdeeds, of a bodice ornamented by a mass of gold, of the small pipe, of the tanbur, of the town pipe, of the two ducks who serve as observers, of the two armoured cruisers Terrible and Power/id, of bitter-sweet, or wild ivy; of pants and socks of destruction, of lotuses with three alternating central petals, of the ability of the Water Witch to avenge the outrage, of the chief the boy dreamed of, of the doom of the *Children of Albion*, of the supreme chief of the Gods of the lower waters, of the normal Miss Beauchamp, when it came to telling her dreams, of the chimney sweepers, day-labourers, and nightmen of Calcutta, of the Regent who presides over the spheres of the heavens, of the servant girl who repeats stanzas of Hebrew, of the southern agricultural confederacy, particles of the rare and of the dense, or of the light and the heavy, of the inner existence of characters, the drag of material, of the named immensity of place inside the seed of contradiction of blood in a dream where world-clogged water of the eye flows, of future loss of soul in the immanent horizon of profane history, of speech of the water in chambers of hearing, saw of look advancing, the ministry of the stars, the broken gear of a bird, the petals of sleep, the sayings of saints, black leather bustiers composed of twinned obi belts, the sadness of the gardening races, the substrate surface of the receding waterline, of the time of exposure of the warp to the action of the discharging-agent of the upper waters, the god of the middle waters, and the god of the upward movement of the exit door, of the year measured by the path of the sun, of the lives of those in whom involuntary functions breathe, of toughness at the lowest level of nitrogen, of various colours and shapes attached to the arrows, of which 12 are megaloblasts, 12 microblasts, and 12 normoblasts, of criminally classified albums of photographs, of marks of the effects of residual pipe magnetism, of the son of the author of the romantic poem *Yusuf*, of soreness and inflammation of the internal surface of the nose, the authenticity of electronic voices, of deities of the Eight Directions, of the method of enlargement of obstacles of Sznitman, of the Lord of the Great Exorcism, the Lord of the Small Exorcism, of the itching of the nipples of the Supreme Emperor, of the baying of the deep-mouthed hound Cavall, of the *Castle of Indolence*, of the ticking of the clock-beetle, of a long, lofty, and handsome bridge of eight gothic arches, of the unmarked construction of the arms of the mountain, of the tree-weapon of the northern god, of the strengthening of hardware products in the eighth month of the Year of the White Dragon, of the disavowers of the non-existence of the penis in females, of the tenacious nature of concentrate-froth, of the fishes of the river that eat of the white fat of Lycaon, of the world's mother-mountain, of the soft, spongy parts of loose texture (spleen, lung, breasts), of the five logical divisions of the cantos, of the masters of the seas, of maintaining a history of hello packets to determine the network (forthcoming in *Journal of the History of Philosophy*) of the congestion-level of seals attached to several contracts, skewing of sample results due to laminar flow influences, of the tribes of mites and ticks, of everlasting transmigration, the veneration of fire, of branching and slowdowns of random walks, of overlapping of erotic complexes, of incessant agitation of the determinatives of divinity, of the loss of verbal function in some active sentences, of the fiery heat of the penance of the King, of the sensual satisfaction of place, of person, the spectral width of the laser radiation on the gently inclined coastal flank of Mount Etna, the development of minor grabens and horst blocks consisting of sequences of event models, of frequent dropping of clear water from the nose, of the structure of the standing sound-wave pattern in the cavities of compression of the records of millions of years, the straight, the accurate flex of distinction, of economy of gift, of the feather-hen of the Egyptian bird-headed moon-god, made of the grass of the uncut hair of graves, and the teller, Tremulous, lord of a strange echo, of future loss of soul, of the anger of the original inhabitants of the castle, of cocks of weather vanes and of the seldom-used fire routes of tall office blocks, of the sum of the squares of the numbers of oscillations, of the trope of the insect in the surrealist poem, of the difficult traverses of the mountain forests, flights of capital, of the use of chisels of diminishing size, the shadow of a doubt of a valley of a road of a death of a hand of Ethelberta of Trelawney of the wells of loneliness of the long-distance star of the silver screen, of sacerdotal garments, of imposing processions of priests, the prostrate crowds of spirit-stricken worshippers, of depth of pocket, the rushing fieriness of lightning, because, by way of, ahead of, regardless, of you, reader.

**This is what**, what seems an age in the corridorlike departure lounge what transpires at the reception of the embassy from the Kingdom of Sin what Freud says about the inversion of a detail in a dream what is the appearance in the snow what regarding the autumn woods what becomes of the slender arms of the nerve cell what is the white thread that we call a nerve what is downside of a gateway of spirits what is a burn in the end of the finger what is the horizontal aspect of the blossoming what is this that runs through the wood what charges through the night to destroy what we see and call language what is what metaphysicians call a substance what is a green bird with no feathers or legs if "the car took a sinister turn" what would you think what is an indefinite pronoun what is an idea what is poetry's interest in time what is the work of nerve fibres what is loosely called existence what puts us in relation with being what is going on in your head it should be obvious what, what is discernible, what is lost, what is this what that language uses.

**It is not by means of doors** that one enters the thing-world. One possibility does not cancel another, which is anchored in one and nothingness; a girl's face in a crowd, one second, is centripetal.

One wakes up before midnight, on account of a dry cough, detecting in the sky the blue of *Beaujolais Supérieur*. In one of the gutters is a blue salvia. It nods and says a poem to Adad, mighty one.

Innumerable angels of events share one feature. One will Insert Word Field, and the other Insert Merge Field. The probability of surviving is one minus the probability of the ruin event.

Kill one of the fiends and run out through the small gap this makes in the recognition that the living and the dead are one. One of those in the crowd is no one's friend. When aroused by the target, one acts.

Tao is one game away from the semifinals. The winner is the first one to complete the circuit. His is one of the more terrifyingly fast decks. He sits like one dead, quivering one eyelid.

A worm one sees out of the corner of the eye disappears the moment one turns one's head in a rotating vehicle. One is really one arm with two ends, one brain with many roots.

One of the most interesting phases is One Yellow, when good things ripen and bad things rot, and dragons create two pools, one with carcass-water forced into the solution and one with it forced out.

Toymakers of Eyyub are one hundred and five men, with one hundred shops. Night covers one half of the years allotted and is spent in sleep. One coal in the stove. One thought fills.

One of Bungo's downfalls is when one morning he indulges

in a sexual act with a violinist in the trough between stage and platform. One is struck by phonemic derivations, and tortured syntax.

Sing of the changes, old one! The firewall holds back death as one long expected. One reaches over and severs the cord, letting one body fall.

One of my students strongly opposes Muldoon's elegy for Heaney. One argues for it. But when an expression evaluates as true and as false, one can use an if-else statement.

Badger wears a scarf and seems to be the leader. This one he tells to go westward: You will be called *Bear*. Bear is angered by this and tosses Badger to one side.

He turns to the one TV camera still operating, and tells us: in the oral round, one speller at a time stands onstage and is given a unique word, receiving one point for each correct spelling.

Two insurgents in the house are buried but so is one woman with a rolled-up scroll in one hand. She processes multiple files from different folders with one command.

One voice notes the experimenter's absence and regrets this fact: The ones in the air, they are human beings.

One Wednesday in November you click and drag one of the corners of the text box to make it larger. Homeland changes from one poem to the next.

One astronaut is chosen to pass through the black hole and emerge in the next universe as God, his body the firmament. I am *Kurigalzu*, the one who made myself appear.

All the buses head in one direction, in a linking of concepts whereby one stands for another.

In a large country house like in one of those films with butlers we do more than transcribe discourse from one medium to another.

This is the real world. The one a surgeon sees pumping in a chest. The person named by the voice as that one is Jones.

One gets the impression the voice-entities are jostling one other to speak to us: The inflection is rhythmical. One speaks poetry. One plays around with devices which get the waves out of phase.

One day the past will come like one, on whom the fear of blindness comes. The one who owns a magic pen is sure to own the ability to write well.

The laser mind focuses on one or two forms of information, the searchlight mind is characterized by a capacity for regularly sampling diverse ones.

THE WAY CONCEALS ITSELF by being nameless
in a sentence so long it contradicts itself
if a spider lowers itself on you at night it is lucky
the symbol you want enters the symbol itself
that organ is irritable which can move itself
remember the line of association controls itself
the beltline hitches itself up over the rear wheel arches
a tornado screws itself on-screen, helix, vortex
the intellectual circle retracts itself day by day
divinity shows itself the more a violent fever burns
so as to deposit itself as a thick dew attended by
the crystal spray-drop leaps of itself
perception cannot express itself eroding
space itself is therefore sphere a mink which
changed itself into a woman brings him food
the right hand shows itself empty the field-
name may be a different length from the field itself

the elementary *rapport* of the brain with itself and
with fire is opposite to darkness as itself
the inner of us is the insect head itself a mask
the phenomenon shows itself as self-reference
the river carves a future for itself
if truth could say itself it would be but truth has no
mouth the lamp's light wrecks itself against the inch
the wind bundles itself into a bluish cloud
and draws itself toward the leaf
the sentence reads itself as we listen the saying says
itself as one draws the body up before making a dive
a knot straightens itself when a single tangle is undone
the moon gathers itself on its hind legs where the dream
seals itself into backflesh slash dinosaur see
the film months after the nascent city established itself
their enemies arrive in force. The city itself seems
in such a fashion that it does not itself give an after-image
there is no sense to be made of the idea that time itself
moves it is not sufficient in itself to interpret the meaning
of a "vision": the explanation is longer than the poem itself
but once the ear has accustomed itself to the noise
the rope itself does not seem to be an aspect
it's an entity that insinuates itself through old wooden slats
and death itself becomes a thing of the past
the empty list ( ) is identical to itself.

**First blackbird of March,** tune slightly different from the year before. The first-person pronoun is drunk with morning's first mouthful.

Pain first on right, then on left side of back of neck on moving head. The first view one gets of Darwin is a dog playing with a ball.

Curl the hair first, then sweep it up in fill patterns. Sever the first joint of each leg: heat the face-end first to a low red heat, draw the skin off to the shoulders.

Put your fists at your knees first, understand them slowly and actuate the cocking member from first position part-way towards second.

Pass silently over motion pictures, the workers leaving the factory, flicker of a first captured world.

Racing to his first day of school, he watches eagles circling a cliffside, the first to speak being the grey-eyed Athēnē. The first passage quoted as poetry is prose.

Contemplate the first card of the suit of Fire, direct a stream of fluid at a first, and a stream at a second angle to induce a rotational sludge flow.

Winner of Best First Novel, with a 200,000-copy printing and a seven-city tour, it describes a Mosso ergograph of the first cantos.

It seems on first reading a diary, or is it actually a collection of obituaries from a first-person perspective.

The First Page refers to the first page of the document or the first page of a section.

First, the abdominal breath, and then the chest breath. Say the first letter is a G. The somnambulist after some effort mentions the three first words.

D has the deal, A is the first player on his left, and then G strikes E. The seal face causes the seal liquid to be released first, indicating a seal failure.

First the quotation marks disappear, then the first words spring like flint shards from the axe.

The dumptrucking moon troubles the streets in first gear.

An experienced, gentle stud-cat for the first service of a maiden queen.

I modified the eyes on my first body segment to low magnification, started my first business creating and selling authentic native sentences.

It was a truth universally iterated that it was the best/worst of times. It moved as if an effort were made to raise it. It was the opening of another war. As a result, the bank, its ceiling accentuated in white gold leaf, doubled its presence. The cloud's mobility undid the state and its airspace management. It breathed high-tension screws, wooden trees, a wet brook, considerable wasps. It was a feeling inherent in the breasts of many, fed freely, and deposited three larvae. It remained in this position for one or two minutes. It understood the schematic diagram of the literature. It contained door keys, from golden Chubbs to too-often duplicated Yales; it resembled powder and was cut into lines. It used stop-motion mannequin-torsos. In its course it received several tributaries. It was dark and not a blackbird, it lacked the nib or the alarm call and had an impatient quality to it; its call was uttered at intervals of one second. It suggested the fur of a rabbit. It held in its claw a helical, unbalanced scroll-formation. It struck the iron bed, so that it shivered into thirteen counts. It was a military instrument of five cords, and its call was *chock*. It was invented and played in the Arabian coffee houses. It had silver pipes, and sounded like an ass's bray. it was a cord-instrument with a crooked handle. It contained paper pulp, resin, sugar of lead, and acoustically excited forces. It had a solid green trim, two front pockets and belt. It was commonly played by shoemakers. It was armed with infrared sensors, pattern-recognition cameras, and the art which explains stars. It entered into the light of the spirit and turned it dark purple. It moved and breathed, devouring the furniture and digesting it into the past. They found it in the ear and prodded it gently. I told them to return it, to impart a walking motion to the foot, raising it, cocking it forward. It was later than normal when I got to the cycle path and the dew had soaked my gauze stockings. The years of seeming it took involved versatile camera movement and military investment. It was a good idea to autocrop prior to running Guillotine. Whenever it perished by the wind, it was destroyed by the wind. In place of locating contradiction in spirit and leaving the world free of it, Hegel declared: a new baby day, it shines and our eyes hurt with it. It was the dawn of Alpinism, it was the tangible environment that gave a sense of certainty to position it. Suddenly, it seems, the girl alien began to weep. A hunter smelt it and pursued it. Its hair resembled the hair of the dragon and its eyes gave onto brick conduits. Its bearded possessors combined the character of the earth, the stained carpet, and deceitful dullness. Its paradigmatic formula was ginseng, aconite, dragon bone, attrition. Its fluid essence located between fragility and violence until its waves dissipated. The swift dog its brother loped in moonlight, its body caught in its clothes, singing *its woof was gold.* The current flowing through it raised its internal temperature with its gear and flaps extended and its wings swung outward. It was deposited on a traveling felt and taken to a wooden roll. It stuck on the upgrading stage and said *please do not turn off.* I dragged it to the opacity property name in the Background Lit layer and connected it to a rear wheel bleeder valve using its snap-clip attachment, securing it to a 360° swivel and tilting it. I clicked it to view its syntax. The store design captured it uniquely. Call it viridian, oxide of chromium, oyster shell decoction. The snake protected its head with the rest of its body, making it ideal for home, personal defence and target shooting. It pumped language through nights. It was tall and narrow, an odd combination of tan shingles and bright red trim. It instantly expanded the room. Fire burnt it. We watched the news and weather, it told me what I saw now: it was stormy outside, thunder lost its way. It produced a hollow obscure sound. It was calling for help and flashing its faulty torch, its light outshining the Foamy Wake. The car stood in the driveway, its engine guttering. Slowly, the arrow reached its ceiling and seemed to pause. I shaved my beard. It fell to the floor, and I picked it up and stuck it on my face upside down, and it grew. It contained the shadow of the person it resembled. The wasp captured the spider by stinging it as it dangled in leaf litter from a silken thread emitted from its spinnerets. It then dragged it through open woodland, over twigs and leaves, grasping it by a pedipalp with its mandible. It took it to the wasp pit and sucked it. It felt oppressed, ate the head of its male and gave birth. Information played over it its unkind light. With its vast pink parachutes full of tableaux of the archbishops dressed in their underwear, it rendered it a difficult task correctly to define its characters. Its contents held the 740 pages of engineering solutions to the Heisen requests and its soft, curved edges gave it a sculpted, sophisticated look. It pierced my effective armour straightaway and it happened because its flowers were that particular blue.

In his belly a whole deer, stuffed full of birds. I wondered who they were: it was told me, they were those who had relation to involuntary sense, and it was further told me, the whole thing seemed part of a different life in which I was successful compared to the people who occupied the whole face. The whole name means "mother eagle young girl" as if the whole half of the body draws together: this takes a whole two hours of my lunchbreak, and produces paralysis of the whole system. Wen, the pride of the whole nation, is off to the dog park for a whole new life. At first there is nothing but the land itself, whole and impenetrable along the line of the whole nine frontier prefectures. The whole side of my head is by then quite wooden: internal beams separated by vertical spacer blocks, the whole boxed in with plywood spyholes. One large area rug in durable *faux* sisal makes the room a cohesive whole. It is a whole section of closely fitted frocks with snug sleeves and off-the-shoulder necklines. It is the secret name that dreams the forest whole.

I BURP and the cat runs out of the room: is this power? In this paper we answer this question. This hiss is accompanied by tingling. This content is downloaded from thoughtworld. This is where light reflects off the tear. This spirit's name was *bearded seal with pups*. Many listen and observe this communication. I won't take this view seriously in this essay. This crawlspace is filled with super-cooled hydrogen, and into this is poured the eyes of a winged warrior. We feel slept dust in cracks or move this face. This whole operation is a disinfo gag: this is a fake drone. This is confidential. This increases the confidence of a young tribal leader. This water is no part wine. This leads to self-destruct of the spinal cord. To counteract this, put your hat on the child's head. This means: a strong one, a companion, one who will save the friend. (This means: the evil one.) This galaxy has one instrumental and one cognitive arm. This adverb of time is not written in waking life. Embroider this dragonfly with raffia and Swarovski. This fragment of the lightning-belt's tail is three-coupled. This was contributed by a woman of 85. This is not a word. This statement is an example of redundancy. The succeeding lay and this are attributed to the wife of the exile. This is what is intended when it is said. This is wrong. This leads to systolic wall thinning. Here comes this little cluster, and the conclusion of my preceding clusters. Repeat this slowly several times concludes this section. Note the nature of this error: it is an overly concrete interpretation, when more than one activity is boxed this box represents a sub-system. The job in this case is blanked down through the die. This directs my eyes. This new sight mounts directly to the optics-ready slide cut. Work did this to me, hard growth in this wrinkled skin. All loss is gone in this poem. Pull the world through this hole's self. This is similar to working on a multi-headed flat-bed. This man is Spider. Spider says: (he starts coughing at this point and is uncomfortable) to live so thinly to the opening pages of this. I find this in many poets. Birds drop on this cold sea within the seashell. This is the subconscious mistaking its mental images. This feedback stabilizes the diode frequency. This carries the gun vertically with no cant. Weapons are allowed in this dance. On this side of Monday we furnish tongues with salt. This remains as a coherent unit for 400m south of the vent. I pucker this frantic and possessive sense. This premium leather bag comes in more than 25 vibrant colours, this area is content syntax. In this hour, we depend on your code, suspended. In this middle distance of my mind's dark, I said, This is the long-awaited beginning of my love. This is the wheel we turn through the eye.

THAT NOISE THAT APPALS me: the unintelligible syllables that predict that that current that in me is frozen in others will flow, that indicate that that which is lost on that occasion is lost for ever. If found it is on that other world to which I am stranger.

We find that he was in that particular graveyard, attracted to the energies of challenge abutting that wall to the little chapel that Madame I uses; pressing that door, we find tools that turn the stage into air, and that that air is our sense-field.

The four paths that are unincluded songs are perceptually close to events that predict adversity, that on the burnt grass stretch to the four winds that cement the casual air in a closing scene that threatens the nuthatch nest.

Oyster beds that are suitable for bivalve recruitment

generate elastic waves that have event memories , and the thatched roofs of god-houses contain hydroponic systems that grow tears.

A Hollywood action movie that hinges on a successful facelift demonstrates that predicates are facets of *personae* in that egocentricity plays a large part. Time-lapse photography lends an ethereal effect that distances the sense that there was a sense to make that made us mean.

The lower the rank of the problem that obscures the control flow logic the closer the shark-god bites, that is, there is no shoal intelligence that manages heterogeneous servers.

Words began later than that inaction we call thought. That a stone falling from a fabled sky is also a sigh that hangs in the air, that the bird that records fire on the sea is that which the moon is eye of. Sigh and sign break that signifying mast of the terminal aitch.

A further chain-process assumes a forked shape that cascades the ash cloud and discharges lava-flows that postdate the paleolake. Then that spirit flows from fingers onto the page that takes control of the pencil that governs the strings that chirrup in theatrical dried seaweed.

That which the cats know and we do not, that thought is action, the circular motifs that recur in megalithic art are that deep eye in the out of the head. A piece of knotted wood that resembles a dog averts the snake that posits death as that that terminates.

Sand is young stones that will grow up to be rock, that orient perpendicular to bedding planes; that is to say, the fragments indicate the channel-fill that drains the stone country.

That does not make sense, says the narrator's younger sister. That dream. That government, so far from objecting to the Water Witch's claim that she moves things with her mind, concurs that this boy's brain is radioactive and emits a faint glow.

That he assists the course of the five thunders that kills 90 civilians in the village of Azizabad; that he in sleep forms one body. That phenomena are true. That you are.

The records show that a variety of launcher systems tremble as they pass before me, that compel the homage of the beholder whose attention is drawn to things that shouldn't matter or that are irrelevant: that the falcon holds in its claw an owl that holds in its claw a priest.

That you lose your walking stick means that the north wind blows strongly. Use design-thinking analysis to enter that state that precedes dreams. Motion numbers time in that it engenders its number.

To jump to a destination that is not adjacent to the current square move in a manner that minimizes real-world usage. The kit contains small wind dynamos with LED lamps that indicate that mechanical energy has transformed to electric.

See that the caps and pivots are in good order, that the chat bubbles traverse freely, and that the bowl swings on the gimbals, that the sun traverses the sky singing OM. The slight rake, lower ride and stable rear belt ensure a rapid draw that rivals the fastest synthetic holsters.

It appears that Self is a blossom that incessantly practises copulation that gives off that musty fragrance of universe, a searched peer is a peer that receives the abstract that lightning bolts, that thunder claps, that steel sleet strikes.

The voice engages in a sensitive work-function that carries a high risk. That's where spider-paths come in. It is essential that we observe that male and female flies have the same underlying circuitry.

The waving and stamping of dancers is a sign that the diagonally aligned space is planted with trees and shrubs that provide structure, that the market understands that the value with which the firm that owns the web page trades floods the network with high query traffic.

That Friday they meet at the Cavern Club and dance to

Lady Leachate. Snore: we make that noise that throat stored in us. His mother states I am the snore that speaks from the animal. I speak for the poet that previously traversed in long lines that many-acred field.

To work with a company that houses sensitive data against that sphere that is death, for that which the shadow searches is the venom that flows from the its mouth that stifles the victorious monarch, that moth-worn star.

**Select these objects** and lock them.

Free these stones by observing them.

Black tripod-beacons mark these.

Do not trouble the earth with these theories.

These block rational desires.

These stretch back to their original form.

These use a device called a river-tree-mother.

The sea breaks on these in heavy gales.

These show bare at low water.

These are called the One, the Beautiful, the other.

We found these in our eyes.

Phosphor illumination from these is distinct.

These give rise to an emotive point of view.

These have bad records, and are covered with scars.

These involve the light of celestial bodies.

These may be found in man without his being insane.

In these cases the buzzers are not sounded.

These question the correlation of identity and affect.

Thought-knots flow from the forms of these.

These amount to 400,000,000 facial images in state hands.

The application suitabilities of these was explored.

These make the logical structure of the diagram clear.
To answer these we require machine readability.
Attempts are made to investigate these fluids.
These are machined with a square wrench.
These represent the entire house of doors.
Achieve home-based business success with these:
insert these at various axial and radial locations.
These come in baby, toddler, kid, and adult.
Unscrew these screws and replace them.

IT IS ONE OF THOSE BALMY SPRING DAYS with clothing ceremonies.
The shouts for help of those whom god loves are distant.
Those who harmoniously follow his orders shall live.
Those who kept journals say his house was made of pearls.
He uses path parameters to ensure those he infects are loyal to him.
Those who find him have their desire for children gratified.
For those who prefer to be guided, the manuals give clear instructions.
Those stars correspond with the figure of a low cart, such as
stone is drawn upon.
Through those lost threads of moonlight, path-length extends.
Those events on the cone are said to lie on the future light.
Those qualities are called the colour and sound of the river.
Those leaves are transcripts of songs. The long legs and short
trunks belong to those in the thickening stage.
Those who are unable to procure eggs travel to *Hui-li-chou*

and return with panniers of opium: those plants weather the thunder state. The shotgun is for those to whose responsive shine it attributed bodies.

Those who climb up will become rain gods, and make third-parties flourish. There is control in the way those arms move.

Theosophy is not understood by those who say they understand.

Those artifacts represent deviations from the real-world setup.

Speech-contents divide into two categories: those that have meanings of a general nature and those that have a personal bearing.

There are those who promise to return from the place where those roses of the living wither.

To those who collect their own ashes, to all those, I say: the forest begins with a tree.

The head and body are human; the legs and claws those of a bird.

Go talk to those shadows boiling on the wall.

ANYTHING'S REMEMBERED localization is in the head.
Panic, because the moon is no longer this nor anything:
click on anything in the window. If you don't
want to delete anything, tap Buy More Storage.
Point to anything in results without clicking.
You don't know anything about Sleeping Margaret's
connection with her inability to do anything. The pain
comes on whenever she eats anything warm or cold.
Lack of anything better than animal qualities
idealises the spiritual newspapers, scraps of lists, anything

bearing words. The pilot isn't bothered about anything
and we tip downwards as he eats sandwiches, eats anything
stuffs himself as we watch. I feel I might do anything.
The commercials resemble more than anything a heavens
with a caption: anything is the explanation. Its
system runs anything from light field loads to full-power
buck and slug. She turns to me and asks if there is anything
like this where I live. I have no knowledge of anything.
She embodies anything but the observer's condition.
Almost anything you do to a fast rise-time pulse degrades it.
Anything that looks like a person you embrace like a wife
since I haven't anything else to do, resigned to
the inadequacy of truly describing anything. This aerial
is useless for picking up anything. I say categorically,
it's impossible to pick up anything with this aerial.
Don't say anything, he is a great tippler. Hej, hej!
Anything moving in the scene is removed, and no
guarantees are offered as to the quality of anything.

**Bright sparks** flashes of light before the eyes: everything
looks red. Clicking the blue-green tab selects everything inside:
everything from real estate to textiles.
Everything the beloved touches is sacred to the lover;
everything disattaches from its proper name.
Everything could be named with enough geometry,
contains everything a user needs to build a stripped
receiver sucking into its half-toothed mouth everything
it cannot name. Do not tell everything.

Accused of murder, she recalls everything about her
childhood. Her fitness tracker monitors everything from
sleep patterns to heart rate to thinking speed, everything
is a great present for the woman who has everything.
Everything you think is true, is in the sense that having thought
it you've made it so, I think. Tonight everything
is so plain: death is lake-space, crystal dusk. Everything
is a warning: to die in summer when everything is bright
& earth turns lightly, everything throws up on itself.
I'm lost in a green word and I know what everything is.
In the identical press of everything, I type up leaflets
for everything from high viz clothing museums to ghost walks.
Then I throw everything in the trash. The deaths
of everything are deaths that have lost their meaning.
I look forward to everything covered in moss.

**Something not seen** that produces existence;
something in her pocket shines
something in the upper chest makes it hard to swallow
something acrid rises in the oesophagus
as if something is lodged. Faces stay
longer and voices seem to mean something
but the pony says: Do not mind me; find something to eat.
A piece of wood suggests something.
That bicycle is something to hold on to, a departure
something to do with local history or identity
something plotted like in a film, all central and beautiful
but something blurs upon the ground a woman
scrapes her shoe on the kerb, sees something, bends

to examine a fallen nutlike something, puts
her two heavy bags down, picks up something, discards
something, picks up her bags, walks on.
Clearly something is moving beneath the surface.
Something set at night, a kind of long search
for something I had lost, a book or a twitch in
my stomach as if there is something thumping in it.
I cry because something inside me feels.
Walking to the study something white escapes my pocket
as I bring my hand out and floats away, something I
only know because it ends in me. I know something
will happen if I stop, a memory of a memory of something
that I've come to accept as something I really did.
A sky free of birds, something sterile here.
Give your eyes something to do, so the world within is heard
like something manufactured for us.
The distinction must be something more subtle than
metadata formats, something to do with work,
troubled nights, something a bit ajar in the family
something that exceeds the hero's self:
all stop in a moment as when something is dropped.
We sleep wrong, something jars us awake,
something larger changes gear: bus, planet, self.

**Whatever suggests a thing** is that thing. Whatever you spend on the treatment, you receive equal value in products. You are to go over whatever the gods give to mankind to own or whatever file is named as your data. What I remember is a misery in me that showed up in whatever I did. I want to find some straight path through this. Whatever crawls is inexact. Our room is one slow sewing machine, the needles join us to whatever is alive. Whatever I do I will have done it knowing nothing. Whatever as opposed to whichever is non-selective. We take whatever steps are required. "Whatever house I enter, flames!" You will feel better about whatever place you're in when these words reach you. The world isn't black and white. It's whatever describes it. Observe whatever floats through your heads without focusing on it. Whatever survives and generates must possess the same memories as are possessed by the living. The tape recorder is set for recording of voice or any sound whatever in the room. The voice calls the names of dead friends and acquaintances; they are free to say whatever they like, to specify whatever they wish to know so that each participant can contribute whatever they want to express, in whatever way, to wander off and try to listen for whatever phenomenon might evoke the observer paradox: whatever they see will be lost.

**5.40AM.** My alarm bell rings
for the fifth time. I am a child or am child-shaped.
I am aware the alarm will go off that it will still be a shock to me.
I am hawk. I think in action, blur, am blur. I
am poem, iambic and ironic
I am doubted, therefore I am. I name therefore
I am the horse that hallucinates time, different from he
who ambled from the shell of an unnamed Pan Am flight.
If I am anything I am a musical amalgamator, grateful too
am I for unnamed librarians, scholars, & webmasters
I reflect on how morose I actually am over a tub of ice cream
& a Tyler Perry movie. Live streaming but am
too sleepy to catch it up. I may not be there yet, but am

closer than I was yesterday. I am so steamed
open. The main thing about Sunday is where am I
going to eat just the way I am. Look at me, hoodouthinkur:
only a little over two months then I am done with you.
I am *so* pumped! Ice cream cones & rainbow teardrops.
People die in the streets. I am nothing compared to them.
I believe that life is a prize but to live I am in love with
automated spam bloggers, am devastatingly depressed
by my child riding the bus & sleeting hardcore. I am
quite possibly the happiest girl on this planet. I am
a praying woman. I am done with driver ed now
I am in a quantum car. I don't know where I
am going, but I'm getting there really fast.
But why am I actually focusing on things that matter
I have a crush on u but can't say who I am lol
Chapters 7 & 8 have been written. I've even edited 7 & am
just waiting on final touches. I lost 0 followers cause I am
awesome, who am I to say something
I am what I am, I feel what I feel, please don't ask me
to change that? So if you're asking me am I confused
I am the future face of the wider team. Tomorrow
am asking harder questions. Hint: know the names
of your bones. Is anyone as excited to see them as I am?
I am not a vegetarian because I love animals. I am
a vegetarian because I hate ham. Him.
I used to tiptoe on Hell's boundaries but I am now well rounded
can't sleep, a strong comma user. I am so excited
& I am awake, but someone I know for real starts following me
I get all uptight about what I am posting
why am I awake after dozing off before 10pm *sigh* let's try this

sleep 10pm *sigh* let's try this sleep thing again shall we I am
the champion at word fued tho Fuck I gonna do how am
I supposed to know I'm only 15 I cried because I am 17.
lol! Guess who am I? I said, yes, true, I always
think I am 10 years younger than I am.

**Isis is deaf** on no side. Her face is a lost mountain.
Chair is to glue as assembly is to wedge language is speaking.
The adjective for inside is insidious as the noun for twerk is gesamtkunstwerk.
I is in S is functionally identical to S contains I.
Language is accountable to those for whom the data is invalid.
The wood is populated with entities: his mother is called the cypress-tree.
Sleep is what reminds us to sleep; or it is the stair that climbs us.
Never is a river. Poem in the morning is tiny on the pillow.
Existence is born of the tense, is born of existence.
The urn of lilies is funerary. Love is death's shadow.
Childhood is driven by an outside world but it is waves that take them from us.
The drag of walking through water is pressure-drag. Mother's hair is mingled with river.
The air is fresh with the smell of flow. Name is edge of hole.
Speech is armed language, hindsight is the least form of was.
Silk is spider's speech. Involution is revolution.
Time is tight: to write a thing is to dissolve it.
Language is the misunderstanding that sense is a possibility.

Doom is senses here, opening a packet of crisps is full of risk.
Event is vent of the particular, silence is the best metaphor.
This burning feeling is rain, empire is graves in the sand.
Food is awareness through space, beetle honey is pulped from brood combs.
Distress is a harsh mistress, the iamb lies with the line.
The storm is the state's elegy. This is a country for old men.
The highest operation of which the plant is capable is irritation.
Self is itself by its surroundings; a cheek-turning reflex is elicited by percussion.
The border is defined by discourses: the line between Yin and Yang is crooked.
A puddle is a quarry for rainbows, self-forgetfulness is rain.
Hard face of the ghost is cloud. Art is thought as thing.
Light is the vehicle we travel. No, sound is the vehicle.
Island is the mind where gravity is a loneliness of matter.
Parking is for ten ants only. The road is wider than time.
Spirit-soaked lint is dropped lit in the belly: the word is felt in the glass.
Thought is heavy, the opposite of the floating is the sunken world.
Fact is an intersection of word and world, fact is a fastening.
Time is the river. It clears the throat that it is.
After midnight, his sleep is uneasy; myth is the tear on his duvet.
A spirit is a protector of properties. Nor is an object created by an allocator.
A roar is in the throat of a thrush: an inner world is externalized in show.
Head is a tree moistened by the past, is this blossom, language.
The water is thick with boy, the ink is of stirred ghosts.

Rest is the resist of the minute, Christ powerer of bicycle lights is discharging.

The spirit is hungry, hard face of the ghost is cloud.

Roar is extraordinary road into the mouth, self is jam in the rock.

Spirit is spirit, but bone is nature.

The face is convinced the light-switch is dark; the condition of the soul is imagery.

Gun is blade of light parting us: in the next room a man is formally speaking.

The freight train is carrying hearses, death is the oldest in its book.

The devil is in the dovetail and is the tenon.

The past is getting colder, sleep is tomorrow's fiction.

The unfurled word is insight, time's bottleneck is perception.

Art is space to the turn of space; to half-sketch is to etch.

A tight ship is a drunken boat, the leaf is the litter of the dead.

Feline life is fine-eared, poem is a sound mind until later.

A union of integrant parts is hard, soft, or cumulative, as is stone, flower, cotton.

The meaning of this passage is obscure or is literally the writing of my name.

Substance is the intimate cause of an aggregate effect: movement is an object.

Dead-soft wire is fully annealed. Half-hard is twice as hard as dead-soft wire.

The night is moving to a destination that is not adjacent to the current square.

An intoxicated traveller is shown to his room in a rustic inn. The room is hung with portraits.

The logic of the peacock is the glory of God. The lust of the goat is his bounty.

The world's descriptive complexity is limitless. A slow wind is time's instrument.

This is now a couple of years later, the algorithm is the output of a solution.

We arrive at something that is not seeable at all: this is sight.

To see if it is intelligence that holds together the universe it is observed.

Is reverberates the issues of its own insistence until what it is is what gives.

Is floats its own cloudless sky above the pool of being.

Is is is, is resolutely intransitive, verb in which nothing happens.

ENCHANTING AND SWEET sounds are heard.
The poets are lined up for their particular
deaths and are given drugs so they can record them.
They are saying poems are to contradict us.
Those white spots are not part of people but are points
of view, separable from body, but not souls. Aflame are
the roses, are the days they requested.
The feelings they have for each other are through arms
but they are generations late. Endless
are their awaited trains. All their notebooks
are incomplete, unfulfilled, even when full.
Their poems are not any more made of words.
They are coughing out farewells as doctors
unplug them. Bass and tenor drums are beaten rapidly.
Clouds are time's rust, but what are these:
dreams, visions, energy, zeal are

indefinitely motive, and in perpetual emergency.
Their poems are the lesser of several million evils
are entirely in mono- and disyllables, depthless
are the mists where in or in which they exist.
All languages are spoken here, for
these are the countries of old men.

**Fearware**

Gods are of six sides and have fevered eyes. The *lung* are mighty powers in the sky. Those up to two millimetres in diameter are called *ash*. They are wingless and live in marshes. To them are allotted all the living beings who are in the ether. Phantasms are afterglow, are not fully bound to the world. Evidence suggests they are generated by portions of the formerly living, who are as the birds are to their songs. Unguents are applied during the darkening half of the moon, poor inhabitants of time are pushed out through long doors. In the outhouses are stored their heads, which are large and plastic, giving them a soft character. The grey adults you dream of in childhood are your own children. The drowned heads of Europe are sealed, our hands are elusive to us as gods'.

**The Future Work Areas**

Many are the symbols by which the future is known, now we are in the time of catastrophes. Flammable and inflammable are interchangeable. Mashed potatoes are white satin at the ball of meat. The orbiter airlock doors are often made of bone. A continuous-time walk will survive to these times that are to come. Warning drums are played for a long time at the start of the dance. These ruins are sets for performance, there are doors built in, adequate light-grasp and width of field of the coming controlled-flow areas. Some cracks are swollen with white crystal suggesting the ability of concrete to self-seal. The pillars are balanced on top, performing no function, precariously. The limbs of the Sun are reaches of dust. Their numbers are depressing.

**A Rendering**

Bosons are ejected from the IN to OUT subspaces indicated by the red line. The pulse and its ramifications are never fully explained. The resulting problems are network design. The first 640K are located at the contiguous address range 00000 to 9FFFFH and are conventional. The Fixed Edges options are unchecked. Custom views are suited to individual preferences. Spider paths are easy-to-follow site routes. They are stolen from rare earth deposits. External tape readers are used for the modular package. Test cards check the operation before the data cards are prepared. Nested objects are Lucene documents that are saved in the same block of data as their parents; random marks are assigned to each traversable region. One or more devices and/or methods for constructing a chat video are provided. Message items are surfaced to create a rendering that constructs the chat. Bicycle Wheel and Hat Rack are abstracted into drawn and geometrical figures recognized symbolically ("understood") by the disruption software. Lists are not synchronized by the spinlock. The evaluated expressions are false.

**Glare Effect**

Fake Japanese paintings are different from Japanese fake paintings. All works of art are founded on driving in heavy traffic. Road rage implies we are different from what we think we are. The two syntaxes are equivalent: the respective regions are *Thanatos* and *Eros*. We are lookers at the still verge. Chance and change are opposites: they say words are the wind that dance us.

**Infrared**

Dreams are structured like TV: slap them and they are briefly conscious. They teach us events are obscure forever. Our lungs are full of night's residue. The eyes we pass through are unwise, change hands. Better instruments are needed, better tapes and interference-free recording. The essential elements are axioms and a calculus. The stated goals of the migration are functional equivalence and client software. Experts in cloudware are found naked and drenched in bleach.

**Bay Area**

Seafront tourist facilities are increasingly exposed. Bent burrows are more likely the result of simple shear, areas of love are drifting. Solutional scallops are common on the surface. Light ice years are associated with a high square-wave moment, but corner frequency and seismic energy are traditionally inverted. Bent burrow fabrics are interpreted as an ethological response. The relevant data are from dead reckoning, seamarks, wave patterns, birds. Note the error: they are produced by overly concrete interpretations of the navigator's abstract. He is lowered and the hooks are withdrawn. The seafloors are shaken.

**Area Location**

Search head clusters are a group of Splunk search heads that share configurations, search job scheduling, and search artifacts. All coordinates are with respect to the bounding box containing human traces. The trees are thorns and thorny shrubs. We are opposite the town hall. Just beyond are places where searchers are assumed to know probabilities. Screen continuum and concrete space are irrelevant to search entity. The glyphs are converted to highres bitmaps. Resonances are determined from the positions of the T-matrix poles as gold values of 34 soil samples are plotted. Events are the preferred level of analysis. Elevation and traverse of the launcher unit are effected manually. The usual scribing points are hermaphrodite callipers. We are drawn on by the sound of water into a compact piazza dominated by a travertine stage-set sluiced by rivulets of spume. In the east, black gates are shut against the sunrise.

## Parent Material

The natives of childhood are leaving. Boys are wounds healing into scars: eyes are almond shaped with heavy lids. Look what their shadows are made of, how they are restless and fretful; Cozen's fractures are of the proximal tibia from ages three to six. The conversations their parents had over their heads are still. They are countless and seem to be weightlifters with developed musculature. They are wearing stylized make-up, their faces are obscured. The symptoms are leonine countenance, large hands and feet. Five are the number of days the child continues to weep.

## Compare

Hearsay particles are high-risen. Utterances are heard better and farther on an evening, and message elements are assigned to those that are to communicate. Membered in the sentences are uncertain paths. Foregrounding languages are featured as phonological and rhythmic. The targets are transposed into the passive. They are low.

## Rare Earths

Transient are the youth and opulence of a stone. Hot-spring sinters are improperly called *geyserite*. Prior to mining, orebodies are surveyed. Moraines are linear bends of drift. Dipping bedsets are referred to as inclined. The prismatic outcrops are caused by vertical fractures, in which earths reaching the outer shafts are positively turned. The traverses follow a natural weathering fault and are fissile. In Fox soils the gravels are in continuous beds, and the surfaces are flat. Schists are caused by quartz-sillimanite knots and stump casts are seen at the northern margin. Tension gashes, minor mud flows, deformed sedimentary structures are seldom found.

## Share Ballistic Knowledge

The basic components are a base, a cross traverse, a sliding square-notch rear sight, and a wheelhead. Cutter holders are mounted in the multiple turning arm. Various handwheels are used for movement during grinding. The synthetic stock and forearm are in a non-glare finish. Two stabilizers are for support when firing. Cockings of the eyebolt in the basket hole are felt as separational forces are applied. Eyeball adjustments for butt swell are made. The stock and forend are covered with Mossy Oak camo. An XFT choke and five Benelli chokes are included. Both are chambered in .357 Mag. Harmful sounds are compressed to safe levels. Afterglow phosphor intensities are various. Phoenix and Sparrow are shoot-down capabilities. Targets are transferred into an inbeam dewar.

**Warfare**

On the moorlands of the tree kill areas, cold are the autumn winds, while in the empty city chilly horns are echoing. Robbers are due. The light is fallen and they are hidden in the sunbright peninsulas of the sword: On the table lies a rapier, and near it are a wine flask and a tall ornate drinking glass. Rival clans are recognizable by their caricatured features. Those who chastise the unprincipled are granted bows and arrows; the hairs of the bow are the hairs of their lengthened bodies. The culpable are granted battleaxes; isolated pictures of the preparation activities are in my mind, sounds are coming from knights riding through the woods where arrows are left as prayers. Unclean *oni* are to cease from the villages. Wars between gods and demons are fought in the vicinity of Ocean, for their sorrows are strong.

**Torturing-instrument makers** are one man.

Uskub are made of the bone of a kind of crane.

Wood-cutters are a thousand men, with ninety-nine shops.

Wheel-makers of horse-mills are seven men.

Water-canal men are three hundred men.

Upholsterers are twelve men, with ten shops.

Unorganic masses are stones and lumps of clay.
The Flute-makers are thirteen men, with four shops.
Stone-draggers are one thousand men.
Spheres are the finger-ends of impersonal spirit and nature.
Players of the coarse flute are eighty men.
Players of the flute with the tongue are twenty-two men.
Palpi are large, and resemble antennae or legs.
Gold-rimmed eyes are set far forward in a field.
Large rocks are the fathers of the little ones.
Eight are the wombs of Aditi, kept in motion by machinery.
Day-labourers or journeymen are ten thousand men.
Coverers with lead are three hundred men.
Organised earthly bodies are of five sorts.
Wealth managers are typically poor at building platforms.
The fixed lights of Heaven are concluded to be pure fire.
Tomorrow your friends are going to come for you.
Coffin-makers are fifty men, with twenty shops.

## Two. Of the States of Existing

MATTER I DEFINE TO BE substance divisible; spirit, substance indivisible. Be valiant that the laws of Buddha not pose as stone.

Be that as it may, be open and operate. Be stone be still.

Let a stretched event be one that lasts for more than a chronon. There will be a village of bones or a pope running to put out his robes.

Right and dead can be transposed by matching control-points of the grids projected from a table detached from the engine parts; it writes scripts pretending to be spirit messages.

To be a by-concept; to be a schistosity resulting from intrusion, be full, as a pot or river; be filled out, as a foot from a snakebite, be stuffed, as the nose; be embarrassed or choked.

In order that next steps be followed, be metallic crimson, pop-art red, chocolate besmeared, be silent; anyone who is not in favour, speak, or be shaken laterally for up to a minute.

The holding of shields symbolizes King Wu's beta program; to seek to be struck by lightning. To be part of the bird's-head pistol grip with which he beats the hornbeam.

For a substance to be body, it exacts impenetrability. The tooth to be cut in the wheel, the bean to be beaten. Placeholder text is to be replaced by verbal feeling.

When will my yawn be in the dictionary. My advice: be the cloud. Let cumulus be your upper edge. Ascend to a vaulted bank to be put to the credit of the deceased.

Be wary of thread-lists becoming empty. For an event to be intentional it has to be in a relation to something else.

The poem should be a bundle of glyphs to be dump-trucked by farmers on their turnip beds.

Culture evolved to be learnable. To think properly of sleep is to be asleep.

No messages can arbitrarily be brushed aside. Be a letter, containing the instruction to kill the bearer.

Nothing can be measured any more, but it cannot be left. Let be be is. Let is be.

**I write alone.** That I might hunt alone in the thicket using angle-of-attack vanes. The *phoenix* are gone, the river flows on alone. Tiber alone, transient and seaward, remains of Rome: Rome's name alone within these walls keeps. In death's kingdom I wake alone at the gathering hour. Tiber catches moonlit stupor, stolen bicycles, father and son alone. For good and ill deeds belong to us alone, until we stand on death's side. But here upon earth the anchorman meditates alone. The I's yearning for unity stems from the alone experience of the womb. This alone with K in the interchange of day and night: alone, not alone. I miss her as I tread alone the winepress of text, when an ice-phase begins and ice-waves radiate with the sound a word makes when left alone. In fact I am altogether unused to this, as it were, living alone. I had a notion of surviving time by sealing myself in a single word that would be mine alone. The coiteration of "lonely ocean" and "alone" focus on my fear in this situation. They sing "In fragrant garden path alone I still remain" without understanding the content, let alone the subjugation. They translate the phrase as "But his terms alone contribute in their influences." An alternative translation would be, "And his terms contribute to being alone." Each suspension-feeder uses mucus alone to trap food. But the calorimeter alone can give the quantity of heat at work. The difference between the volume of both the water and solid and the volume of the water alone is the volume of the solid. Leave me the hell alone, alone or jointly with you. Live

die suffer enjoy. Alone is the state of mind of a mined state,
through which I walk.

### The area

being a mere fragment of the once perfect lobe, the journey
being facilitated by a
being of battered moon. The bone
being three parts cut through is broken, the whole skin
being turned over the skull. There are feelings
being displayed on the face. The ear inflamed, the pain
being partly cramplike, partly stinging, the eyes
being brightest, each bleeding
being preceded by paleness of face, with the material
being required when demand exceeds the of a child volume, a
being in a place for the first time, stepping into a pool
being its adjectives, the stamen filaments, the slit
being who determines the length of a child's life
being workers' state of shock when, exhausted with
being, silence exacts its answer, white light-plane high on
being passed through a prism, previous to the engine
being put in operation. The receiver
being on the hook, the supervisory lamp lights. The subjects
being in jail illustrate a tendency noted by Freud
being alone with distant memories may be rendered:—"Ah this
being cannot exist to the eye
beings flicker in and out of existence
being insensible to external objects
being drunk" here the ideas, instead of
being slow, arise with rapidity, as hair after

being shaven. By 1800, however, the cocked bonnet
being for the dead on the intercalary days, the usual note
being a nasal chung, his trust, when the disembodied
being returns on the evening
being quick goes to the east, the milk
being the rain, controls the power which Indra derives from
being, which is divided into several compartments, body
being of the ocean, the souls are extra-dimensional
beings that attach to our bodies after birth. How badly she is
being bitten. This call is
being recorded for playback, the word power
being in the up position, the downward force of the spring
being naked, having a chance of
being between. An exclamation indicated
being. One of these was a woman-
being, or was satisfied that there was such a
being. Your true
being sleeps inside you, enjoys steady-state behaviour without
being attached to it. The persona
being fatigued by the questions, said she would try;
being of a different nationality, the vesting
being wrapped in a red handkerchief and placed in a tumbler
being tossed successively into each numbered square.
Being is that part of the I concerned with
being a statue, a
being on the edge of persisting through the head
being surfaced through the interface by participants, so
being a father is an exercise of memory, imprecise materiality that is

being, the printed part
being in contact with his hands. On a mesmerised half-crown
being put into them he had difficulty opening them, saying
beings applied a clamplike device, the writing
being very fine would have been taken for that of a lady
being captured, he felt extremely guilty by the black
being of corn-soot, at other ancient sites
being written in reversed direction. His
being brilliant in this way like a tree
being contrary to all other basic experience. The energy which is here
being young, his son was succeeded instead by his nephew
being left in the woods of Was, my
being the endless chain unceasingly causing.

## Three. Of That Which May Exist

If you can keep your headset when those about you are losing it and shitting on you. If you can embarrass yourself publicly, making all men unfriend you, but retweet their criticisms too; if you can give a fuck and not be tired by shit, or being fucked about, don't deal in fucks, or being canceled, just do what you were going to do. If you can bear to hear the truth you've tweeted shared by losers who don't get irony, and don't point this out to them; if you can grow old and watch your pension value decline, month by month, and your pension age increase, and not invest in crypto. If you can search to see if your ex-partner is online and not IM them, or if you can correctly implement subnets, and have a filtering point on each, if you can count to a hundred, but not much over, since you don't have much time, if you can fill the unforgiving minute with sixty seconds' worth of browsing, on work time. If you can work out how to screenshot what you're dreaming and post the images on Reddit or whatever and have your card details refused, and start again at the beginning and fail to give a toss; if you can switch news channel and see that all of them are weighed by interests, and be unsurprised if it's the petrodollar or geopolitics or colonialism which says to them: "Invade!" If you can draw a layout cell without insetting a layout table, and tell which of your trousers are machine washable, if you can wear night-vision goggles and see night visions while being forced to work in slave conditions because your passport was impounded, if when you arrive in your new country you see it as a start-up op; if you can play the game to its logical conclusion, and even then get ripped off; the payoff may only be a remedy for your 3-year-old's night cough. If you can see that some are vulnerable, but everyone at some stage will be. If you can be not prematurely exploded before your start-up ideas are meta-coded; if you can avoid being forced to live in a refugee camp, spend your last few notes on a border crossing and have your mobile confiscated, if your main worry is not about global warming, but how it will affect which stocks are best performing. If you can wear long lashes, and extensions which last for up to three weeks. If you can try a lip plumper or collagen-filled lip colours and go natural with clove-filled lip enhancers in mauve and pink, and make sure it appears on a clickable link; if you can ask a trend guru to come up with a blueprint for the quintessential restaurant, if you can wait an hour in a call queue and still know to which company you are speaking; if you can do this through a futures contract, and pay initial and additional margins, if you can introduce a pathogen and go viral, if you can market a product that has no use, whose sole purpose is to confuse, if you rank high enough on YouTube to be an influencer, and you don't influence people to buy useless tat; if you can decolonise your mind and remain aware of the historical layers that rind your skin; if you can see history from the perspective of the defeated and laugh at the shallow victories of rulers, but also then reflect that if you have the luxury of reflection, you too, in some way, have inherited this from some other group's defeat; if you can still read the poem that was voted the most popular in the UK, that seems at first sight chained to old ideas of manhood and empire, then you can look into the sense of "man" and "son", and discern the irony in the fate of K's son, then you'll be a reader open to the poem's chasm, for no one can be such a man at all. If you can list a set of arbitrary or unfeasible targets, and set the stakes as whether your male offspring qualifies as a son, if you can make these targets dependent upon a creaking sense of empire, then you may not have been a realistic father. If you can detect logical confusion between the earlier use of "all men" and the "man" that you, the reader, is not yet, you need not feel excluded. But if reading it you can also sense that K's poem is a poem first of all, you'll see that the rhetoric only indirectly addresses the poem's inner theme; if you can entitle your poem "If", it is in a condition that cannot be fulfilled, because to be a "man" and a "son", under imperialism, or perhaps always, was more than a burden, white man's or not. If you can see that the conditional is not existent, that there is an aching loss upon which the poem teeters; as with all poems, it says indirectly what its main point is, that there are only conditions and trying to become something that you are not will fail; and what's more, if you can use K's poem to speculate on the childish and destructive dreams we all contain, if you can read the poem as the insubstantial wish of a child; if you can do these, and all I'm asking is for you to sit and read a poem, yours will be the Earth and everything that we've left you of it, which is not much, and—which is more—you'll be alone, and remain so, my son, my soul.

**Today I'm writing a letter** to you instead. Last night I decided to extinguish my head torch, but instead I set it to flash mode; placing three eyes in a row with no explicit statement instead of teeth having an entire jawbone indented like a saw. A pair of infuriated monster eyes in a cage employ a rolling, circular knife, loaded with straight attack-power instead of strength. Instead of an advert there's a poem above us but the train stops prematurely or we get out at a stop too soon and instead we get into a plane and we are going to some southern European city. Instead of the cross, the albatross. I mean to go and ask it to come in but instead I sleep and when in the morning I look out it is just cigarette butts in the doorway. I get up with the intention of turning the radio down but pick up the phone instead and it tells me instead of seaweed albums or pressed flowers, start a fashion for pressed street-rubbish, which would reoccur in the novel I am to write, but instead of noting down external appearance I am given illuminating parts of psychic life, so instead I flail about with the most slippery of words that will talk to me, once, but not right now. Instead, there is music, a stranger's friend is talking of the hatches on maps they used to have instead of contour lines. Language is a skin, I have words instead of fingers. We drive around and clearly there is nowhere for the coffee she imagined, instead we turn into a vineyard. I cannot see the source of the bleating, instead a couple making speeches instead of love. They could not find the Palomar object but found, instead, a 21st magnitude object 4 arcsec south-east. Instead of the completely soldered joint between the inlay and pontic, the writer has used a small squared bar of ink. What I really mean to say instead is, come back won't you, just all of you come back.

**By a still lake** they are all leaving perhaps
following me because no one is in front perhaps
news and gossip are the final form of history perhaps
lord of the moon's excellence we travel perhaps
through perceptual models far from page-edges perhaps
not less numerous, which few readers perhaps
will at the first glance see, clearly profile-cut, perhaps
and the dog with me and breath of ancestors perhaps
by the sea on this pier there are perhaps
many people. She tells me she wants to be left in perhaps
a small wagon or private banking hub perhaps
some wheeled ordinance a bicycle perhaps
a stone in shape of a person with a soul perhaps
try and move an arm or even blink perhaps
keep riding and I end up in a large building perhaps
it is a form of afterlife, on the steep slope perhaps

in front of a large school we play basketball—perhaps
in some way I am in charge of it—it appears this is perhaps
nudity on the steps of some important perhaps
neo-classical building. It seems this may have perhaps
been a field by the edge of a town where perhaps
I did some secret performance, some activity—perhaps
physical, athletic. I have a friend with me who is perhaps
a professional dancer, coming to watch. The ritual perhaps
starts inside a circle with an initial radius of perhaps
10 miles. Perhaps
I take part, feeling ill with some chemical poisoning. Perhaps
this goes on at some other hotel perhaps
German youths play pranks with fireworks, perhaps
trying to find my room very late in the evening, perhaps
by now I am on my own in a flat, perhaps
I just moved in and hardly know anyone, perhaps
destined to die because of its qualities. Perhaps
only in the space of a night turning on perhaps
the central moment in Lacan. As the child learns, perhaps.

**To see in a dream** a capon, or to hear a hen cackle, indicates sadness. There is no correct way to construct a note or group of notes. Hire new salespeople or build new platforms in object-deletion or distribution to decrease from penal servitude to strokes of the light or the heavy bamboo. Or you can embed A in the ruler line with a cord or chain received through ear loops. Draw the skin flap distally and insert and tie one or two stitches to attach it to the nail bed or click the layer visibility icon to turn it off. Accuse of or for? escape from or off? wait for or to? Socket of bed or arm of dream. A detached stone, or a single blade. Headache, violent on walking quickly, or ascending stairs. If desiring to enter south of the border, a fence or designated territory functions as a preserve or safety zone. This folder has been deleted, or you don't have permission. Opens mouth or curls lip showing teeth, snarling, nose licking or tongue flicking. Jogs or shuttles. Diverts eyes and shows low-level anxiety signs: sniffs ground, scratches, urinates, or occasionally immerses head and neck, or foot-paddles in soft mud. He could not decide if he felt sated and stateless, or insatiable and stately, or kept a reckoning of the soul as alien technology: software or virus. Downstairs I am sniffing a glass: whiskey or apple juice? Or suddenly the language laughs, or twists or puckers her mouth because the origins of words like gag or nah are articulatory or imprisoned in sand, or in the limestone regions of the tibia; or in the swelling uplands of the brain. Certain characters are hung or fastened over the house-door or the towers; and on this understanding is figure of taste. Nor is the same as Or but with its output inverted. Wits' end is the laugh or gasp that must evaluate to true or false. The pulsed A and tonal B calls can be produced singularly or in phrases or songs, by a catch in the light or throat. Grabbing, or symptoms of light-headedness, or nonorientable motor responses; draw or suck the juice or essence out of a thing. Mirror or reverse the direction of a closed fireball, snowfall, lava, or nova. Take nails or smeared stones from the river. Pound hand or fist on knee, table or chair. Pound knee, table or chair with fist. Be swollen or full, as a river after rain forebodes a great war or the pest; or build the roads wider, with the crown to one side, as when attempting to weave a mat without knowing how, or with pea stalks or with down or hatcheled flax or metal shaving or a bundle tied up by an old woman or a person peering out from a hut-door. Converge a sequence of variables or a work-party, by way of tribute; proclaim, in the morning, or when closely thinking. Distribute wine or spirits to the soldiers, or their servants, or agents. Or, he will say, the horse heard me, knowing the penalty for falsehood is a nonstandard address form. Use an electrical charge to draw fine jets from a solution or melt between a pair of relief or printing rollers giving indistinct or undefined chilliness. Mark the shape on a piece of metal or scribe and flatten it between the rolls till it is 1 or 2 on the metal gauge. Anneal into a storage type of an oval or rounded form, apply bright pink or corals with a Kabuki or a rounded blusher brush. Charge incidents with pity or fear; imbue red or water with new qualities, allow for expansion or contraction of the top or side handles. Options include black with Agent 1 grips or stainless steel with Nighthawk medallions. The past is eternal, or internal, or in the sparks of hooves or a cigarette thrown from a window. Some landing pages ask searchers to enter their phone or email, or when the unseen novel object is hidden in a locked barn, blood smears are examined from 5 to 10 minutes, or thin blood smears from 20 to 30 minutes. In the twelfth or highest mansion of Heaven lives the Great Spirit. Make a list of words that describe wind or fire or the cells of the grey substance in the spinal cord or the sensory ganglia. The neighing of a horse or the braying of a he-ass is a favourable world-disclosure, carries biases and prejudgments that characterize every sensory of hearing or ear. Two magicians or angels are sent by God to teach men magic. Two light syllables, or a single heavy syllable appear everted or bent outwardly. Skippers take on an inexperienced man or two as split-share men. Is there *culpa* or *dolus* on the part of those who navigate A's ship? Slip into shirt or trouser pockets, slip onto belts or over a wrist. Wall-to-wall carpeting or a room-size area rug maximizes square footage. Spring or early summer for dwarf onion or woolly head clover. Dream of evil white pill-size or slightly larger intelligences, like grubs. They inhabit doors, or hatches on yachts with weakened or harsh respiratory sounds on shedding blood, breath held or gasping, ensouled or embrained. Slow deaths, or the symptoms produced by the slow-death factor or factors, were observed with survivors that had received sublethal doses containing the fast-death factor. Rubber or robber barons. Max Miller or Max Müller. Err on the side of error or tear on the side of terror or roar down the tide of mirror. It speaks or is spoken. Angel of history: dyslexic or illiterate? Read poetry with a microscope, a periscope, or a telescope? Drive a lamb or Genie, read theodicy or The Odyssey? Terror or horror? Death or dishonour? Cloth or dishwasher?

Entering a new market a wealth manager faces otherwise
otherwise the material leaves a small border of afterworld
frequent drawing pains in the otherwise sound teeth—
I have been otherwise told to never go into those words
hydrogen-induced cracking otherwise stepwise cracking
otherwise permits nondelimiting indirect arguments
a statement P at a point on an otherwise blank sheet asserts
the conjunction of P otherwise on the sea, at sea, in a ship
in a field, forest, desert the hunter does not look, otherwise
he would die, the equal method returns true and false otherwise
it is used as the query object; otherwise, the user is asked for
an identifier at different points on an otherwise blank
sheet. A leader of the Society of the Harmonious Fist, otherwise
known as the Boxers, produces moods otherwise inexplicable.
Run the compound, otherwise he will freeze all day
in the office. Otherwise, you wake in someone else's coffin.
You have forgotten every address (affectionate or otherwise)
you were summoned by as a child. Otherwise, one morning,
sleep, for otherwise you are not quite real.

**And Kung gives his daughter** to Kong-Tch'ang although Kong-Tch'ang is in prison. "What! are you here?" Although I am not. Although the throughput has doubled, the old file system still uses 4% bandwidth. And he gives his niece to Nan-Young although Nan-Young plunges deep to a single, although manifold and corporate, equilibrium. The behavioral work varies, although it is seldom actually poor. Although this is not reported by most participants the women victims state it would be unlikely for them to last longer than a film, although it feels like one until the chase ends up near a tidal channel, although geographically I feel it was situated in the I. of Wight, although swimmable-around. Up to the stage one comes very much like Janis Joplin, although apparently it isn't Woodstock, although the details elude me, something to do with local history; I notice a museum of glass, although it is full of books, not glass, so we arrange some kind of affair although the books are still of importance, I remember them vividly, funny because in reality I phoned her last night although I must have looked stupid. Although my family is quite faceless and diffuse, it is definitely them, and we are driving in a mountainous backwoods area with my cousin (although she fades from the picture, although there is a lot of water maybe it's a canal of cast bronze with a removable front although by the time I have unconcealed it it changes to bluish bottle-glass and contains soil although now I can't remember what relation this has to what I was teaching. I go out to look for the bus and although they are not worried I can't remember getting on the plane in which there is a bar a level downstairs although it isn't crowded and I am terrified we will crash into the ground although no one else seems worried and it pulls up with a jerk so we don't crash although by any reasonable logic we should have done. I am involved in some kind of struggle although that merely means my cousin sleeps at the crash site since he has lost all desire to run and the night of the play goes wrong although for me it does not seem like a problem. I love the bit downhill from work although the flyovers are uncomfortable with people throwing flick-knives at each other although they also look like can openers. I must have half woken (although there was more than I remember now) and I'm in the woman's section although even after being told off I can see nothing wrong with that. Although this experiment is not intended to be a research project, it manifests as almost human, although like in a movie I try to kill it then reason with it, although in the end we reach an understanding and it crawls off, its expression saying that it has an idea, although its words do not answer to that idea, although it brims with what it was.

**Whether you wish** to allow your hard drives to turn off or
whether the child switches to the right lever
whether Margaret knows that Sleeping Margaret is
here whether sensation survives
whether large or small, hard or soft; we ask
whether S knows that his ticket is a loser
whether each element is the depicted object
the flesh vehicle takes me whether I like it or not
whether it is unmistakably John Berryman
or whether John Barleycorn who must die
whether cognitive interference is interchangeable
and whether to talk to him. I can turn my
intention to a committed cog-wheel whether words
repeat the same meaning every sentence, whether
funny or sad, whether the thread examining the list
is the thread asking whether he was asleep, he replies

*Yes* and whether no precaution or every
is taken whether the search includes the glove compartment
whether people in the vehicle can be quake predictors
whether to open the feed items in the same browser
whether first-order logic is undecidable contributes
to the proposition expressed by whether photography is real
representation works its way whether we wear coats or not
the soldier decides whether to detonate the head
whether the rhythms of words are sudden enough
whether on a bridge or high gorge's lip, on a whim.

No one sees them now except as a memory, similar to the regular view except this time we are living in a house not a campsite except a composite, except there is no separation of bodies except through language, we are the same being, the same organism to an extent in a gang a bit like an early punk group except we are ten and aren't doing music and we brush against the flanks of the Dining Room, empty except for a claustrophobic table. Every room in the house except the bathroom is filled with bookshelves, and all expression flavours in this book, except JavaScript, offer an alternative expression syntax that makes it very easy to read, and so past the allotments, except the allotments have now been replaced by furniture; the place I come to rest at is a version of the Lloyd Thomas Building in which I stayed my first year except it is much higher and in a square forming a huge inner courtyard and I alight on the top and all the kids flee in panic, except looking back now I realise no monster appeared at all, something like a remote part of Australia except in other respects it could have been Mexico, where they don't speak English, and they are showing me a video, like one of those early travel narratives except with me as a wanderer who leans out of a window as it gets dark and I shine a torch into the water except it is as if I am the torch, so it is impossible to see the shadows where the light is not; on my own on this very small island, the rock is not marked except by breakers in a heavy swell, on which I am set naked, except for a rag that covers my loins, except there are two lovers the other side and I shine my torch that has a kind of tremulous motion, not possible in real life except during brightness-excitation, into the water, in Africa, except I have made no preparations except for a few seconds to consider what might be the best footwear, and I climb up and then ride down this great fairgroundlike water-flow except it goes on for miles through canyons, and things are nearly back to normal, except I am still, reading a statement about corporate responsibility, except the word had been written corporeal, and I run up the hill, except not running in my usual way, sort of loping, with crutches made of edge-cone singularities, except I do not know how to explain this. The bones in my face shift tectonically, except thirty years too late. The sound that wakes me is a swan clapping the water, except I'm miles from a river. It is two conscripts storming the stairs, except I live in a ground-floor flat. It is a neighbouring state's motorized cavalry, except we have no neighbours. It is the summons of distant church bells, except it's Monday. It is the couple next door arguing, except next door is boarded up. It is my partner getting up for work, except she's been gone some months now. It is the phone in the livingroom, except they disconnected it last week, except I'm on a train going to work, and then the same in reverse, except I'm on the way home.

**The Tao that** can be expressed is not the eternal Tao. That text can be changed. A convolutional code can be represented by a tree diagram. I can code an if without an else, but it is illegal to code an else without an if. Rectilinear construction can be summarized into a suite of methods that can be mounted to a framework. I can add, reorganize, and rename files in the not-yet burned field. I can enjoy the running water and enhance its functionality. A five-axis model can grip a blank part. Rocks can be represented by a few simple hatches. They can neither stop their movements nor moderate their exuberance. I can supply the operators with operation-ready aircraft. They can be sent back. Read the story by Wells: a series of gestures can travel through the mind's mud. It can be a door not noticed before. The structural field distortion can be avoided by realizing this. Self can be taken out of a shopping bag. The medium can make the thought-graph of the object presented by the sitter. Scribing and breaking can be accomplished with minimal loss. A maliciously shortened route can successfully disrupt flow. The time-dimension of a state-description can be made explicit. Potential gradient-curves can serve as a prognostic of fog. Tuscan pork fat can be outlined in fawn, fawn sable, mahogany. A caulking gun can eliminate cocking of the wrist. The mother's request and its inversion can be done in the frequency domain. Forget, if you can, that our time is an avalanche. I refer to the edge that can be crisp of toppling clouds. I have a doll which can produce water. An event described by a verb can have only one terminus. Discrete-event models can avoid the unrealistic assumptions of analytical. An innocuous act in the existential world can be lethal in reality. Errors in dosage can leave a prisoner conscious. A particular can in no wise exist without a general. Unlike any actual house I can call to mind, this one contains cable corridors. If I can draw the 5, I can catch a king of any denomination. Long-range enthusiasts can engage targets at two miles. Longer sequences can lead to a combinatorial explosion of appreciation bonds. A lifted corner can break the tension of the solder. I can position my holster to low-ride or high-ride. The execution-path can be changed through conditionals. The effectiveness of a protocol can be assessed by the process distribution. The resisting line can slow the eye's advance. Tremolo basslines can sound like vomiting. I can tap facial databases. I can walk through force fields and collect weapons and ammo. Digital adjustment switches can be manipulated while wearing gloves. Feet can be rotated allowing the shooter to adjust for cant and tilt. The long positively charged Kloop can interact strongly with the click-yield. An unrecognised crab burrow can cause havoc with the integrity of the sample. The mesial boxings of the upper and lower premolars can be conservative. The tomorrow operator can fill the air with its emanations. Can cause bleeding, jaw-shatter, cancer. Can be said to conform to the interface, or conform to the type. Your shadow can appear on the shower curtain. It can be seen by dragging a corner of the box with the black arrow to make the box larger. I can see your face in the rear view.

**He could expect the following** sequence of events: it could be the son is drunk as the voice of one who could be his dead brother draws him into the cemetery; he captures the voices from the departing train; his entire nervous system could be separated. He could not break himself of running after trains, though he laboured, but he made it home, and could sit on the sofa and stretch a cast structure and be happy. A certain kind of mobile life could be lived in a world of events, he thought. Cloaking devices could not occupy the same space as suspended matter, their engines could not breathe smoothly. His thoughts in this case could not be regarded as associations. If he could only find the end of the passage where cry could be the contentment of a mother bird, where spinal fluid could leak into the eye making him feel he could rush out, but he felt faint, could not get into bed nor sit upright, but when lying could make every motion. All he could do was laugh quietly: then the opening xylophone solo could be manually released. He could hear the dance-sticks clatter on the cedar boards and the moon-rattles whirl, and he could see smoke curl from the smoke-holes. The spirit-lamp in the house on the headland could affect proportional logic, but even with mirrors, he could not see inside. He saw towers that could topple out of an eye, he could compare the sound to causation-cascades. He could survey his new lands through the swine's eye sockets and come to terms with the canoe people; they could look through his walls to cause his death. He was legally dead, and could not look, like other men, upon the sun. He could see slight movements in the upper part of his arm, feel the muscles quiver up and down his back. He could not find his body, could not associate. He then saw a face, but could not understand what it meant. He believed he could stick his finger into it, that it could be partitioned with sliding doors. He could see the swirls and clear spaces where he could fly, could reach over to one of the greige and taupe consoles flanking the camel sofa, could feel it then, a downiness in front of the mind. The highest to which he could attain was the plant sphere; such a blossom, when self-dependently subsisting, could not continue. When attackers saw they could exploit flaws in the maintenance computer and had taken as much as they could, they could not pry the words from his mouth, they could make no edge against the sky. Before he could put on his own clothes, he was made to parade naked through the client base. In the distance in an outer set of woods he could see a light. It was as if this hill could continue indefinitely, until he could scarcely walk. He could rest here, there would be no mud. He could identify areas of thinning and thickening, and predict flow-paths. Studying the movement in the cluster metal as it drew from the blank-holder could be of great help. He could identify areas of clinkering. Sabot rounds could penetrate a demon's hide. He turned away and shut the door, and on the stair wondered how many times he could have proved his worth.

Line 16 mentioned a cedar forest, the traverser of which could not see the sun, he recollected. Such information could be used to generate more realistic event-sequences, but this was not his focus. Her extended arms or legs could not be made to descend by darting the hands at them. On producing a letter to ascertain whether she could read it, she said, before it was opened, that it was not signed, which was the case. She could not, however, distinguish the others, and desired to be awakened. Now, he had taken good care that she could not have a glimpse of the paper, only a series of inner acts could delink the chain of deeds of which existence was woven. He rode after it as hard as his horse could, as costumed trolls traversed the surface of what could be another planet. If glory could last forever then the waters of Han would flow northward. In the queue he could feel the hunger of the people behind him, voices that could be his children, but no joint could be moved. It was not known if controls could be implemented on a chined forebody. He saw neither past present nor future, but what could never happen. If AI could write poems we would not understand them.

STAND BY THE WINDOW that I may speak to you
from this brightness a sharp image may appear
beams from your car may probe the bedroom wall
of the child you were, you may recollect
Egg Rock Light may be seen westward of Winter Harbour
the pre-fetched may not match the modified instructions
the media player may be disposed in the housing cavity
from which access to the engines may be gained
your multi-joint arms may be of non-woven material
black zone lines may develop in the light areas

the device may include a trigger-assembly
which may be positioned against your body
your chisels and punches may be driven through iron
jerks may spread to the finger flexors
out of which a hard-cased black fly may spring
resting against a high-backed chair may reduce tremors
smite the dust of the land that it may become lice
all you may see is a rash that looks like a fern on the skin
it may consist of operators in curly brackets
drums and half-drums may be played for kings
the error may be detected after several clock-cycles
or let us suppose the earth may be hollow
authority may take a suitability action against an employee
compliance professionals may collaborate with architects
the spirit broken from the body may suffer a different Hell
a single dance may result in twenty or thirty new songs
poetic statements may not be discovered except by automation
a dialog box may appear to warn self-report measures exist
a suite of events may result in evidence of the events
the valve may be put on end-for-end without being put on wrong
pieces of gasket may remain in the glands of the gauge-cocks
you may pat the buttery dough with a paper towel
the Bolognese's coat of dense hair may appear bristly
open landscapes may offer an escape from sales management
positions may be defined in terms of absolute locations
inputs may attach higher importance to links from web pages
your dream is not favourable, it may not be removed
dismay may compromise security
the *acute* and the *grave* may stand on any vowel
you may use the information for the untended purpose only.

**The day might work out beautifully** if I was not afraid. I might partake of accurate dimensions, the light briefly settle on me, the hill of what might be next, dynamic predictions might reference magnetic drum memories, tones might be compared to a painter's palette, what I hear might come from underground. I might describe the world in some way that might change things. Flowing, the heavenly sea might darken the framework and the roar of tumbling waters might inspire pilgrims, they might introduce a human virus to swine populations, these thoughts might be turned to account in what one might expect to find in a discourse of this sort, the profile might claim the persona is a MiG pilot, each point on the sheet of assertion might be called a point of assertion. A spirit might remain in the frame for less time than the sitter. The spirit answers: I do not want to do that, for I might kill you. If the chairs are heavy, he might bring only one chair. The mighty might fall, the fallen might rise, that it might be part of the other dream: though the fish enrapture the ice, called upon they might rise in chains of syntax, mouth thanks and head for the waves of what might be next. What dangers might the traveller anticipate meeting? What might be the consequences if the traveller just waits? if the alarm hadn't gone off I might have caught a terrible disease. A portion of lung might be in a condition of inflammatory congestion, the percussion-note over it might mumble. Under us snakes might free their shadows, a full-size porcelain head might speak at any moment. It might ejaculate some unrecorded matter, seminal, testamental, generative. The ambiguous pronoun might also refer to the penis, by which a callow youth might be transformed into an archangel. The development of e-poetics might help to alter structures that entrap socio-aesthetics in the academy. I watch over mortals as mothers might do—as one might waken after death, she breathes again, she might.

## Four. Of That Which Should Exist

I OUGHT TO OPEN THIS with an apology
mother ought have eaten the tooth in a piece of bread
the vessels ought to be of gold, bell metal, or lotus
the eight attitudes ought to be inwardly experienced
translators ought to be sensitive to foregrounding
receiving links ought to be a crucial strategy.
Kosti, here is Kennedy. Kosti, I ought to like it here.
Ought often expresses a relation between agents
and actions; it is not the naive view that ought
always expresses this relation, ought also has
an epistemic sense, the deliberative ought:
the subject of inquiry about what we ought to do
because a proposition ought to be the case.
The meaning of ought is indifferent between
there ought to be world peace and you
ought to see Squid Games. Agential ought
expresses the relation between agent
and action when that action is what the agent ought to do.

THE PELT SHOULD BE COLLECTED and left on the stretchers. Its skin should be cased pelt-side-out. The armature shaft should be turned until the number 1 appears at the peephole. The upper end of the body-wire should be cut. The test light should light in the LOCK position and go out in UNLOCK. The pawls should be depressed, and rendered by argon washout. The sailing directions for Bass Harbor should be followed. Duck Rocks tripod should be seen, vessels should pass north of the whistling buoy, not in the way a sentence should go. The sandpaper should be folded over wood so as not to spoil the shear studs. The parties should turn to the north during the day, and to the south during the night. Their biceps should finish in line with their ears. Should the switch fail to turn off after a pulse operation the contactor should be a safety device. The indicator should remain on as the forks lower and turn off when the forks are level. The cache should result in uniform execution time. System shutdown applications should pull data from the server. High velocity hoods should be late in the dryer section. A botanist should accompany the contract administrator. Frequency shifter engines should take up the suite of values embodied in the trailing shock. The fruit-bearing shoots should produce more cock-to-cock conflicts, occasionally screams. You should explain to your team how the shoal should behave. They should be covered with veils lest their breath should offend. The red ball should fit the tube closely. Execution of the fake should be sharp and crisp. Paths should be defective in that they lack inherent endpoints. A void field should be disallowed: this method of examination should not be used. The cursor should be positioned in the text editor. The spindle should be lowered by means of the spindle nut, the hold-down clamps should be bowed slightly. The aim should always be to finish the job in one heat. The input LED indicator should be used to check this. The policy community should receive the events data, then the menu should appear: the sheath distal to the injection site should be compressed. The compliance office should not be within the offices of other executives. The clock should be independent of time. A system of corrugated-board standards should encourage optimum allocation of different box contents. If the packing is adequate the carrier should regard it as a burn hazard. You should not copy it or disclose its contents to anyone. Eyes should be bandaged, and the magnetiser taken from the blister pack.

It should fit snugly; integrity should be verified using a hash function. Turquoise stones inside the hole feel dryer than they should. Sleep should be irrelevant, unnecessary, and unsatisfying. The past will not be resisted but should. Shoulder the present, push past the inner monuments. The phrases should be taken into account in their entirety, should hurt, should contain you.

**Space is only the future**, the curtain
drawing, finger on the light. Only in sounds
of winds in the ashes, only if broken and remade
as it rises, for it can surface only
an inch, and then inserts in skulls only the blue
pixels. The oneirocritic has only
eyes for the second hand the only reason to use
a navigator tool is if your bolt unlock button is only
an ignition circuit or the box is only temporary
only remember a small part of the prophecy
it only remains to cite a few symptoms. Retention
of urine which passes only drop by
drop, or mucus only alleviated by clearing the throat
or only thrown out by hawking
grows darker and depends not only on
wavelength, only follows the course of buried cables
only eye shadow with shimmer on the upper lid
now ragged and suffused only by optical modulation
in a domain with noise, the norms are only
dimly relationship-driven only
onyx leather illuminates the side keys only
when it times out the only source of illumination is the keylight

you are only two nouns and a verb from a paradox
only the waters of the river of tears flow quickly
I walk only a few yards out of the city into deep odour mist
the forest assumes grace only when entered by axes
visual stimuli differ with respect only to flicker
gray molecules persist in a primitive state only in rods
I move only by not attending to the medium I pass through
the output is 1 only if both inputs are 0
desire has only one house
any opinions are those of the author only
hear the voice only thoughtlessly
Raven only reverences the ancestral flying fish
they are the ones that only imagined the sea before
only use kill for debugging or to terminate threads
the galls contain only milky liquid; the floury eggs
each contain presentations that differ only slightly
electrons only complicate the clocklike mechanism
a repulsive core only rarely collides with its own wall
subsequent heat treatment only aggravates the trouble
produce space-war sounds with only few elements
if the cat uses one paw only a guest will arrive
there's only in the end the walk to work the need to fulfil this
but I see only chilly mist and withered grass
picture quality isn't the only bright spot
we differ from stones only in having anus and mouth
if you enter steering wheel in the search box it will only know
that each discourse's shape grows only in time
for in this world sleep is your only friend
in the only corner of the courtyard that the sun
catches, only my head, then not that

it's only the night which gets up to leave
give me only that leprous horse in the corner
a lull broken only by the cadences of the priests
the 5am call contains only the echo of your own hellos
those are referred to as voice phenomena
the only strength I have is to tie my beard and hair together
space is fear and love time only a word for what is left
remember there is only loss only not.

**An object known** must be the subject knowing it
must insert what the words missed, must be read by
the light of what we don't know, saw through woods we must
exist or not. We must be equal to draw of breath
a black stone in the forest must be very old
it must be that the time of seeming is coming to its end
an organisation must be concerned with forward flows
we do not say differences must be reduced to likeness
the navigator must make allowance for tidal currents
must design the gate-drive circuit to ensure turn-off
Lancelot must run through crowds, bearing messages
must traverse on bare hands and feet a bridge
the dwarf answers: surely, he must have tumbled in
procedure must be followed in all cluster-formations
hardness must be controlled to avoid hydrogen cracking
you must count up the pieces to see if they are equal to
your age. If they are, you must change your name at once
a wry medicine must be taken
I see a cursor-arrow and death must follow
you must know we are in the Hall of Audience of Hell

says the priestess: one must particularize the rain
must scrupulously delineate what is not there
when a child sees its first swallow of spring, it must spit
where there is a baby in the house, you must sit
variations in attentional glance must not be interpreted
keys in search-trees must come from a domain of total ordering
peers must be reached peers, but reached peers
are not searched peers, the body must set out on the same day
film reels must be synchronized to audio reels and logged
hepatic ducts must be searched by needle-puncture
dry gloves must mate directly to the suit and seal
the discourse must bypass the thing
this must be how it is arranged in the later world
the large boss must be preheated to a good red heat
must listen hard to hear the day through the night
my son, what is promised must be fulfilled
where a contrastive meaning must be excluded
we must run for that tree, it is overleaf.

**Despite the never-ending** widespread news, the poverty and northern closures, despite the rumours, despite the hundred dead off the white coast. Despite the million in hospital, and the one running after them. Despite the telephonic day or night, despite my body flying away, despite the lizards crawling into the altars where the potents are prepared, despite the intrusion of doctors' maids and Egyptologists, despite the old *Spiritus* carried in by art lovers, despite the nest of spider-kneed beggars, it is heard. Despite the producer's reluctance to keep filming, despite the sun just up, despite state-of-the-art spirit roads and a bathyspherical cabin of glass and plastic, despite anxious cries from the eagle, and despite the eagle's rappings on the flanks of the whale. Despite your compound predilection for ignorance, despite the inclusion of prefabricated sentences, despite the struggle with language to raise a head, to find its place either in or out of this world, despite our remote arms seeking this palace of wind, despite the message we cannot suppress, despite the rise in crime, the fall in love, despite the anxious moon blocking our view, despite the rain, the sun.

## Five. Of That Which Exists by a Quality or Choice

Even last Friday's to-do list seems alien. Weakness in the head-joints, even when sitting. Great drowsiness in the evening, even when standing. We can make an aircraft fly by and we can even make it bank. All sounds verberate, even my voice. A metallic cast over the sky and that even with hours to go before twilight. It retains that hew even though paler. The forest is so dense, even the power of creating is denied. I watch the gates lift, and even watching this I am on film. The ducks still appear agitated, even to the celestial ruler. Even Army of the Dead's cooldown resets, though not every group will take dimness of vision, aggravated even to blindness. The kind of rain that even with the wipers going rephrases the modularities of event-life. Even the dolls have peel-off skin. Even this high-level data carries with it wet streets, certain leverages, earth-piercing ripples, air-driven sprayheads. Even at work there is an unsteady chance of change. Even the sound of the alarm is ancient. Often an individual is in more than one database, or even more than once in a single one. Even finite phenomena exhibit infinite complexity. One thing Larkin's characters want even more than happiness: to say anything even to the air. The wild ass and even the still-burning cigarette are still met with on the borders. Even, in the tiny distance, a photograph of you. Even as Hakala in the darkness searches the frozen bodies for documents, he maintains his even temper. Even if nothing is conscious, loss accrues.

Sentences occur which shine as full as mist, part of a system by which ghosts utter never-seen text.

The lapis-lazuli stones which you promised to the Weather-god are brightened by the cold air.

The feature, which is in General Settings, is inclinably mounted on a crankshaft which engages two separately driven caterpillars.

Raven's moustache is a seaweed from which eggs are gathered, to eat of which brings wisdom.

Since languages are media in which we immerse, their meanings are the objects for which metaphor stands.

The mallet is applied, which, on reaching the bone, is turned at right angles, at which time the emanation is transformed.

Fine sediments are typical of maar lakes which over a few hundred centuries grade upward into channel-fill which generates screw dislocations.

Bots hatch as morphologically simple fry, which have the body and head of serpents; discourses are boxes in which to arrange them.

Music is the mechanism which catches the blackbird chanting the psalm which begins: song cannot be heard.

Which are states that have enlarged thought-objects, which are states that are content-rich.

The boss, which is placed in the brick mould to symbolize the sanctity and efficacy of the western fire, masks that which it destroyed.

The sculpted symbol is approached by the spider, which allows it to tunnel open space; in which it suffers still heat and stormy cold.

During the ten creations and destructions which precede the present, spider spins a web which spreads over the river's reach.

Flowers have faces confined in a great lake which belongs to five sisters, which the descendants of Noah carry into the uttermost parts.

The gorgon calls in an airstrike which is performed by systems of the weather-gods, from the day following the day on which those hands pressed the auto horn.

The word means the sore which heals in vain, which means a way, a path, used to refer to the wheeled vehicle of discourse.

Torque wrenches have large teeth which contain two pairs of contra-rotating, profiled tooth-shaft assemblies which accept the ore.

Egg whites, which are composed of soft tissue of waterlike density, are supplied with discharging agents in which children must be bathed.

A manifestation which cannot occur due to brand recognition forms a celestial object with which it has no immediate connection.

I come to that conclusion which the rope speaks which is in the end a vision, to which are attached conditions.

The thing which he carries turns, swirling like a great cloud, of which I am largely unaware. The rope fractures the wires of which it is composed.

I can't remember which house I left my son in, blessed be the paps which he sucked.

A concentric glass cylinder, which revolves by toothed wheels and a hand-worked crank, allows searchability. The eye which turns receives a white light.

Along the way through which the robot traverses are signs which represent ideas in her language. No matter which way she turns the source of the voice eludes her.

We are framed in a narrative poem which repeats "the sun rose" frequently, in a mood which swings between glorious vast periods of time.

The bottom cone drives the take-up shaft, which drives the lay shaft carrying the lay gear along which the quarry road progresses to the present-day exposures.

We obtain a transaction which we must replace with an open world which is still in the making.

That which river rages is people scattering to their workplaces with umbrellas upon which teethed ripples are mounted.

I wish to convey a certain quiet naivety which is like that point at which my throat wakes me, about which it is not necessary to write.

Speech is a lump in the throat which induces hawking, so which direction is the speech.

My current emotional state, which is a blend of anxieties and blunt, beaded lightning with a sodium base, into which the raw elements of life drool corn starch, sucks.

The book describes a history of loss by which we mean pictures of sleeping monitors, by which we mean these pages.

**Language is the ruins of god,** for forgotten things can be remembered in syntax. For Lacan this process is not modelled on transform properties. He monitors the father-in-law for signs of turn completion. For when art chooses god god flies. A new apparatus for the study of trembling plays a role for the application. Down-gaze palsy for all types of eye movements indicates bilateral lesion or video game joysticks. For the direction of this world, five Budhus are appointed. The gardens at Jo-run are full of nightingales crying *Kwan, Kuan* for the early wind.

The fields give space for replies. Factory-install a concave surface for mobile crushing plants. Fault-trace a flow grit chamber for turning the edge of metal by gaged shears for insertion into sheaves. Provide a springboard for product-developing wounds, hair follicles and appendages for redeployment for burns treatment. Maintain constant optimum velocity for effective grit settling and an effluent lagoon for wastewater in duckweed-covered static ponds, aching for the return of lost constellations.

Use coals for eyes. Make snow man; use stones, broom for field of association. Meet flammability standard for sleepwear, for a rich man: more riches, for a sick person: die for a mouthful of dust; change a garret for a grave. For some, pearls bring tears, opals are worst for all. Soft-boned hands are for leaning on. For the protection of men who carry ice, supply waterproof shoulder-pads. Use stick for nose. We walk for several miles. Nothing, a conversation for which content items are conveyed. Choosing properties generates connection pages for the adapter. For a cold backup, remove the side panel, copy.

For ages still might fair Nara flourish, for here love is identical with existence. Carry a stone for fear of snakes. For due comprehension of the passages, ear-tune video channels. Hastily collect what books you need for the evening, connect to keyboard via the snap-on soul form (a standard device for connecting legacy systems). Provide hard and soft platforms for real-time evaluation. Vehicle officials run searches for downed alien aircraft for illuminance levels. Look for Hoteland Conference Centre, where movable accent chairs and side-tables allow for flexible floor plans, featuring zinc-plated shot and nickel-plated heads for corrosion protection, adjustable backstrap grip for close range, target crown and rear slide bevel for increased comfort, with limitless modularity. The optimized frame features palm swells for fit, concealable for everyday carry.

Office worker writes chirpy birthday message in condolence card for grieving colleague. Data on the postings for each index term is unavailable, as is a machine-readable mesh for use by indexers and users. What made April a cruel month for Larkin was a TV attack by Eagleton, long-listed for the Man Booker, who faulted him for his fear of human involvement. The routes for regional pain relief include epidural block and operatory transformations. Embody with an androgynous starched, standaway silhouette for pieces packed with understated allure.

Days are for packing events into for they are symbols of gloom. Play me the dance you made for the barge-master. For me. A gilded cockerel boat for the abbot, a gilded launch for the king's sister. The poem contains ninety-six verses written for eight suited *gangifa* playing cards. The story of the river's search for its lost noise provides a figurative expression for locating stillness. Henry brings suit against the railroad for his injuries. The suit applies pressure to the body, pinch-hitting for the air pressure necessary to prevent rupture.

**I read the wrong books,** only chose what would make
no sense. I assumed wrong when I assumed
nothing. Objects were infinite; the varieties of wrong were
not. The child felt it had done wring or wrong. My cash
songster said: I'll prove that might is right is wrong.
The doctrine that the time was wrong was
directionless. We left Henley and took a wrong turn.
What did not go wrong stayed still. A song
fell into my mouth the words came out wrong
arriving at the wrong house and finding it open
the animals had the wrong sequence of features: who
would correct a song or find in flight something wrong?
I taught the children all of the ways to do this wrong
by placing the ceremonial things in the wrong god-house
to find white fowls, with the feathers growing the wrong
way the wrong explanation fit she wore
the wrong head but the right face. The last remark
probably referred to the wrong Song Dynasty.
We were wrong to expect we could dial M for mother.

The roulette wheel spun to the wrong number.
There was noon in here. One had done me wrong.

**We published your dreams** in the form of daylight: we didn't quite get the details right. I was sitting urinating at 1 am and couldn't quite penetrate what this meant. The character writing this was not quite me. A quite fragile network of airline movements, logistics chains, channel frequencies, quantum accretion and crank sequences held the stone quite horizontal. It is quite possible that a lecture about him was relayed by various radio stations. He looked in a complaining sort of way at the noose, as not quite certain that it had designs upon him. He was dead, but not quite stiff. He was pleased, highly chuffed, quite pleased, chuffed, pleased, dis-chuffed, disenchanted, quite filled up within, as a full barrel, or river. Quiet. The word was so nearly personal that the possessive was quite admissible. The threshold voltages of the erased cells was quite large. The violence of this quite blinded Leo's second eye. I could no longer quite grasp why there was disorder within the group but once the crowd dispersed I was quite regretful to see it depart, although I waited quite a long time and slowly realised she was going to leave me here all day. Two Australian women quite liked me and I explained to them my collection of masks, all of which were just quite subtle carnations of what I looked like, yet even so the character writing this up was not quite me, and writing this now I cannot capture what was quite so exciting. There was a fire that and not quite accidentally I was the cause of, and this made her face look quite different, structurally, and was quite exciting. We devoted lives to making runways on which we never quite ascended. The crab had some flashes of brilliance, but it was quite a long way from intelligent. Disturbed by some quiescent energy not quite visible on the walls around me I knew I had to spend most of the day inside, not quite contemplating work but aware that at some stage one had to make preparations, and in all this I was not quite me, I was on the point of being a different person, the keyboard interface quite overshadowing my face. The football ball was thudding regularly, not quite regularly, against a wall. Covering it with kitchen foil could have quite a rich effect. Lexical deviation was quite common. We found quite suddenly the road dead with souls. Quite so. Quite right. Quite quite.

**Why is there a rush** the children don't understand why we have weeks that is why my mouth bleeds words in the form of the start that runs through a Naugahyde chair. *Why yes*, she said (in the dream to His Majesty): Why did you not give the instruments. Dear Papa: Why should tame folks wish to be wild, why do you lead me back to carnal life. Why are hands and feet cold during fright. Why Pope's name is distinguished in literature. Why can't something be both. Why is summer foreign. Why had she brought me to her mother's home. There are two reasons why a recording device is employed. Why I love this set of handpicked nail polishes. Why does my son only communicate with me by text. Why flare your nostrils why all my spreadsheets have stains. Wake in the light unsure why the alarm had not gone off. A voice says: *Why don't you open the door.*

**Discourse tends to consist of** a because therefore structure, rather than a therefore because structure. Global regulation furthers the interests of capital rather than continuing from three trains, on a railway. For this we need to resort to the behaviour of material as continuous rather than discrete particles, giving it a rather appropriate light rise. It extinguishes harmony, rather than noise, to constitute the spirits' song rather than if, for example, your queen has rather poor eye colour for her breed. It suits rather the raven to contain the personality of that animal. This slight feeling that people at work would rather I did not exist, the pedestrians who choose to be maimed rather than halt. The image of the record, rather than the actual paper, is required. In the distance the poppies seem insufficiently real or rather too unreal, because we are now in the position of real-time content; a look-aside, rather than a look-through, *cache* controller. I think rather of those show homes on desirable new estates, which introduce a range of rather esoteric super-premium bottlings rather than the Gold and the 18 Year Old, but I would rather be on intimate terms. I arrive sooner than perhaps later rather than thinking the fire can be slept in, working rather at the moment on the more distanced projects (see the adverts and trailers as childhood and youth then the film, which is one you are rather not interested in). The agar produces a discrete nodule, the size of bird shot, with a rather large faint areola leaving a small scar. Absence of pain rather striking. Sequences can be edited in shooting order rather than show order. In Xu's version, the word *chilly* is applied to modify *horns*, endowed with sadness rather than coldness. The sequence lipstick effect refers to the tendency for consumers rather than large buyers to refer to liquidity. It is rather a distinction between two ways in which the same thing is regarded—between considering it as it stands, namely, boxy rather than high-pitched, while the breath sounds weak.

KNOWING AS WELL AS merely believing a proposition
as well as the *nebulae* described in my letter is
certainly well outside the negotiations of evening, but
sleep well. Do not tell me the heavens
as well are a wheel. Talk to people much as to toys.

Feel shame's foundation rub on the chief's wife as well
as to and between the dead, who have well
guessed they got it wrong. Tell light to eat well.
Popper explains it well as the searchlight theory of theories
as well as ability to solve nonroutine problems
represented by *ensemble* average as well as the Web.
It would be well to leave your clothes there,
in the city in the well of the head letting
all the Wood, Brass, and String as well as percussion
play as well as possible, change our past in the room—I
well recall standing by the harbour when I first visited
Orford in 72, flesh and engine configured in respective as well
as integrative performance and the well loss unit was feet.
Select perfect peaches and wash well, place them
well in the relaxed metal-removing processes. Say
we are both well, the world and I. It is not
heavy, breaks down with no tools, and carries well.

**Chapter One. How** the moon fell into a powerful sleep. How Finn went to the Kingdom of the Big Men. How King Wu overthrew them with fiery *yang* arrows and called the two boys to him and said, *How is it you call me father?* How the bugs were invited by the monkeys to be there. How accomplishing the showman's plans helped me become a bright light. How my mind got my finger to squeeze the trigger. How fiercely we drove, after our deaths. How in answer to the question how many spirits are present, the table tilted twelve times. Illustrate how the meaning of this term evolved and show how it is appropriate to this poem; how silence should be observed, and solitude sought; how cleansings should be by water or earth, how evacuations should be effected. How the sipping and spitting of water is performed. How figures are structured in the eye. How flattened and stretched I look, how hard it is to realise how held the light is by the sun. How the sun feels in the arctic of explanation, how to make this sayable, how the light changes us, how hard it is to travel through the thick, the moment. Only at 4.40am does it hit me how hollow my current situation is. How many of the dead follow me through media. How many miles am I from here. How many whispers make a shout. How many Newtons in a Milton. How many maps make a tree. How past sleeps us. How would you rate your experience, ask later how ash feels in the finger, how this is flow. Tap the storage icon on the settings-screen to see how much space-string can be configured. Management needs a clear sense of how the board wants management to proceed. How to gracefully accept feedback. How excellent are the sayings of the poet! How r u? How was ur day?

THIS SECTION DOES NOT SEEM to relate to glass in any way. Look out of any window. Do you have any wasp in your neighbourhood of the strength of *Pepsis*? Any instance needs visual bounds, based on icon, transforms, and the impact of any overlays at the page top, in advance of any input-operation. Things happen in any order at any time. Check the system logs when any or all switches are closed. At that point, any progeny viruses will migrate to the network-services. The pilot-lamp lights when any answering supervisory lamp lights: this prevents any cardinals larger than any given large cardinal at any downstream location. Seven points of light are absent from any known sky. If any readers can make any sense of the enclosed note, we would appreciate it. In this respect it is like any ceremony connected with water. Turn clockwise and watch the reflection of any light on the bit as an eel, stone in the river, or any viscous asymmetry. Break open the door of any room in such a dwelling and suspend the spherical crystal along any two diameters. Air-stones are available in any store that has aquarium equipment. Sleep does not afford any rest, accompanied by itching eruptions, without any redness. Think of any card in the deck, and direct any loose hairs onto the curler. Any bag containing a non-transparent item swollen with blood is susceptible to sea nymphs. These are great grabs for any death-knight; as far as the voice reaches. A silence is not indicated by any motion, less is indicated by a motion, more is not indicated. If any orb, sun or planet increases in weight, if the ninth of any month fall on Friday, identity in bodily resurrection must, in any event, snap. Stop making any sound in any graveyard or any room where a body is, and avoid the touch of a person who touched any of these. Nothing in all this reveals to you any internal disorder, but they do not any longer conceal that when the child vents anger upon any object it is because matter, in contrast to birth, lacks any urgency. The dry unconnecting brother, who Z says sheds any element of the maternal, will be reset. Any dead people will resurrect, but the game can be stopped at any time, so as to remove from it any wrinkles or folds. Drain the bed to draw off any postoperative leakage. Avoid shadows in order to mitigate any odour. Lock onto any subject. In any of them we look for the defining act, or objects have an air of a decision that can be made any time. As most diamonds were small enough to be concealed in any orifice, this chain behaves like any other. Any storage unit is a negative feedback stabilized integrator of flows. There was not any coding drift during the years of fieldwork. Object philosophy questions the utility of any model beyond its immediate company. Any questions?

**Misturn contains** both mist and urn. We see both the sleeping form and what it dreams.

Head-ends serve for both reading and writing. A good metaphor breathes in both terms.

Soreness of roots of upper and lower teeth, violent humming in both ears: contents of head seem to issue through both occiput and forehead.

Dr Sleeping with right hand mostly but sometimes both together, makes stutter stop, which turns off both the shock and the shock-signal.

In swinging both hands in an arc spirit is both image and goal. Hold with both hands the wind-wheel and the water-wheel.

Both cockle and curl are due to unequal tension. The scarf or overlapping sutures withstand both wood and stone.

I endeavour to draw up his left arm, but both arms and both legs rise. Fields need to be separated by spaces, punctuation or both.

The selfish fool and the sullen fool are both froth. So saying, with both hands she wipes the wrist clean of *ichōr*.

The claused shell casing traversed both hemispheres. Brain matter protrudes from both wounds.

Both badger tracks embody deviation, of which both translators have different understandings.

Translators should convey both surface and deep meaning and employ foregrounding theory both theoretically and practically.

Literary studies and poetry are both products of broad shifts in economics. Tactful use of lighting addresses both aesthetic and functional aspects.

Sediment concentrations for both clear and foul outlets present both wretched and narrow views.

They both enter the same name and password. In the

evening, they experience twitchings in both of the lower extremities.

They are both estranged and thrown together. Their expedition inland sees them beset by expansionist native creatures, both created and natural.

Both parties assess ongoing conversation to make face adjustments, both activating and repressing.

We compare both coherent feedforward and interaction inputs. Results will be found both in the result region and the region region.

Where there are drawable areas in both region 1 and region 2 , results will be left both in the result region or the region region.

Exist through both gates. Both are locked.

**Each sentence ends** badly. Each breath slices death. Each individual day is not how days are. Each hour testament strikes the malleable clouds. Each day staff members log in with Healthy or Sick; in each map there is a hole through which they may tumble by looking, and each morning something small has been taken from them. Each of the respondents is handed three innovation cards. Each player tries to capture an heiress. These entitle them to a bonus from each of the other players. In each bottle a new state. In each instance, the webcam and shutter-glasses display different images to each eye. Each interruption is registered as an event. Each morning I look out for Wittenham Clumps. Each second counts, each leaf enacts the fall. Each time I take an apple as I run past. Each night the house turns into a Baltic lighthouse, where spray-clouds chase each other. Preselect the colours to appear in each window. Each smolt has numerous successful movements. As they become tight, they find they can finish each other's poems. Each incident scores upon the consciousness. The sounds gradually increase until there are crowds on each side of the retaining planks, each detachable face-frame getting stiffer and stuck deeper, as if each witness stands alone. In each joint a set of eggs is formed, and each is terminated by a double claw. As the crankshaft rotates, each arm oscillates laterally as each scarf is printed with hundreds of joints, each crowded with eggs, each with a crooked hatch known as a stave. Each day your history is wiped. Each child indicates threats-per-second. The pointed crest of each is iron-red, dotted with gold, outdoing each other with clashing trees of each creation. My rotation by half a turn is a symmetry for each of these views. Each circle is faster and also less noticeable. Finish each sentence with suitable feelings. I drill a small hole in each side of the box for the arms and two in the bottom. A succession of feeble stimuli each reinforce the other, each increases the effect of the preceding as the control card copies each instruction to local memory. Each application (more properly service user) has two queues, one for each direction. Each consists of the torso, gloves, boots, helmet, and undergarment. Turn each comma into a line break and then alphabetise each paragraph: each column-inch *yang* and *yin* trigrams displace each other. Type a field name in each cell, each in turn stops at the order column of each field to be punched by skip stops. Each piece straddles casual and sophisticated. When the men approach each tree they throw pieces of stick at it. Each room in the pyramid hums a sealed tune. Each song-wild lark's flight finds heaven. In her last poem each noun is death. Each verb is be. Each water drop shows the sun his face. Chimneys line the hill, each surrounded by piles of bones. Disambiguation-protocols are for each possible realization. Each day is closer to the next. Eat each peach. Eat the rich the *Reich* the reach. Each day's beach recedes, reseeds.

If the event has a terminus, it also has a path, either implicit or overt. The Northern *Song* Dynasty can either move ahead, or decline. Your spouses have either left you or refuse to understand. You die either without knowledge, or your lifetime's experience proves useless. Monad or Nomad? Either state binds us in the unperceived figure. Slurry sieves are either froth-pumps or pre-preg. Experience either a difficult lawsuit or a dangerous disease. The white ball may be dropped by either hand. My train goes through a narrow corridor with bare rock on either side, then into a row of either office cubicles or changing booths. I keep thinking S is lost, but he is either slightly ahead or slightly behind. I am either a serial murderer or sharing a house with one. We have either foot on the ground, are trending either up or down, from month to month or hand to mouth. My out-breathings form clouds of either water or fire. To discard either the 4 or 6 of hearts renders the other worthless. If the client requests it angle the spindles either out or in. Either run the words together or separate with underscores. Either change the current directory to the directory containing the file, or convert either platform to ethernet. You can either draw the table with Draw Table, or insert a table using the table. Either open your primary file or create one by opening a new file and saving it under the same name. Watch a 1930s spectacular, either Nazi or Soviet or Busby Berkeley, either in a light-dark rhythm or under continuous light. There is scarcely a difference either in plane or scale between them. Figure 1 shows a water stand probe holder designed to read either side of a Bendix coupling pump-screen with six channels. It may be corrected by either reducing the overall lens size or numbering the junction point in a program flow, either by means of signals or by physical transportation. Rotate either the hexagonal pattern or the alignment key until an axis of symmetry is reached. Use fuzzy rules without changing either the rule syntax or inference engines. Crystal Reports is unusual in that you can write either of two syntaxes: either a fixed percentage or the minimum guaranteed amount. It cannot be asked too often: Is either subject-matter or form the chief interest in your work? Either the property C, or the property D, is present; but they are not jointly present. Either of these fails from the standpoint of hostile intelligence.

PARTICIPANTS WATCHED THE VIDEO and imagined themselves in such a scenario. *Ikarus* was the source for inventions such as interpolation, auto-tracing, auto-kerning. All such were terminated by selfhood. Such a broad pulse-width exceeded bodily self, and the word self precluded such frameworks as subjectivity. As they predicted nothing, such dreams did not require an interpreter. Wire ropes fractured in detail at the fastening, and such tendency was not lessened as size increased. Such a rare form of traveling wave was the *K-complex* of sleep. A collection of unique simile bodies (such as ground shaking, ~ sound, downslope creep) was broadened to include such discourse as metaphors, such that the object referred to was the subject referring to it. The loss of one attribute, such as a limb, generated a tamper response such as a self-healing programme. She was such a dreadful serpent that horror and fear seized the ship. The engine's relevance construct evaluated operational measures such as sweep rate. Such moments produced vibrations. Another proverb exhibited such connections as It'll be a good one when it lights, improved by the use of associated characters such that a file name similar to the primary file, such as *Training_letter_primary.doc*. Bishop's suit wasn't designed to take such punishing heat for more than a few seconds. 200 of such dollars I purchased for ten cents. The resulting corpus included exchanges between dyads such as professors and students, employers and employees. On-task interactions, such as those taking place in the classroom, were excluded with variables such as hedges and intensifiers held constant.

They fled into such arcane figures as *Styx*. As such, every reading of every discourse may be minimized by judicious use of structured objects such as arrays and records. The goal of the proof is to prove the existence of a configuration c of S such that the behaviour of S provides the framework for the design and study of such.

## Six. Of That Which Exists by Addition Or by Consequence

THE CAMERA HOLDS the image for a full six seconds
using the serial port connected to a second computer.
In the second exercise, keep your knees stiff,
moderate earth noises are heard 30 seconds before shock
the second version narrows the imagination: who the caller
is still puzzles her when the phone rings a second time
at noon on the second day the whale submerges
as the experimenter talks about the second I, a voice interjects
the leaning of the second half of the sentence is not clear.
The second sentence expresses another voice-entity's
disquiet. The first concerns Dr Raudive; the second
the phenomenon itself, the blown petals that for a second
kept the shape of the tree.

APES AND ANGELS and archangels and gods and Isis and Osiris and dogs and cats and mice and man and beast and worm and foul and fair and square and cube-root and branch and line and plane and simple and compound and adjective and adverb and phrase and fable and able and will and representation and diversity and inclusion and just and ice and easy and hard place and rock and roll and butter and jam and tomorrow and tomorrow and today and always and forever in the here and now and day and ageing and loss and gain and again and now and then and in time and tide and sea and sun seen and approved and moon and stars and stripes and checks and balances and object and subject and verb and agree and disagree and collide and collapse and accident and emergency and merge and edit and rub to and fro and shampoo and conditioner and styling system and research and develop fiberoptic front and rear sights and expose and shame and pity and pretty and *chic* and duck and drake and josh and joke and jerk and hand and fist and palm and arm and leg and foot and length and breadth and butter and tea and Q & A & E and I and you and me and her and him and ancient and modern and night and fog and mind and spirit and blood and bone and joint and several liability and contents and preface and front-matter and back and forth and third and last and final offer and accept and bow and arrow and target language and source and stringing and drooling of melt and quench and pour and serve and weak and sensible to cold and rain and shine and smile and laugh and cry-emoji and logo and logos and word and deed and dead and buried and born again and again and ever and anon and drag and drop and click and collect and the ring and the book and the brotherhood and the hinges and brackets and the door and portals and the stair and the wide and long white and blue and black and red wires and wireless and home and hearth and earth and heaven and hell and high water and open and closed and cramps and coldness of limbs and dissociation and incoherence of expression and impression and weld spatter and thermal distortion of aggregate sludge-pumping station and final settling tank and metaphor and metonymy and the dancer and the dance and the dreamer and the dream and horse and rider and park and ride and up and moving and power and fury and ants and aphids and elders and betters and aiders and abettors and abattoirs and meat and potato and weed smoke and coffee breath and Lords spiritual and temporal and dungeons and dragons and belt and braces and relaxes and a clear vision and an oak and an olive and need and desire and postage and packing and track and trace and dogs and cats and a pause and a breath and quick and easy opening and closing meat and veg and salt and pepper and heaven and earth and keyboard and printer and creating and selling at kiosk and exhibitionstand and product and process and terms and conditions bring and buy space and time and motion and audio and video and integrated voice and data and ATMs and profit and loss and administrators and agents and accountants and advisors and appraisers and appraisees and assistants and associates and acquaintances and attachés and actuaries and advisers and advocates and auditors and agonists and antagonists and addicts and alcoholics on antidepressants and anticonvulsants and the skirt and belt of Sun, Moon, Stars, and Celestial Dragon and heroes and antiheroines thalamic and hypothalamic a tooth for a tooth and a nod for a wink at slow speed and high torque headache and burning that waxes and wanes at dawn and dusk by night and day high and dry or nice and easy for friends and neighbours associates and adherents authors and artists adolescents and adults far and away in forests and lakes in sun and moon with spider and web for ages and ages by addition and edition by accumulation and agglomeration and clause creation and destruction definition and metadata by trial and error through arteries and arterioles over land and sea present and correct acronyms and abbreviations flushright and flushleft an officer and gentleman in sackcloth and ashes over and above and out and about in shock and awe and drum and bass warts and all hand and foot with ifs and buts in a time and a place in this day and age drive a horse and carriage with a heart and a half through attitudes and assumptions assonance and consonance of allusions and associations far and away every now and again for forever and a year through green hell and thicket and high water via *adagios* and *archipelagos* aldehydes and alcohols antigens and antibodies antiquarks and antileptons apples and apricots agents and friends and enemies wheels and axles exes and adzes and axes the allies and the axis bus and connector and all that jazz and a wing and a prayer with an O and a hay hoe nonny and uncle Tom Cobley and all all.

**With certain worms** there begin the first head-brains with an odd flutter of tongue white fields seed with white words with suggestive plosives, the first colour to begin the face with is the red of cheeks with pineapple cubes with ring-pulls and ring-pull catches with distant hills with congregations of the dead hunting with 3,000 dogs moving in a deliberate manner with tails cocked their eyes sparking with the love they hunt with.

Ants surround the dead bumblebee with petals with decorative side-pillars and a moulded plinth-top with a one-piece folding base and four heavy-duty castors upholstered with fabric and trim from old-world weavers, a straight grip with a Schnabel-style forearm to attack the capital with a massive Cabernet and with short-fused beehive shells the Void punches the beach with heavy blows beginning the sentence with the adverb creates a sense consistent with fascination with the women's arms downed with light brown hair.

On their return with the hostages they are greeted with the Indians blowing feathers in the air they then kiss their withered feet with the declension of death with speech symbols and extended tongue with a white cross tightened with holy wool the respirator with a tight-sitting facepiece coincides with opening a fridge door.

The poem fills with words and sinks to ding the swingbinlid with a tomato tin with bent legs paw the ground with fiery eyes with good complexion with a hard-cased body with multiplayer skins with side-to-side head-bobbing and neck-stretching with blue beards streaming with large thin pods drooping through green leaves loaded with loose bars a measured *chock-chock* variegated with orange and margined with black with offices in France and Luxembourg reveries in sleep with anxious dreams and fantasies of efforts to urinate with a copious discharge with a red gravelly sediment boiling over with a black froth.

"The Sisters" opens *Dubliners* with a dilapidated house with a new satellite dish mated to an integral bedding-block with a single tool that rehabilitates worn jaw-crusher liners with welding rods interfaced via pin-connectors with an attached chain of inverted lotuses with one central petal with a beaded lip and scalloped border richly emblazoned with heraldic bearings with straight combed-back hair cinched at the waist with a stone belt.

The ladder of myth begins with the symbol of the centaur and birds of heaven with triple-banked teeth clothed with long hair with a hard-holding styling gel with the trident of Siva her head hung with snakes with dense clouds of steam with critical strike rating with conformity with the principles underlying men and things with clove-filled lip enhancers in pink and mauve slicked with oil and pepper to conceal a compact grip with fingertip operation with pre-drilled mounting plates with adjustable eye-to-scope alignment etched with a Maori warrior motif with an internal guide-rod assembly with the object of committing an outrage.

The exclusive abstract camo pattern with warm tones of sand and dry grass soiled with septic wounds due to a bullet traversing the frontal region obliterating the eye and mid-face sprinkling the torso harness with holy water with minimum wearing parts the anti-theft windows resplendent with moonlight with family letters and journals braided into the narrative or retouching with a fine paintbrush a song filled with new words a cup filled with old wine drawn tight with an icing bag fitted with lung tissue with tooth-shaft assemblies in the dark with inadequate lights covered with creamy fur attached to the trunk with free running cable that concludes with the opening air of wistfulness where the earth is gilded with yellow violet.

The day is bright with love and riches for the unconcerned a boxy shirt with hints of iridescence finished with diamond grinding wheels lined with moist thick clay with belching comparing the observed with the expected frequencies with sporadic gleams of slow-conquering sun with each lateral traverse of the cam carriage a child with a beginning letter stands wearing a familiar ending pattern to make a black-painted house door littered with place names derived from indigenous peoples with grubs emerging as the box installs flush with drywall with two sets of figures.

The sun is a massive peach which the government feeds with the hearts of citizens whose light still smashes through the window with atomic force with a handle to the moon armed with alpine stocks with ham sandwiches and seltzer wasser but the read operation conflicts with the write operation for that chain of causal phenomena terminates with death.

**It is the opening episode** of some expensive crime series, events take place that seem unrelated. A fetish, a decayed splint hat, an old broom or some vast salvage equipment appear.

Some plates increase in curvature during ontogeny. Along valley axes, some profiles display overthickened A horizons, with some interfingering.

Profuse bleeding at the nose causes loss of the capacity of pronouncing some alphabets. Some then discover wells by dreams.

Some confessions: I urinated into the change-dispensing slot at Docklands Light Railway, c. 1993. I climbed the stairs towards some receding love, I presented my closed or extended hand.

The laughter lasts some hours, and after that the patient is delirious. Some thoughts come out like song.

By white offspring some understand the white clouds attending the dawn: some see red-blue glows, water-clear. Fertilising rain enables men to offer some love-odes.

A poem is an island of light in some forest, made with lamps, in which moths of thought are caught. Some are classified as non-thoughts.

The explorer emerges in some site of pilgrimage: she reaches the top easily and kneels. She rearranges some shells on the grave.

There are fowls with black flesh, some with black bones, and some with black flesh and black bones. The broken machines whirr with some new dislocation.

Linear systems feature some form of edit-display based on the time codes of the edit points. Some have additional effects, such as poems spontaneously corrupting.

Sales management leads Sword to traverse some familiar ground. He makes bows, carrying some in his hand and some in his quiver, and opens a cache. He puts some thought into it.

Some dishes, such as the seafood symphony, bring the *chef* from the kitchen to layer assorted shellfish. Some of the company become excited, leaning forward.

You notice some letter-boxing when the full-screen assets are shown. Segments are controlled independently, allowing some parts of the screen to darken while others stay bright.

Loud as hell, I want some milk and cookies. The act of requesting causes some burden on the hearer.

Some autobiographical gestures remain oblique. Some plot point sticks in the mind of a child.

Some events later, pour some of the milk into a fiery oven. Some separation may occur.

Some of the projectiles are boxed with the casings. If the coverplate screw is painted, chip some paint from its head.

The transcendental beings require some form of energy to produce these effects, yanking you suddenly in some unexpected direction.

Some of the voices make announcements and comments in the way radio-transmitting stations do. Some of the poems have shadow poems.

**Work grinds but also polishes.** Painful cramp in the left anomaly, also when boring with the finger in the ear. In previous ages souls also adhered to other animals, and also bathed in the hearts of the deceased. They change their position frequently, especially when sitting, also when in bed. Also use margin-bottom, margin-left, margin-right, to change margins. The spirit-ancestor also called Mountain Luck Lad is also the father I wished for. At one particular point a certain rhythm and also a voice is audible, which also amplifies the interference-noises. He also infuses old books or analog devices, also tastes sweetish or bloody. A river flows and also a river's name flows, and smooth also is the muscle-phantom. *Horus* son of *Hermes*, and *Caleoibis* son of *Apollo* and also fund managers expand into new territories as also the journey of life-in-death which also suggests the hue of ripened rice ears. *Windswept willow catkins* is a rough description of the breeze by concrete unit to emphasize it is also a lexical deviation. Intense reflection prevails in the spiral garden but also in the window and its angled swings. Metaphorical statements that are also teleological include the wind searched out the cracks in the cabin wall. I also make a series of boxlike wood constructions resembling coffins. In my small way, says the fly, I also no longer remain. Each keychain has a powder-coated sling-hook, and its heft also makes it suitable for self-defence. It is also a device for scribing titanium. Death also puts in its appearance; in time the tomb also rots, although the end-teeth of a handsaw will also do a good job. East or north-east winds bring frost and also drought. The look on your face is also to look from your face.

**Evening all.** The keys to all knowledge are contained in the Dot, the Line, and the Circle. One produces a second, two produces a third, three produces all things. All three signal darkness, the self and the other. The unconscious builds from all discarded words. A girl is born with all her ova, the seeds of their ends. All sense starts as wounds, all trees extrude fingers, all seeds are teeth. Silence is the message we fear most of all. All states and tastes reside within it, exceed emission from all other circuits, but we are all script, the apparatus squashes us into foam, loam, ball, all of which is controlled using a smartphone. All along all I need to do is sleep but the rain exposes all exceptions, all of the lost names, all are bound into each other. All of these wooden shower-hutches have doors and they all open at once, revealing my collection of masks, all of which are versions of what I look like. The self appears in all theories of the personality. All the possible switch-combinations are shown: clouds, rivers, the wind, televisions, rocks rolling downhill, power stations, industrial areas, and, most of all, houses and office blocks. These have all been judged alive, and all pass swiftly. The dead-colouring of a face is to be done the roughest of all; edges easily fall and spill and the fire burns all night. All thought is operated through a hidden window, and all the thought-patterns flatline when permeated with dry fallout. The barrels are constructed of aerospace grade stainless and oversized in all dimensions. All include time-dummies and a quadratic, because all control-flow is determined by hard-coded values. All start with an attractive profile that draws the victim into a potential relationship. All active listings are taken down. These are annals from which our data are all derived, all the activities required to move a product from point of use to disposition. Calling on your gallery files and all your skills, you fuel the halls and chambers with beauty of all description. You sweep onto a balcony and see Bali in all its thralling panoply. Your thoracic wall widens, all thrilling with sensation. All the laws that bind you are composed of all events for which the interval between you and its origin is the class consisting of Socrates, Plato, and all other *maîtres à penser*, but all biographies end sadly, all that blisters is not god, is flesh, is glass. The books are all large and leather-bound. They contain 643 individual *tanka*, all dated, and all accounts-payable invoices. Incense sticks, spirit money and bamboo roots are distributed among all present. All that now remains for the medium to do is to hold the two slates under the table on the medium's right, and, by scratching with the fingernail after the manner of hatching, to pronounce all dead. All this is before you, all that lay behind you; and, as for the present, all other states relate to the worlds of sense. All are marching toward the dead. All languages spoken here. All is incline. Venice collapses all along the Istrian coast. A metallic noise sweeps away all before the eye. All ports are aspirated to remove any air and to ensure that blood is easily drawn, and then the sea and its galleries all became silent, all the while threatening to tell Mother by right as Commander-in-Chief of all the Emperor's armies. He follows their sheep-bells all through the night. A drink, then, to all the unknown of history! All answers return us to a core of void, end all sessions by right-clicking the Current Connections container and selecting Terminate All. A mysterious energy pulse destroys all technology. All the events spread out in space-time are "fixed" all at once, so that the principle of energy actually applies to all reciprocal actions. Disperse the material elements and all emanate into secret places of ice. Then the sword will traverse the world, laying low all things. To all of you, named and unnamed, I give my thanks.

**5.25AM.** Again I do not sleep. I shove off the canoe. Bear comes again and tells Badger to go out to hunt. Badger, worn out with fatigue, goes again to hunt buffalo. The arranging hands of men, the dulled ego, caught, lost, caught again. A few minutes of quiet, a woman sings a crying song.

6.05am. I again dream of the pony. Refastening it, the rope is again tensioned. Through this world I am traversing again another wind blows. The translation "the songstresses sing the song composed in vain by a captive king" has again not retained the foregrounding language.

7am. Again it is the working week, and it is not long before the clock again weeps and I listen: wheels are once again set in motion. Again, the experience of typing with a damaged hand. I have caused concern to His Majesty, and will not enjoy the company of my sister again.

8.12am. Pain again in left occiput; axons having negotiated the ventral midline turn again toward the brain. A convulsive laugh for ten minutes, then again weeping; then in alternation. The pain comes on again during breakfast, also stitching, then again gouty tearing which forces me to take to bed. And once again they're undimensioned shapes from which again the waters of the sea retire for a time, and again return and produce inundations.

9.03am. Drag again to erase a little more. To turn ortho on, press F8 again. A color stop, and then click again. The control unit assumes again the main spindle speed. I again address you, and would hesitate, but for my body never to rise or spirit fall again. I will travel again; I must go on.

10.15am. Try again. Try soft mauves, light onion pinks, light aqua, over and over. Late breakfast. In another half-hour downstream I come to el'Anab, where again there is an enclosure of grassy heaps strewn with stones and ask again: *Shall I stand here?* The sun again pulls the canoe.

1.12pm. It's in my mind again to steal. I stopped stealing for a month and then it came right back in my mind again. Pictures come right in my mind and I steal again.

2pm. We are parked again by the beauty parlour. Z has gone into the shop. S says he once pooed there. We can see the top of the receptionist's head, we see him go into the parlour and ask to use it again, the woman's head rises.

3.42pm. When Europe comes round again, it will be a cloudshape from which to keep flying out and back again. Should we meet in the other world, the roller should be revolved backward.

6.25pm. Again take the ball from the cup and hold it, mouth upwards, in your right; then, slowly and deliberately invert it again as you place it mouth downwards upon the extended palm of your left. Cover with a sheet and turn over again, leaving the cake right side up.

7.10pm. Retire again to the sea, and pass the night in the deep. The striplights come on again until evening, and in the night I am happy, because of the avatar masks they bring back again.

9pm. We relax in the bar and become again like the people we were made from and look again through the hole we smote into that empty air. Only then do all know that King

Wu will not again make use of his army.

By and by the house shakes again, and the ground with it. The people in the house again hang their heads, and, looking back, these same shoals coagulate again as if no more than a breeze had passed.

**The head is broken** in many species, the dogs make many different responses. This is the language that many animals run on. Many machines (inscribed with peace in many languages) fly their words to us on multi-lane motorways and then single-lane bicycle bridges deserving of many adjectives. This year started many years before in the appearances of light, and as a result, the complaint-line of the stucco manor with its many rooms, of which many doors are open and all lead to dark passages, hardwood floors, mahogany map cabinets, shelves with many poems, many with short preceding prose commentaries, has logged so many mass-marketing fraud complaints that many of the staff resign. An anecdote starts under the breath that ends up in many life stories, but there are so many sentences to revoke before getting to the core. We should not keep the worlds as rigidly apart as many imagine may be necessary. Many of the calibres have various bullet configurations for concealed carry, and many other applications. Many people wear my clothes, have come years later from some sports event involving collaboration between many life forces. Fill the screen with as many transactions as will fit into a sea of many fingernails, playing. In many cases magnetic dampening occurs. He rebuilds a failing mental institution that integrates nostalgia, grief and many other delicate feelings, but trouble enters on many levels as he tries to help a beautiful young epileptic. Searches of the error boxes identify many likely candidates, which suggests many of the unidentified sources are pulsars. It is fitted with many extras: twin fog lamps, wood-rim steering wheel, modified gear manifold. I am bleeding from many hands the poor dead stones stated, the many children move like fear in the spine, in many iterations, both now and as the family grows, but many things happen to the body, its manifestation as us, as anyone who will fit. We are many, we investigate the settlement of structures in the palace of many windows that stood for years without movement. The slopes see many dead enemies added to the soil and there are so many emails to delete, many mansions, many words.

**Hence a confused or disordered** state of the departed, hence an ambitious new discourse. Hence man has no sense of them, nor are they under the disposal of the will. Hence affinity of film to dream, hence, set up, erect, as a post. Hence, decisions turn out to be suboptimal, hence the target is damaged or the degree of damage is increased. The faint firedamp leads days hence to *Herren-Moral*, the fiercest, and hence king, of all the spiders in this country. Hence, draw or suck up or away the liquid from among the solid food in a plate. Its colour is dark red, hence its association with Grandfather Fire who corresponds with time; hence conditions you with firmness and hence return home, hence put back in a disfigured or nonfigurative order. Projection-lines diverge, and hence cannot intersect. Hence, they pool their resources and resolve to work with fresh meanings, hence the mechanisms that enable henchmen to impose their world as universal, and hence legitimate. Many years hence we could open these letters and decide, but for now we might be perceived by members, and hence members' responses are poorly correlated, hence no need to reframe in language the various and intricate sublimations of civilization, hence this woman running towards me in the park. Hence it seems like a mistake which we have tried to explain. Hence sending spores through the smallest apertures, hence thriving on the corpse of monumental languages. Hence the crank-pin will revolve, or the traveller will decrease and hence if one chooses a large flange number, the length of the traveller will be more, hence the name, which means *Glue place*. Hence, the faint odour of choice trajectory of tragedy.

I often write about what I do and it loops like words often appearing at rhythmical intervals. I'm naive with my actions and that often entails life-world practices forming what often become theories. The hills rise into a place I often dream, urnfield in mist, a picture photocopied too often. I half open my eyes and more often than not elicit the sublime from the mundane. I do the work, often quite well, but know that part of me is beyond it. Often during these reminiscences my eye dims. I often ask the same question I asked before and I often ask where am I going and I am often walked past by all kinds of people. Singular calls often occur during lunging dives or bouts of surface behaviour, and often recall to mind a flashing brightness. My old apple now makes an ominous hum, and often will not start up. Dropping asleep I often hear the grass in the orchard. I often think of death but cannot think the thought to the end: it would be thoughtless. Photos are often spoiled by people blinking or grimacing. Discourse is often diffuse and aimless. I often want to cry out against it. I often find I have odd lines that suggest something, and much is suggested by a kind of meaning that this phrase often assumes.

So much depends upon the scholarship of the dead, they fall so thick the living cannot leave.

The steeples are empty and so are the people, marked with radiolite so they may be located in the dark.

I am incapable in my stagnant career, so I move to the

crest of a hill, mine for certain locutions so rare I'm not sure they were ever said.

This world is so new it is only an intuition, so long in the past that the ruins are already absorbed into the future.

The girl is taken to Spider's house, so he makes his wife sing in the distance, so as to be distinguishable.

Decorative detail has been so flattened that it complements the wall textures so the merchandise stands out.

Make a small slit in the house, so that when a person holloas in the slit, it makes a roar so as to recall the late *Song* Dynasty.

Cricket-song gathers into the disintegrating and integrating motions of its axis so that it takes flesh in the Introduction to *Lohengrin* which I mention so frequently.

Draw text so as to replace undirected lines with arrows of implication so that spatiality is not part of the field.

I insisted on seeing them, so he unbuttoned his coat and took them out; red rhododendron blooms. They attach minds to plants so that they can forgive us slowly.

OUR TEARS SOFTEN death's blows, therefore draw them softly.
Poetry maintains the absent object; choose, therefore,
each season, the present fruit and therefore time stretches
what we cannot see must be true therefore initiate
a naming of every thing and action and therefore
penetrate the necessary: reality remains opaque therefore
we are conscious, our observations therefore are important:
recalling the Six Dynasties we therefore write this.
The first clause is dependent on clause 2 and therefore
has a small serrated crest and therefore may be considered
a subordinated clause. The status of a truth-claim is therefore

a dream of death. Therefore man has Mono for Android,
and kills out of terror. Therefore man walks erect,
forever alerted: therefore invent fire and flint weapons.
Therefore perform language's song and
therefore celebrate deeds, arms, the man.
We wish that we may also perceive things. Therefore,
the star takes our heart. Therefore, the star gives heart
that we may not hunger. The star calls *Tsau*. Therefore
summer is the time it sounds. Therefore write
till this world is therefore changed. We listen
therefore to the Pleiades as earth unsounds, the pages die.

**While thus suspended**, the table vibrated, raps were heard. The wire contracted again, thus moving the paper.

Thus in a year the trees' wounds healed over. Thus peculiarity descended from generation to generation.

The girl spoke thus: Let us for a while wait for him. Coyote thus: Here the sand will bury you.

Thus these twins were counterparts of the original gods of day and night. Thus existing and nonexisting mutually produced each other.

*Please listen.* (Thus he came close to her, embraced her tightly and kissed her loudly, then spoke). Thus, the silent massy range of columns north and south end in mist.

We found it thus represented among the wielders of thunderbolts that the series of disposable legs thus produced was called a cluster, thus prefiguring the revolving door personnel system.

Thus was recounted his manifestations, enhancing overall impact altogether and thus freeing internal machines from the incest taboo.

The state of wasteland or half-wasteland thus remained an area of significant research value and thus was not funded. At night, I often sat an hour out thus, attentive to a dull insistent roar—I questioned my grandfather, what things it could be that spoke thus. He said to me that the stars were the ones who spoke thus.

**Mr Wood and myself** make the movements together.
We beat our hands together to make a drum
bring the trigger-assembly together
a sound like leather rubbing together attracts the attention
we lie talking after dry-weather therapy, breathing together
flowing together in incompatible tones and styles
together with sense-fragments of the target text.
The eyes move together on calibration tracking.
Stand with heels and toes together and eyes closed.
Feeding is effected by bringing together the halves of
the nut. A fly rubs its hands together and looks at us:
we murmur about our untethered future together.
How work both throws people together and estranges them.
The poster shows Dean, Bogart, Monroe and Elvis together.
We enjoy stillness together on each side of the ether lake.
Draw the jaws of the pulley together, and the rings clamp
the rope. We toggle close and feel discharge together

**My head turned** because I heard a sound. I turned my head because my ears were affected. These are confused modes because they twirl and have a hard edge. He hates the moon because it reminds him of the sky. He is sad to this day because of the loss of the child. Because he knows I desire his mother he desires my downfall. Because of the goodness of this Lady and because of her loveliness, and because actual drawing on the ground involves bodily actions, they lack sequence. It's because of this my foot grinds down. The subject will not lift because the screw is turned out. This creates a downiness loop, because physical illness cannot be more general than itself. They are poor because of the state of their noses, dry and short. In the east,—a red serpent because she appears in lightning. In the west,—a white serpent because she appears in a white cloud. Silence is unheard because it is disauthorized discourse, drowned out because of the very shudder which it gives him. He hardens himself because she had given birth to the fire spirit. She who is irrational because she keeps buying assets as if their prices will rise forever; but very faintly, because you can't lighten a deep colour without spoiling the picture. You can't just run out of the ring, either, because you will take massive damage. To be caused, to be cause of. Because the activated ability goes on the stack last, it will resolve first. The misaligned syllables draw the foot towards the centre of the form because the overall distance between their left edges and the left foot edge, as reflected in the number of violation marks assessed, is not Hamlet's object of desire because he rejects it with all his being. But these are not all equal chances, because there are more kings of all denominations than there are queens of hearts or fives of hearts. Because including cycle-time directly in an optimization-model complicates things, a gardener standing nearby points out to us that there is an insect in the grass and to be very careful, because of its contents, despite its low PageRank. I'm thrown into the debugger because of an error. The veil draws the Western eye, because I like to enter the world of the dead. I can't wake up because I'm not dreaming because my kids tell me when I smell, even when I don't.

**Every shop and every house** has its idol; to these incense must be offered every morning and evening, also to the nurse in the subways of every night.

Jerking pain in every position, especially in the tendons with orgasm of blood; every other day there is hilliness.

A food pellet is released into the cup for every second correct response. If you set this option to *Every 15 Minutes*, you receive rustling in the ear as of straw.

Nausea at every meal, succeeded by a short stitching ache projecting different dream events at every opportunity.

Every morning the old woman takes out the shining thing, and every evening she brings elkskins.

Every time the hasp is released, an unpredictable seal number generates echo request packets. A trees' array-list contains every location used to hold a stem.

As every stone conceals fire; every lash brings off a portion of the skin. Every time players perform actions, they increase threat. Every time you level up you get an unlock token.

In every book white is black. In every edit-trace, there is the real presence of event-sequences.

Abstraction is impossible and every thought clings to the concrete. Every subsequent note you play with that voice will use the recorded curve.

Elliptical distribution-patterns inform every aspect of the school. A mysterious wind awakens thoughts of oppression and splendor at every corner.

Every time he puts a log into the fire different things run from it. Various groups of instruments play every note, while the other groups glide.

He is convinced every name represents an object in reality, and has existential import.

The user generates a search request about every two minutes. The sensor can search only one cell at every instant.

Every worker is asked to informally audio-tape five hours of off-task. Details must be perfectly executed and the composition be in balance at every level.

Life is exempt from every restriction. It is easier with a set of knives, and this 13-piece collection is sharp in every sense.

At every renewed contact with the voice-phenomenon I try to gain deeper insight. The list lists every location that is searched.

## Seven. Of Similarity and Dissimilarity

BISHOP MOANS LIKE THE GHOSTS I suppose on earth
warm air causes the narrator to feel like dreaming of
flight and waking in a plane as the days pass like
men loaded down with days, our talk, like smoke,
disperses my son trikes over to my knees and pipes up like
a flightless bird words stand like petals on wet black
acrylic nails, like an embodiment of
irreconcilability this exists like the h in ghost
cog driving the wheel, clogging the artery, like
a froth aroma like scented bath soap
it feels like weather torn from a newspaper
there's no scape like a firescape, the Wi-Fi
network is like a 7th sense spanning the planet
the text is like it is drawn over with a real highlighter
the get-well-soon balloon trails an umbilical, like
one familiar with your skin it touches you like
Beethoven's quartets that lie in the cellar, like
H. said, potatoes, his poems on reality like
a paraphrase, like treasure maps with wind cherubs
what felt like rain was static on the stereo
like rain, gentle enough to nourish growth,
to extenuate like a cloud
seeps through me like last tomorrow's rain.
What is like coincidence is a shattered mirror.

**As cells pass through** the aperture they are perceived as out of body (as reflected in satellite images of light density at night). As the film's spectral villain lures characters into plasma-viscosity, a poem works as a biography of an *alter ego*. Think of film-time as an approximation of poem-time. Structured as dream, a poem reads as a history and explanation of memory, a film as a dialectic as the two flow into each other. Was it this that gave me the sense of cyborg-assemblage as I woke? As I unpack, one of the screens lights. I feel the shopping as disembodied spirits working as category controllers in the chilled ready meals and frozen foods sector. Evaluate the poem as a reflection of the character of Pope. As when your traffic-guidance app fails in a foreign country, and a new roundabout system leaves you in a nowhere: as the driving frequency changes, the flames on the surface respond. In this case remove the batter head by loosening the tension rods as you did with the snare and toms. The display model of face cream appears as fear generalization. A method expects an object as an input parameter to serve as a container for the layout cell. Show a simplified representation as you draw it. Expansion cracks, as found in bread-crust bombs, are absent. So as to assist our readers we give the text here: Three small black squares appear on the lower-right corner, as circled. They are seen as creatures inhabiting time as birds do air. As they rent our love Mesa's ability triggers as a precaution against blasphemy. As for the defeat of the Gods by energy blasts, as the war winds down, National Presto turns back to the civilian market. The discourse present in the rotating light sources, as dazzling as a flash of stone in the river, wavers as we drive off. Flow manifests as movements of trees as evening darkens the fronto-nasal canals. As soon as Mimic's ability resolves, as well in the dark shadows of the face, as in the eyes, eyebrows and ears, the spinal segment loses stability, slides forward and aggravates the trunk. As it turns out, he possesses an inactive second brain that he trains to similarize objects to 20 decimals, reassembling them as strings. The emission arises as matter dragged from adaptive-feed-back-control produces chirping in the ears, as of grasshoppers, blown cinders, cylinders of air. It feels destitute, as a man of stock; wanting in sense as a bell ringing in the head. Write on a scrap of paper, as you read, all that seems strange. As a child, you come to the lagoon for the storage of swine-wastes, where light crusts. Yeats flaps and the steam rises as if the masks rot from his face. The conditional returns as an optional value. As you wander, the rain creates a photo-negative, as blue and as pure as a lotus petal or as dawn on a wintry sea. Often as I near sleep I think I am a device, closing or opening apps, the will of the dead manifesting as news, shifting without ascension, body to soul as anchor to ship. The to-do list emerges as a compositional method in New York School. *Ogun*, possessor of stocks of iron, suffices me as a divinity. He is esteemed in Scandinavia as a middle god and as a constituent of thought. As his throats pulse in the dark, he manifests as emblems of time as receptacle, body as root of brain. The knights worship the leaf as a sign of their perseverance. As clouds build, crowds dissemble that were once a human being, light as down, downer. I sing of the changes as the sun dies, the mind to the body as the sound of a lyre to that lyre. The metacycle of productive capital repeats as a *repertoire* of tech imagery as the fever of high summer ashes the grass. Sounds as of a distant football match come from over the high walls, unfolding as utterance. As I approach waking, I start cleaning up the mess I made earlier in the dream. The gradation of merit of waters rises as follows:—sound as from eerie rivulets, light, lemon-coloured urine and cow dung as a poultice for toothache, the river as deferred arrival, buzzing in the head as of bees; as the sight of high denomination notes or pubic hair, as voice eludes the speaker, wring thoroughly, as a wet garment or lemon; grow upon, as *fungi* on a tree, intend, as regarding some future action; feel certain, as about something to happen, as a field of variables defined as cool to the feel. Slit, cut a slit in, as from sliminess, as an eel or stone from the grasp. Gulp down, swallow whole, as a draught of medicine, as when a lover is considered as a lesion of the intelligence, for as the body moves on the feet, long as battery life and strong as storm wind; faded, as a withered plant, in a sweating manner, as liquid through a tiny crack an hour drops, as a black dog, as a toothless woman at a tough piece of meat, as a sleeping-mat appears as an object of anxiety, as a baby puts a finger into flame, as she speaks, as she lies winking her eyes, she hears the dog coming home, the snow as a silent apology for previous wrongs. Literary criticism as a refined form of ancestor worship. The ocean as a time-containment unit. As the rain hurtles to its certain destruction on him he wishes he had a raincoat. Pope draws silk from a restrained spider with a variable-speed reversible drill, coaxing as much as 100 metres in a single session. As winter passes, his snowlike complexion becomes ruined as yellow pus appears on his face. He sees poems as preposition-engines, structure as projections of syntax. As you learned in a previous lesson, the initiate can look at them as at the letters of a super-sensual alphabet. As cancer takes hold in the villages, statues pose as stone, as is the heterogeneous nature of quality. Click the refresh-button as needed. Enter two youths, dressed as travelers, with staff and knapsack which they carry into the woods as an offering to their insectlike spirit friends, parasitic forms of life known as thought. A tempest overtakes them as they enter, as we move through their spaces, oblivious. Insect as *Shekinah*, shrilling as the frost-wind. Dracula's amulet is matched by a close-up of the village woman's crucifix as it spills out of her shirt. Book-collecting as a way to recover my father, piece by piece. Atavistic gesture as a pang of knowledge, the rolled moon as felt surface, blood as culture medium. Poe's "The Raven" as interpreted by Buddy Morrow and his Orchestra. Pope as the raven. Nature as artefact, as seen-through. Therapist as catalyst: I see the album titles as he flicks through them, but when the air is thicker, as in the night, he is as clear and correct as possible. As he falls asleep he murmurs as from a dull instrument stop me from sleep. As the poet says.

**Repeat the same process** on the other hind limb
that same scene the ambulance highlights loops through trees
on the same motorway, imagine a baby crawling
that in turn plays the same biological function
the beam paths do not occur at the same time
we rejoin them later in the same sentence
clinging to the same grammatical tingling
of the ears; afterwards, tearing in the same;
the triangle performs the same function as the circle
this same process of turning the heads is still employed
on the same principle that the brain is alleged to work on
produces quality fake data with the same provision
press the same keyboard shortcut to reverse the setting
the loop runs at the same speed, reading it it runs
at the same speed as when the cache is turned off
scrapings are performed by the same two individuals
the resurrected body does not enjoy the same *persona*
it protects hawthorns and loves those who do the same
it plays the same tune twice over, drops out of our hand
at the same time it keeps up a kind of monologue
self-feeds from the carcass at the same time
and the roots of the hair are commonly of the same colour
errors are the same part of speech as the deleted word

under your vest is a red ball of the same size
at the same time transfer the concealed ball of
the same size as the red handkerchief invisibly to the left palm
the hand now takes hold of the same end of the wand
opening a dialog pane with the same progression of commands
the feature allows two views of the same presentation
at the same time creates ample space for retail
the crankpin travels from C to A in the same time as the piston
representing the same time in the revolution
maintaining the same viewing window and footprint
offering the same benefits and design as the pulmonary sac
the emotional engages the same muscles as the reflex
after lying down on the same Saturday for several weeks
each slot will pass the phototransistor at the same velocity
this experiment is frequently repeated with the same result
the ruined landscape Slothrop traverses is the same lake-front
the indicator stands the same when detached from the engine
a bowl of the same type dates several hundred years later
shows the same Samarian particle syntax
the law of nature stands in the same relation to (a) nature
by the same means we ascertain the truth of the sentence
spirit hands are from the same elements that our hands are
at the same rate that waves break on a shingle beach
now the same twitch moves to my elbow
opens the same kinds of clauses as the simple relatives (b)
the same voice continues: to prevent simultaneous
access to the same file the packet arrives at (c) and
the same procedure is followed, each month
we receive an urn of ashes with the same
or similar message: A fool sees the same tree.

You are reading a discourse about referentless and syntactic words. For example, one cannot write about language without referring to things. Imagine their absence: a discourse about about. About how about abouts. What about does. As it is about to be thought, about jumps into the water about 11 miles SE from *Western Ear*, 3 mile WSW from *Gully Ledge*, real bullets whizzing about. About the time that *Mount Desert Light* is dropped, *Saddleback Ledge Light* is made. It is roily about the places where herring spawn. About 2 o'clock a light fog drifts in. Flocks alight on smooth streaks in the water inshore of a line of netstakes that extend about a mile out. Something ageless about having time to think, cogging down to an abbot whose cross-sectional dimensions are about 1.5 and, throwing his tail about, forms ripples. He is rather thick about the middle, with a Vandyke beard, and bouncy is the region about his ribs. He asks about discourse, to which you reply: about about they were all masters and as masters mostly wrong. He gathers the ropes tightly three times about his robe. A violent aching about the lower part of the axial slice brought about by shuffling the feet on a sand-strewn floor obliges him to roll about until steadied by clutching boundary nodes. He wakes about half an hour after the mesmeriser left and mum fusses about getting things packed; what she does not like about consciousness is the wall between it and sleep. It is about drift, about losing purpose. About death, yet if we don't die life will. She is working on a poem with this title. Without looking at it, you ask what the poem is about. She can do about one narrative turn per poem. It lines up, it is about itself, short-circuits possible metanarratives about voices. Is reluctant speech, uneasy about naming its object, leads into a thought-spiral about her relationship. The ambiguity brings about two distinct renderings. It is safe to feel dreamed about. You construct a 1,000-head swine barn about 40 feet from one of the turkey houses, about which restless abyssals creep, using their probelike tongues. One person might have vague or incorrect ideas about backup internal batteries for power outages, another person might have illusions about the object as it wraps its leaves about their brittle spine. In a note scribbled on a letter he sent to her about some poems she had sent him, Niedecker comments that she is about to insert the tines of a fork about the margin. The scribing-blade head is revolved about the stem by the finger. These heads, between about ten and 200 in number, are generally mounted in groups, with about ten to the inch in the axial direction, frequently turned about the Z axis. At 2 in the afternoon a light fog drifts in, an anxious sweat breaks out. The myths are about to change. The number of true descriptive remarks that can be made about concrete elements of existence is not finishable. I take up an essay about what prisons paragraphs are. Be serious about the stuff a doc team should be serious about—like developing a content strategy; a great deal remains to be explained about what we do as a species. Attempting to reach an agreement about the meanings of various images and statements, data about your purchase becomes part of a system, yielding information about you as individual and as boundary. Monophonic sound accompanies the 57-minute *Carmen*, about a soldier suckered into a determined market price. The thing about language is it holds and makes visible. Typical access time for moving-surface memories is about 20ms to reach a sector of the disk, but the moon is unclear about stars, so it writes about them.

**The sun rose, it seemed,** round a corpse, we seemed
as statues round whose base some river runs
that important area round the mouth emitted waves of sound
the soldier turned buried dreams round in his mind
his arm turned round on the stud, giving motion to the great *jinn*

who ran round the room like a noun complement
he passed the wool thrice round the needle loosely
the segment formed a nervous ring round the shaft of the hair
he felt as if a handkerchief were tied round his head
an interior space circumscribed by a single round arch
and set within the shrine and round about it
the dog ate fish and put its bones round the waterpot
emperors wound round with long green arms
last year's cloud come round again
it was cold all year round but especially cold seated
ivy bines snapped round the ankles, to run still and through
half of three turns is 1.5, which rounded down to one turn
to spend more time chasing him round the garden
at the end of the Tunnel of Love I turned round to find my arm
round one of the skeletons. A poem is a park in a city
where things can be thought not through but round
round a corner a flight of birds foregrounds language
I invite her round to discuss reader-response theory
the knob comes off in her hand, and the room swims round
her: a fiery silence now all round us rose.

**Sediment creeps faster** than *Leviathan* maintains burrow structure. There is no better way to illustrate downslope shearing than in more sloping areas than silt-loam, exhibiting more *Thanatos* than fatigue on limestone beds. The turning of the clock is worse when lying than when sitting; a tiny hand—smaller than any adult's—amounts to no more than an aggregation of fragments. Call it something other than metal cords, four tones deeper than other cords. I write to feel bigger than my job. My theme is wider than the page. Asia's wealth-market more than doubles. It comes in less through the eyes than the ears. It's easier to indulge in abstract thought than to play dolls. She's less than 10. She's more connected with the singing shaman than the others. She's lighter than falling down. She plays in more perfect time than mortals. The piston travels slower at the head than at the crank. The voices of politics are more click-through than a fountain's. Thought is longer than lives, narrower than roads. She is no bigger than his thumb but with a perfect face and detailed dress and hair and gives club-quality sound in a gadget not much bigger than a paper clip. A god-house's thatched roof is longer than the online moving surface. Diagonally placed styling mirrors make it look more enigmatic than it is. Its density and weight are greater, even, than the human heart; nearby objects traverse your visual field faster than distant. Choose a word more specific than this.

THESE SEQUENCES CAN ANYWAY FOLD into structures
from this sphere onto an anyway oriented plane
and I say what time is it anyway. This he says
is laughing matter or laughing gas or anyway I'm aware
I suppose the erotic side has been scarce lately anyway
even when we are together, anyway at 1am I move
to the study. I'm awake, well, functioning anyway.
Can I go back to bed please? but anyway the satnav
directs me to a flood, I drive through anyway,
it washes the car. So anyway I'm walking to the bus stop and
this bird flies 2cm from my face I wanna shoot pool anyway
lol is it really that hard to find a MickeyDs anyway durrr
whatever. I'm not going to rant. You all hate me anyway.
Its cool, I like being told no. I'll do it anyway! Tonight's gonna

be a good night my tweets under investigation anyway
to try & creep in I dont argue over trivial shit anyway.
I turn my worries to God. He's anyway going to be up all night.
What emotion do you think this is? Guess anyway.

**The structure of** meanings fractures in whichever version
whichever way the fall is described;
whichever writer rebels, rebels to give users
the freedom to use whichever system they like.
Vacuous Quantification Deletion deletes whichever remains.
This returns either eternity or the current date, whichever is
greater, selects whichever of $net and $gross is larger:
the owner is paid whichever is greater, a message is sent
to whichever communication medium is selected.
Choose whichever syntax is easier for you to type.
Whichever group of cats I meet, I rarely pet the smallest.
Each one moves whichever way it sees.
Whichever theory best accounts for the data is correct,
just use whichever one reads best in your code.
To try out whichever Error Console you use,
create a small error, whichever, the realising
subject is whichever person precedes the verbal root;
whichever follows the root is interpreted as realising
object. Use the shell installed with whichever client you use.

**Woke up confused:** tinnitus in the other ear. In the one, a white handkerchief; in the other, a red ball the other end of which was attached to a blue silk cloth-clot. She was the other girl. She was not allowed to enter the other reality of concentrate froths. As the cloud crossed, it permitted her to reflect other borders. Mother-goddesses prevented other devices from connecting to hers. Brushing her teeth, she heard the people on the other side striking wooden shoes against each other. Other participants with an acute sense of hearing later confirmed the audibility. Life was an egg at one end and a remote desktop at the other. She inserted the other gold tooth in a beakerful of brake fluid and the target and carriages came into contact with each other, accompanied by a thumb-twitch that spread to other muscles. On the other side of the coffee-room the man-being abode. Other spirits came and caused paper jams whilst the other who was of a solar nature shared light. They slowly approached each other, vibrating their antennae finely and alternately. The *Bone spirit* flowed from one nostril, while the other was blocked. I filled every other glass with water. Over the willows, the fine birds sang to each other. Other features included easy-adjust volume effective for high-volume dove hunts or other upland game. With two windows open, one Unix and the other Netscape, add hard and other block devices to ledges and other sheltered places. She named in one ear what came through the other, a womb: gateway from other worlds.

**There was nothing left to burn** but time, thought the ice. The shadowless light ice and the sky appeared to meet but that was an effect of the mountain. I shouted from the balcony but was inaudible to my headphone-wearing son. Perhaps death is impossible but I doubted it. My throat felt constricted, but without pain. The probability distribution was a watch ticking but internal, telling me nothing but what was agreed. Ice creaked and jammed but held. My French in the dream came out as Spanish but I only realised that on waking. Her *debut* book was all but guaranteed. The review was favourable but I could tell it was a terrible novel. I bought her flowers, but once inside the house they smelt of urine. I did not touch her, but I did not withdraw. I longed to embrace her but my limbs were wooden. I cried out, but desisted. She was insensible to pricking, but was moving her limbs. After holding a sovereign, I put it into her hand, which closed on it, but relaxed when a piece of iron was rubbed upon her. Iron abolished the effect of gold; but friction increased it. Eat an apple, she said, but you did not feel like eating an apple. But you ate it. Space was full of voices but had few ears. The poem of the wind existed, but not the world. Time was but the excrement of its own mother. Spider shot several arrows, but in no instance did he hit Eagle. Power co-opted language but language disarmed power, power appropriated language but language invalidated power, power used language but language disused it, power demanded but language remanded, abused/disabused, confused/fused, forbade/bade, buttered/uttered. No additional data entry was required, but if there was, the system prompted the user. A triangle symbol [Δ] designated the traverse, but also the triangulation station. Time code identified edit points but was hidden from the editor. The rat like us knew but did not remember the sadness of leaving a mother's nipples. Composed wholly of small tubes, sometimes branched, but more frequently simple, it was a model open to energy but closed to information. Kindlmann's technique favoured a solid, but not booming, 16' pedal line, and a reverse distribution network, ending in a *finale* of ruffled gowns in what seemed to be waxed raffia, but turned out to be trash bags. The seal replied, anything but Canadian Club. Came home tired but then the butterfly-dotted lawn. Sang before waking but waking forgot the song. It was a disappearance into an invisibility called necessity. The ice tried to shine back on the dream, but failed.

## Eight. Of Selves

**We arrived from colourful** wasteland. We chose to construct the robot from wood. We each picked up a log and gave the other, till he rose to a sitting posture.

We were mixed up too much in what we were, we rode the silence and exchanged vows through layers of purpose to come to what we decided after much effort must be an answer.

We worked on small *kunstwerks* and found an individual direction. Onstage we debated with the audience about the issues we raised.

We landed fast as a flash, but not as bright, and crept into gardens of forking paths. We watched remotely operated systems drop into hedges and sense.

We met in Departures, and were placed in a diminishing series of rooms. We drew a pair of axes on the glass and compared their positions.

We had some tea with the relatives. We walked around the gardens when the rain stopped. We understood her son had died, and here was the poem.

We had lost the Empire, we ripped flowers from Yeats's grave. The shapes we formed when we thought of form were pre-worn.

We were bored of the way things looked, so we tried a different channel. The keyboard stuck, we still keyed into the night.

We skirted Book Cliffs, traversed the Axial Basin and followed the weathered gray-yellow rock to Sky Lake. In that mirror, there was no progress: we shone, briefly.

We shelved for a living. We left with the feel of something underwritten or overhead.

We watched light arrange the oranges, we shopped for the things we needed, and flowers. We traveled night's machinery, looking for a tunnel's end.

We came to a lock where effluent was piped in. We traveled decades to the shores of a black lake and stood at last on the summit we sought.

We got home to find our hamster missing. We immediately resolved the promise by calling defer.resolve.

We slept by making fragments of the self. We smelt the book we needed, and had myths to hand.

We pulled the rubble out of the children. The trees agreed, we had trains to catch and a world.

We broke into other people's smiles. We were living on fast & dislocated time: film time. We affirmed without denying the contrary of what we affirmed.

We emerged from sleep only temporarily. We gained access to the consumer world. We felt it caused dryness of the tongue.

We watched the news to stop it breaking. We moved through myth to get to work.

We noted the following points in common with *Travelers in a Wintry Forest*. We presented an overview of Ant-Miner.

We avoided making an arbitrary choice of priors by imposing a rationality requirement. We compared forest yields using a ř-test paired by searcher identity.

We had little knowledge of the systems we maintained. We had short lives and attended to their ends mostly, nor did we have time to drag the shining body to its face.

We compiled the boot image and flashed it to the device or created a new mockup for the user interface. We found a flaw in the new security matrices.

The sun rose, we moved into a world in which shades hardened. We hung on in blue light to the importance of knives, teeth.

We made for the far parades. Eventually we approached the sea, it seemed as we trailed out that we had behaved appallingly.

We performed electrical and mechanical studies under vacuum at 4K using a platform we refered to as a feedback-stabilized break.

We climbed a few steps to the reception area where chairs excited the motions of our legs. We wanted to be shown content in the form of posts for this thread.

The wheeled eye of the horse says *we'll die*. We rearranged the words to make a home.

From morning till night we piled up ashes and scraps. The poem ends We heard them weeping.

**He was of an excellent and pure smell.** He wore on his head the skin of the dog, showing its teeth. He comprised in him seven individuals; four constituted his frame (trunk) and three went to form his side and tail. He was a mocking boy with living eyes and he was a pummelled and a punched boy. He was warm with a sucking mouth and quick bladder. He was dead. He was everybody's friend. He was further delineated as standing, or riding, on a flying peacock. He was subject to fever once a month. He wore a greyish coat, black vest, light pantaloons and slippers. Lions he slew from his open chariot. He opened his mouth and said to his mother. *He he*. On three occasions he mounted and mated the shoe of a person entering his pen. He dreamed. He broke into satanic laughter, he tore his clothes and hair and cried *Ka! Ka!* He drew a canal which he called *Triton*. He heaved a sigh, he asserted God was the Infinite Man. He insisted he saw him blazing at the end of the bed. He sang, I am a spider of spiders, he entered into the coherent Goldstone phase field where the Great Being lived. He passed water into it mellifluously. He was warned of an approaching attack by the sense of weight in his limbs. He struck his knee hard and wild turnips fell into the basket. He said to his mother. In the dream I rubbed my eyes, full of daze, and called: Bring my sister, bring! Bring my human soul. He went into a storeroom and brought out a whale on the end of a sharpened stick. He thought his breast burst, and he felt heat in his scrotum, and on carrying his hand to the part, said that he had been cut. He groaned when his right nipple was pinched. He lived on air, changed his bones and washed his marrow. If he dozed he woke agitated, pulse rapid, tremor of arm and lower limb. He imagined humming sounds. He unzipped the satchel and pulled out his spirit heart. As he opened it the leaves made a thick crackling sound, unlike the rustling of paper. He put his thumb precisely on the condition of the previous day. He buried his face in hair. He parted it in the middle and wrapped up two long strands that reached to his feet; he wrapped them with bark. He hesitated to risk the leap. He felt thick. He gave the steed a drink from the bottle, and he had such strength that with one leap he went over the fiery kitchen-ground. He wiped his tears, touched the king with the spear, stopped crying and said to his head slave. My father is he who is indifferent to me. He spent his steel like farthings on the sea. He moved his great shoulders restlessly, closing and unclosing hands in hungry fashion. *Hyoh!* he said. He instructed an Imam to journey the world and select forty of the choicest descendants of Huang Di. He asked his wife to bring a basket. He asked his wife to make a hole in the ice. He took two sticks and stuck them into his nostrils, he blew, then he blew them afire. He deepened his kiss of comprehension. He felt in his dried-up sack, he brought out some tobacco, he felt in his dried-up sack and brought out a coal, he blew it afire. He blew out the smoke four times, till he threw a cast of his spear, and made two pieces of her. He was then with some difficulty awakened. Nothing had annoyed him, he said when he awoke. He mounted his horse, and commanded the helot to take his wife by the plaits of her hair. He saw that her skin was downed with feather-fine wisps of white-gold. He presented to the tombs of Asclepius money in abundance, and he rolled in the *hex-enbesen* and the wet laughter of nymphs. He sang hymns with *Belal* the Abyssinian. He threw himself on the soft ground. He elevated his horns downwards and make gollup. He rose as a pillar of smoke and bent in the wind as smoke bends, he streamed as bands of black smoke, and out of him darted flames. He laughed a mirthless laugh. He lived deep in the mountains and performed feats, riding on the clouds, moving mountains, and ruling the birds. One day, he walked on a steep mountain slope when it suddenly began to rain. He cried bitterly: *Ka! Ka!* He was infuriated, and since rain is caused by the dragon kings, he made use of his high-voltage mode. He traversed the Jordan; he attacked the city of *Ai*, and was dispersed. He repented his deeds and fell into sadness. He stirred logs and soon got black meat from them. He took an iron kitchen poker, about a yard long, and, holding it in his right hand, struck upon his left arm till he bent the poker nearly to a right-angle. He went out to *Hori*, to look at the wing-flapping storks. He returned by way of *Sei rock,* to hear the new nightingales. He imagined himself as a disembodied pair of hands. He spread the cold smell from the fridge through the house. He spent his days badgering librarians to order his books. Called over the phone he asked if he constantly keeps the wound of the negative open. He played his tongue in and out of the mat of hair, zeroing in on the suction head. He raised his head further, past the proud vault of ribs, the rhythmic rise and fall of breasts. He showed a white drop-waist lace gown, bell-bottoms. He then adopted an assumed name, declining higher affinity conformers and he delineated in his poems an increasingly specific housing cavity. When he opened his eyes and no one was there he cried. He rarely opened his mouth and spoke telepathically. Under hypnosis, he said two lights descended from the sky and landed nearby. When he drew up the Three People's Principles and the Five-Power Constitution, he hoped for political attainment. He contemplated the ornamental appearances of birds and beasts and the different suitabilities of soil. He imagined orgasm, a process to which he gave visual form in drawings. He got up and as always went downstairs, ground beans, scanned the morning news and started his coffee. When he went upstairs to take his shower, he found Z still lying in bed. He touched her. Then, using a felt-tipped pen, he joined the top line of dots. Keeping his pen on the last dot, he unfolded her. He mistook his dog for a shadow. When he settled in his Hi-Leg recliner he read Dick's account of numerous laborious traverses of Caithness in search of sections of boulder-clay. He had his Wikipedia page withdrawn from him. After swallowing the elixir he ascended to enjoy immortality. Before taking leave of earth he bequeathed his head comb to his son.

I FEEL LIKE I'M finishing my dad's life for him. As if with no intervening time I am at school. I realise I may be in a situation. I dream of broad and isotropic rivers. In the book there are terms referring to the I and its components—I show him its singularity, cook breakfast, carve the boned lamb, shave, jerk off. In summer I notice facial irritation and drying out contact lenses. I say do you mind if I ring off now. I ride home, read a poem, order a box of maniacs, listen to furious Latin. The I aspires to nothingness. I install a *modus operandi* system for the State Police. I follow a small path south through the woods. I mark a stone, drawing two curved lines from its neck. I desire to shed my responsibilities and dance. I stick in traffic. I create a decision tree. Whenever I look up I see bright spots. I want the whites of my eyes to roll up and fill the evening cloud. I hear from the sky a wondering voice: I notice distinctly the movement of the keys of the harmonium. I become chief flautist to the queen, entering rooms forbidden to money; I kiss the bronze statue of Joyce, warm from the Istrian sun. I watch the exterior minicams as the craft accelerates and feel jittery, like I have to get out. I don't like to hear my own clothes. I have a cynical side and a cylindrical, which is on the side of history. I finish the last and best story in Welch's *Brave and Cruel*. With the voice of fire I cry. I am a creature of clay, kneaded with water. Visions of spirit-forms I am familiar with. The spirits often sing I hear them sing. I am going to *Kalaskigan* to have the Indo-Aryans make me a shoe of gold. I explain to dinner guests the grades of flying dreams. I have not prepared anything to say, but let me say this: from a teleological view I believe identity theft is a state of being. I knuckle-tap the tub's cast-iron sides. I think of release, pacing of breath, the catch and springs of locks. The apple I pick on the way to work is a Trojan horse. I am pushing a trolley, or is it a pushchair? Let that which I say pass; I am at a loss how to render exactly the meaning of the compound. I do not have this problem outside the office. I am wide awake, golden, and smooth. Sir. I do not want anything to eat, for I am part of Mother-Earth. I experience the feeling of an everyday experience. Slight laugh. I get control of my arm and swing it, I hold my other arm down at my side, and the violin plays. I speak the ritual incantation to the illimitable east, to the weak water in the north. Exiled the city, I try hard to sleep, to obey instructions. I am hailed by a person but I do not understand the import of the hail: Yes, I am your son; I have returned. I have a superb reputation, *resumé* and references. I forgive you for writing "If". I have strong connections with an intergalactic consciousness. I find a presson nail stuck to his underwear, brass knuckles with his name in black gold. In the lulls of illness and exhaustion, I send out certain chirps. I remember distinctly the movements of the nurses and physicians. Waiting for the favourable occasion afforded by old age, I travel the shore at different tides. I would like this to be about syntax, the clause, and then delete line breaks and spacings so I have a flow of uncomma'd text. This I think as I straighten my tie sewn round with bells, jangling when I move. I have lived in it all my life, have been from Rangoon to Plymouth in it, before I was a year old. I rub my wand, the repository of all magical power; then I am suddenly obstructed. I touch myself and find it different from a woman, and I call a policeman. I open the door, recede inside, and he slowly follows. I am walking an underground corridor with iron swing-gates at regular intervals. Full of questionable identity, I worry inessentially. Don't expect this to be a memoir, I can't be contained in discourse. I call the emergency number, and a voice tells me of the permission form I need from the NHS. Feeling a smothering sensation, I am seized with an impulse to laugh. I am pursued by ghostly feelings. After the sovereign is removed, I rub the palm with promotional items, and it closes rigidly. I put my thumb between the fore and middle fingers. Tomorrow I travel. I miss the bus and I look at my ticket and it is for a plane as well. On this flight I have wool socks, summer underwear, an orange anti-G suit. The effect comes slowly: if I place my fingers and thumbs in position, slowly, and not till after many mistakes, though at last most accurately. I rub the palm with the poker, and the friction overpowers the influence of iron. I never want to show my playlist, it might be embarrassing if I show what I listen to. I play a Magyar folk song commencing I see your face in pieces, and I undertake the rebuilding of terraces. Push the soft hem of the night into my mouth so that I stay quiet. Grief is all I know and joy all I understand. At a beach on Paros twenty years before in meditation I met my innermate the Rainbow Woman. I venerate her thrice a day. I cannot find where the sex class is going to happen and I wander over into the arts wing. In this life I celebrate my former life in which I anticipated my present life. I create comics from my own photos and use the pen to create speech bubbles. Through painstaking mastery of the classics, I have risen high. Sighing deeply for the fallen flowers, I wish to leave a lump shining in History's archive. I wake to new life with the morning breeze. I will take in hand afresh the unfinished embroidery; I will introduce into my song a yet unknown melody. When I am asleep I come in my mind and then I wake up. I describe an encounter with the plant as resonance in the skin. If I stare hard I see my vast and craggy knees. I see them leave their egg cases, clustering out, and as I try to push through they are caught in my hair and then behind them a wall, total, I try to get to my children quickly, am pushed back. I feel disappointed that I rose to the bait my child laid, that I had responded with anger. I, pundit *maudit*, am black ink, I am straight with the world. I am writing you a letter, it begins.

**Who rotates with their mother,** and parallel children, who functions to entice the others from safety or base or home, who places a tablet of stars on her knee, who consults it, who poses the riddle: who alerts the stars, who knows dreams well, who has their dwelling among the tombs, who is not sick of devices, who observes justice obtains rain in due season, who occurs as no name, a scent on the seat, who cries with the voice of the frost-wind when the corn has aged, who loses face in the dark wells of school desks, who becomes a fit performer of sacrifice, who can tell who works harm to mankind from those who work good, who returns from death as certainty, who harms by looking, holds, who acquires wisdom through lifetimes, who is drawn in a range of skin tones, who for years carried a penny given by an old lady who had been without experience before marriage, who dressed in men's garments to follow her lover in the shape of a fawn, who gave him the epithet applied to a person who refuses to reply when questioned, who has not felt the attraction of the sphere, who feeds on the flesh of the deer-sun-god, who breaks the chains binding them to the revolving Great Bear, who in anger slays the good *alter ego* of the evil Red Thunder, who sticks a poster up denouncing Wenting: The scalpel of Lu Wenting serves the traitors who delight to sit in the dark and trace glowing embers, who go about with reports of other people's sayings and doings, who exhibit skill on the occasion of the Imperial circumcision, who one day invites to a feast all who play at night, who with their train amount to the number of 3,000 men, who still has a fist when his hands are open, who is allowed to enter the castle to sell wares, and on entering slays its defenders, who finds the hidden king on spotted Arcturus, who is cured of all human ills: who knows this, knows the trodden paths, who in her second birth transforms into the sun-physician, but who was first born as Sam, who sleeps inside you, who compares her horse to an elephant, who is the wielder of Fang's sword in the sea, who is the unknown wolf, the beaked voyager, who is the tree left by the wood-chopper, who takes image-quality seriously, who furnishes the Aunt with drugs and charges them to her, who is the I of other poems, who belongs to the god of fire, who rides upon the wing of *Thoth*, who chops wood to quicken a torpid liver, who come as a wanderer to the shepherd's fire; for who carries out the plan carries out the dead, who draws a map to their house and takes tea in a thermos, lamented by the deities who were the cause of their destruction, the infant who catches my eye whose mother spills change in the shop who I offer to help who when I say to her it's not your day replies: when I have the child it is never my day, who walks across the Stygian swamp to break open the Gate of *Dis* who is the head of the sharp-witted, the shell of the user who owns the file. He, who, by the clashing of the two stones, engenders dreams, who wants a no fuss point-and-shoot, who is writing in the voice of William the Conqueror, who was shipwrecked in Normandy, who is the digger, digging over the world as if rent from who knows what object from the dead-things world, who wears a removable shoulder pad, who writes for Chinese pavilion, who doesn't need a little extra light for Instagrams and selfies, who once ran the world passport bureau, issuing passports to people who wished not to have or who were excluded from nationality, who listens to your last communication, a strong team player who traverses products, sales segments, and timezones. Who, after slaying the serpent, unpens the seven rivers, who bears a black dog and a white cat, who belongs in no world, who must not be left alone with the controls, who draws a simple curved line to stand for a person, a refined poet who scrawls crass graffiti, who imagines a longer mountain than this, while who the musicians are and who wrote the song remains to be known by we who crystal are, who are indivisible and inner and of whom I have no direct knowledge, who is on the other end of the phone, who are fragile mechanisms, poor puling stomachs, miserable dust who outlived the former times of disorder, who waxes the moon, who have no spoken lines, who disclose their presence with an involuntary shoulder jerk, who dwell in a seclusion equal to that of the dragon's shrine in the underworld, who prefers to be knee-deep in Code view, who walk, who run, who sleep, who smile at the Saxon hierarchs, who laugh at the Norman line,—Who follow the mighty *Hu*, kin of the warrior-princes who sank in the bloody tide, who mouthed inarticulate words at the latter end of the binge at Fleubaix, who burned twelve Welshmen with fire in Piggots garth, who was parted by the separating arm of a woman, carrying faggots, who leant from the moon, who worked in the secrecy of abandoned towers, who slept still. The stars move who are impatient for love.

**A toddler was chasing** pigeons that wouldn't fly from him. His head seemed to him compressed in a frame; a painful sensation compelled him to scratch, as if he had touched nettles. At the gate I missed him to the point of crying, of wanting to rush back. To bounce him to the rhyme, the rhizome. Sans made a deal with him, enabling him to penetrate the control tower, to shanghai a couple of rock trucks. I grabbed hold of him and started to shake him and he lost consciousness. The electrode caused him to turn head and eyes. When I caused him to vocalize, he said: I didn't make that sound. You pulled it out of me. Dreadful wounds were inflicted upon him. He did not turn from the enemy, but tears poured thickly out of him; Water Witch drove meteor shafts through heaven to defeat him. He saw the local high resistance anomaly coming toward him through the wind and placed his sea-shimmering shield in front of him. At last I sent him to sleep, and, standing at his right hand, drew up his legs by tractive passes into the reclining posture, and this made him elevate his frame. I drew him to the couch and laid him into the sitting posture. I lifted a long power-wave towards him then replaced him in the recumbent posture. Out of the way for this man! I am going to cook food for him. A clamping device seized him by the shoulders, causing him pain in the back. Dressed in black with a cloak concealing him, Eno met Hassell in person after his summer '79 performance; then visited him at the hospital and secretly instructed him in loss. In front of him the ten canoes of people laid their clam shells. The music box slipped from his hand and the lid snapped shut, startling him from the edge of a doze, causing him to rupture his hardware. The Dun Bull scattered him, bones and body; carried with him his chine and his thigh. Then he stood to the west and yellow lightning struck him. Finally he stood to the north, where white lightning struck him. Once again, Larkin's crude correspondence had turned, like overrun artillery, against him. It revealed him as wine discussed through his body and spoke through him: near the beginning he used Q to designate the unknown, though usually this letter stood with him for the square of the expression after it. Turtle asked his wife to roast him and season him with sesame seeds, each seed in fact connected him through her poems. His cycle left shimmering wake of leaves behind him.

The events that led me here flowed through me. There were many of me all laughing my head off. The dead stole the moon into me, it didn't hurt. Not me individually. Please tell me the poem the poem tells the reader. Let me stress it seemed to me the dark approached hesitantly, trying to smell me in order to make accusations as a crowd passed me, unitary, as if they had all just seen the same movie. They described to me that temporarily unified world. In front of me, sleep's hazy itinerary, my son came to the house, and said "Da –, excuse me, da –, excuse me." He led me left down a turning, a gorge, framed into me sounds. The situation at this point struck me on the upper surface of the table in front of me. Heath sat at the piano telling me of his sorrow about the children, then cheered, and gave me money for ice cream. "Father is dead," he told me. And those fruits tasted by me: let me display their wounds. A green insect on the wooden stairs unfolded, aware of me as of a change in light. A dream told to me in 1967 by a young man of the Kwandú moiety: a child came to me and begged. My mother turned him away. A friendly-looking shepherd dog came to me and she stroked it. It took hold of me tightly but did not quite puncture the flesh. It didn't seem to have bitten me out of anger. The dog was me. She trained me to fetch. She rewarded me with meat. My paws took me into a nearby park. The meme reminds me of me. Two twin girls came up to me and said they could read my fortune. They took me to their mother's house, which was in a part of the city never before seen by me. The house filled with people, and an older woman cautioned me to pay attention, she was going to read me. A roosting hive-mind eyed me from the roof-eaves. Images filled me as daylight fills a room, me thinking a little about work as a way to spend a life, giving me one more go at doing it again, but with match-grade accuracy. The ethnologists threw me into the sea then listened. The bell of a boy's voice asked: Will you not let me help you, father? You gave me dawn and sunset and newly born ghosts. He breathed his spirit on me, his feet led me through Mondays of truth, where people kept stopping me to comment on my chunk method. If Henry, in lines one and two, was the speaker, would you be angry with me for what this speaker told you? The amateur god of the garden was me. The sense of me, what me dissolved, the mauled centre of me, and you, my wife, in a silver kitchen, frying me bacon and gold, dreaming of me lost in a quarry with my brother, who could climb out and leave me. The giant said, Come with me, boy, I am your grandfather. He broke and gave me bread. He placed me between his knees and pronounced over me the menu option that hurtled past me into the evening, untold.

**The man who will throw himself** under a train
occupied himself in the morning in throwing himself from
side to side. He went off by himself and stood on a hill.
He sat down, and threw dried grass over himself.
Coming to himself toward noon he boiled into music.
He introduced himself to Renfield who, in medium shot, raised
his hands. This quickly cut to a shot of Fler himself.
This allowed him to see himself looking.
He prepared himself a whisky in the stained-glass bar.
He styled himself the Universal Pacificator King,
assuming to himself the rights or qualities of God.
He took himself to where Grizzly Bear & Blood-Clot
were skinning, tied himself like the chief's wife, dividing

the clam shells, keeping the smaller part for himself.
He untied himself, went to the chief's wife, and untied her,
declaring himself the Eminent King. He boxed
the papers, addressed them to himself in Tennessee. But
when he woke he found himself sitting on a rail.
He scraped himself in the armpits, rolled the armpit wax
into a ball. The thinker himself, in becoming, roused
himself in order to resist the movements we wish to give him:
Only the greatest makes himself small enough to enter Hell.
He is involved in a procession, himself walking briskly
down the road, with scarves with which to hang himself.
The man under the rail bridge built himself a small home,
took a book out of his apron pocket and wrote himself
notes, returning his attention to himself.

**Felt myself losing** self-control, found myself inside a shell lit by glass tubes, cried out to myself words of amazement struggled to wake myself placed myself in relation with energy, found myself cycling through long valleys, let myself down rung by rung into the shelved well, saw myself in a mirror recognized myself as out in a field in November, a first-snowflake version of myself I could never satisfy myself I saw felt bodies not myself or unfound the wresting angel in myself. Forgot my laptop so mad at myself never asked if I needed a day to myself, secluded myself to watch tv, old & sleepy eating graham crackers updating myself on the latest oncology studies got myself some Hello Kitty slippers, when alone I take myself seriously with this hat on, locked myself out of my apartment in my pyjamas, spilled coffee all over myself I thought to myself I had to catch myself treated myself to a pink iPod Shuffle laughed so hard at myself ate pavement leaving the fabric store stood at a podium uncomfortable calling myself a writer a word criminal can feel myself giving up text updates eating lunch by myself 50 minutes on step machine and cross trainer impressed myself my hair and eyebrows did em myself *pat myself on back* I ought finally to express myself: found myself snoring on the sofa, swam myself into the ground but couldn't bring myself to say definitively he, god, is left over, he wanted me to take an axe against myself so I directed myself into the trembling dark: saw myself (I was there) in a blasted dingle, forlorn blue scattered copses oozing the mystery at the heart of intention and blinking roots, so consciously eased myself while on the train into a kind of sleep, and reminded myself that I had ingested mycoselves, so knew constantly that a rose by other name was energy waiting to come out of a mouth, could be collecting myself in the parking area, shot myself in the foot, placed myself within the field of meaning provisionally speaking.

**Writing** is the descent into the abyss of oneself
of driving, of constraining oneself to norms
to find oneself slowly achieved as a conquering image
another person begins to take hold inside oneself and
flowers define "us" for oneself, for the tree and no metaphor
imprisoned in the nurse cell: oneself, one
begins deceiving oneself, and ends harshly
carrying the pip's point of evil within oneself—one
has the right to demand the unexpected from oneself.
Walking is a way of leaving oneself to return to
oneself, a way of erasing by asserting
oneself or asserting
oneself through erasure—it's a way of absorbing,
but so much is beyond and outside oneself,

it is easy to persuade oneself that backbone is stone
to assume for oneself the qualities of matter.

**We settle ourselves** comfortably, applying ourselves to our clothes warm neutrals like beige are still ourselves, bird-shadows flock over us as we fuck slowly ourselves from each other to find ourselves on the edge of a muddy river we needn't concern ourselves with how to fragment ourselves in order to examine closely each aspect let's call ourselves the *Febreeze* brothers feeling so fresh what we have done for ourselves dies with us; we're alone this weekend and have no idea what to do with ourselves. The firemen look disappointed we put the fire out ourselves. Rorty waits for creatures far more ancient than ourselves, thinks matter is just indecisive, until it comes to putting ourselves in the world impetuously, stomach-equipped stones, trawling for things to fill ourselves with we come to figure ourselves as eyes travelling down the discourse of straight streets turning upon ourselves and meeting for the last time. Plant is overture to ourself. What we have done for ourselves dies with us; what we have done to others shows we should love ourselves or not, hinge upon ourselves, make night. We are the birds who call ourselves names.

**The plot of the play** is against them and their search
for answers structures the meaning of them and leads
them to a gruesome discovery. I have seen
them through strangers' windows and walked in
to keep them from falling, the apricot blossoms
from east to west, the view between them.
On them I unscrew the lipstick and draw
a pair of lips, and put a cigarette between them.

I have seen them, in their anguish, unable to cry,
dug them their graves in the warm soil.
I could not distinguish them from hands of the living
—demonstrating them to be veritable spirit hands.
Call them now the hard and the soft,
ready them by cocking to the opposite side
of the body upon taking an observation of them
as they arise in the mind, so take them into a waterpot
and the spirit bones enter them with rainwater;
for them there is a troublesome course of births.
Take ants, and rub them on the body
plant and water stones to make them grow.
The longing of the clouds communicates to them
it prepares them for the higher kingdoms
to see spirits and yet not communicate with them.
Call men, animals, and wild beasts, speak to them.
Capture a blank number of them alive
turn them into thunders and thunderclaps, cut
their heads with large teeth and give them a feed-size
not connected to the narrative that unfolds before them,
returning them to you as attachments.
Rest them on the shoulder close to the ear.
The days carry with them the memory of children
looking at them from the height of low field strength
to capture and confine them in a single water-jar.
Give them bones to clear, a glass of wine a bowl of nuts
dot them with bright neon pinks and greens.
Boys pick silver flowers and stick them in their hats
from their faces you'd think them agents of grace.
Stop at this place, and have them cut long sticks.

Fasten them to thwarts by winding ropes around them.
Stand them, with supports, around the graves.
Count backlinks and rate them by their importance.
The light from the spheres tints them with the spheres' colour.
The long process of removing them from their machines
negotiates them bedwards, rotating
them through wide and graceful arcs:
Stars discharge. We draw from them answers and power.

**Participants were told** to watch the video and imagine themselves in such a scenario. The flames stuck themselves to the houses and sucked life from the people, and in themselves constituted insanity; the proof is, the English threw themselves into the river, with outstretched arms, themselves liable to *a priori* connection as the tulips amassed themselves in a disposition of arms extending themselves upwards, as stars like Jean Harlow draped themselves over sinuous furniture causing themselves to be borne in chairs to the Waste Land, while the leaves swept up themselves, the poems stepped in and introduced themselves, describing themselves as better versions of themselves, squat quatrains looking for queenly sonnets, drew fluid to themselves even before the precise forms of the buildings themselves were distinguishable, entangling themselves in us and moving through our rooms picking clothes as the clouds rained themselves away. They came to themselves lying on the retaining timbers. After they had remained there for a while, they forgot themselves. Then they came to themselves lying on top of the planks. When they came to, they were afloat on the ocean, with no friends but themselves. Dr Raudive had been visited twice by American engineers who themselves gave little information. The experimenter invited voices wishing to manifest themselves to do so. The voices themselves demanded an *anathema*. They were preserved in the cupboard until they learnt to multiply themselves, and joined us in conversation. Each night they stood on chairs and examined themselves in a mirror to see if any hairy object had started. Birds named themselves, words came out of themselves, woke into our heads, snorkelled themselves into dreams, as when on a long drive, your partner, your children, one by one fall asleep, leaving themselves in your trust, through hours in which thoughts pull themselves out of their bodies: they become words.

**Remove yourself** by pressing the pound key. Sometime later a subtle ghost, yourself in memory, yawns. You ask yourself whether this is the patient you believed to be disordered. Keep your legs, knees and heels down; throw yourself into a sitting position. Put your hands at your knees; raise yourself keeping legs on the floor. Take yourself to your house: it's yourself you see behind the door. You edge past a shelf of wind: it offers some give, so you urge yourself through the walls—underfunded, miscast in the role of yourself, younger. You do not feel yourself.

**When a person dies,** someone sorts through their stuff
I tell her they were someone I knew through Facebook
after collapsing, someone puts a blanket over her
every time someone hits the hourglass, the fight rewinds
she hears someone call out hoom hoom far away, addressed
to someone who does not exist
I read the word JavaScript as I overhear someone say
there, in the moonlit woods, walks someone
saying: I race against someone along the island's edge

someone more well founded would not have done this
someone among us is evil but no one knows who
but it is someone else and the van keeps going
someone keeps offering me drinks but I don't want
much someone starts pinching my hand with force
later with someone else I go to examine the breath-sounds
someone has put thin paper between us and the objects
if there is someone trapped there, we cannot hear her
we merely hear what someone else tells us
a man on the far side shouts. Someone is calling you
thinking in sleep of someone who has no thought of you
someone steals the bicycle I stole, there is no fire
nearby but there must be fire in someone's mind and I say
(with the madness of someone who answers the radio)
once you hold a contract with someone they are yours
someone knocked him off his bike and he does not mind
someone piled barbecue gear on a disused trampoline
yet someone else not twenty streets from here
begins telling you a story about a child who hears someone
calling his name. She heard this is a town where someone
like her could garden in her front yard, suspecting someone
is confident someone will bring help and states
as much, to strive to seek to insert someone among us.

**She showed a collection** of gentle, eccentric dresses. She stood with the expression of one victorious in battle. For years she produced crazy poems, praised by Ashbery. In her silver chambers she reclined. She was as light as the next object floating away, she put up ironwork in her eyes. This proved she was a person and not a dream. Shirt-clad and light-clad she traced through many dark paths. She had two teats, Kathantara and Brihat. She rose, she came to the Gods: they kilted her. With the Paintbrush tool, she created a chard forest. She suffered from spread, which she defined as shift-invariant degradation. She washed dishes and imagined the dishes were orphans. When she saw the king was in distress, she grew nervous. After she was beaten on the shins three times, she revealed what she knew.

She feels herself masculine; she lives in a small shop somewhere in London and she doesn't know London well. She says will you ring on Monday. She hopes to be all right on Monday. She's got her feet in mustard and water. She is *chic* with a little scarf and a lonely smile. She puts her jittery ink line and layered washes of colour to rose. She does not realize she operates like modernist discourse, she speaks river, she is fluent. She is current. She is identified with *Vik*, the Word, and she leads to the gates. She comes to the trees: they shear her. She comes to the Fathers: they kill her. In a month she re-exists, the fire she enters spawns bombs. She is treated for infiltration of the tips of the lungs. She twists from the blows, and creates the impression of a phone operator. She rubs her mouth with ordure. Towards evening, she feels sick at the stomach, and her head turns. She becomes heated by taking wine. She turns from one side to another. When unable to sleep, she is unable to open her eyes. On rising she feels she has not slept enough, she constantly has to move her feet. She complains of a jarring sensation which thrills the right arm. She fancies she looks red, although she is not. Several times she vomits black coffee-grounds. She cuts wounds in the rose tree. She bends and breaks the flowery twigs. What she understands she disapproves of. She expresses tears at parting and sends me the transcript of a galvanized sheet she recorded at her therapist's suggestion. She gains her first knowledge of shear wave arrivals. She installs a holding-tank to feed two vibrating screens.

She impersonates the king's dead daughter to avoid the paperwork of adoption. It is she who is the primordial no-sayer, and during the night and morning she receives the ministrations of Revs. She takes her station in the air's mid-region. She sends me a picture of my mother and strangely she is smiling. She wears a high standing lace ruff, open at the bosom. She gazes momentarily at her exposed skin. She makes peace between rocks and has a digging-stick and moves it before her as if hunting. She is a water and rain serpent, she is intimately connected with the cult of the sun, she is mainly water and rain. She casts a farewell over her shoulder to the camera. A chain of images moves as she says this. She shows some Seventies looks, a few slinky Greek-goddess gowns. She wears a pin and carries lucky bones so that sheep flee from her, and she eats their food. She works with black and white, injecting shots of bright pink and yellow, and shows sack-dresses and reimagined motorcycle jackets. She is also the goddess of the waves. She brings them so close that a surface seems to form between them, an edge, an iridescence, as she calls it. In an incantation she is associated with the river-god, ugly and malicious, and skilled in witchcraft. She begins to perform actions that suggests an end, without effecting one.

When she does not see the dwarf, she will understand his deceit. She will leave the floor followed by whistles and claps, holding a fistful of bills. She will notice the clock stand at 3.33pm. She will slide the sheaf that contains her body soundlessly.

**If a family gets into a new house,** somebody will die;
somebody might have a fiddle, or maybe harp.
Somebody says So let's sum up our conclusions, then,
and somebody else sells shooting accessories.

Somebody gives a dramatic *Howl*, maybe *Sunflower Sutra*.
Somebody takes the trouble to compile a vocabulary.
Somebody stole my pants. Psychiatrist: I can see you're nuts.
It is as if I had become somebody not by becoming another
person but by becoming somebody who splits.
Z fears that somebody is in the house by the pond,
she then reflects on the fear that somebody who lives
by the pond on their own might feel, aware somebody
wants her dead. Can somebody shoot me the info on how
to transfer souls and then somebody else comes in
and does it in a day. Does anybody know somebody
who knows somebody? No one knows such a person.
Confusion arrives from somebody you don't know
when somebody touches the aerial, the noise is horrifying.
*Tschock* seems to be somebody's name on
somebody else's typewriter, I'm displaced because of
a slight variation in space between keys: somebody help.

**They emerged from the fog** on all sides, leaning dottily on sticks, beating little wings. They prepared to fly leather cocoon coats to us.

They stirred limbs and built pyres of selves and they pierced the soles of their feet.

When the detectives located the killer's apartment, they made erroneous motions of their heads.

They turned poems into documents, they held shreds of selves, they rhymed their eyes. They shared a sensibility with early filmmakers.

They returned luxury planes to their owners. They coked into coherent masses, their zincs reduced and volatilized.

They went to the ants and told them that people were saying that they could not fill their sack.

They were painful upon external pressure. They felt pithy, enlarged and dense, they suffered from loss of life.

They went up the hill in 14 red and black strings, and they were the strings of blood and death.

They tuned the violin in my presence, and they forewent being touched by spirits by seeing them.

They resembled small grape seeds. They frequented about Cairo and many other places in hedges and bushes.

They were the dread of the civilised people. They confined the folk culture to clay mouth-organs and knuckle-bones.

They were classed into the necessary, the voluntary, those needful for cleanliness, and the secondary. They had faces they could not talk with.

They halted for the purpose of refreshing the sick man. They slept repeatedly with his wife.

They appraised the property according to the best of their knowledge, but they disliked divulging their ideas on this subject.

They smelled of hard-run horses and ancient sweat. They first wounded with their sting, and then conveyed the lubricant to their mouths.

They saw the waters come out of the earth like clouds, but they had not taken care of the exits of the waters, and returned to the earth.

They gave the youth a military suit on Sunday, they threw him into the river to clean him. They threw his body into the realm of the Symbolic.

They passed like rain on the mountains, like wind on the meadow; they carried on their wretched trade in heaven.

They were filled with sadness at the sight of the bejewelled chariot, which they drew to the edge of the fire.

They drew the cage-system's structure underwater, they were involved in that destruction.

They varied between the Miami and Bethel soils. They differed from the Fox soils in occurring in cross-bedded pockets.

They were told they would watch a VR video from a first-person perspective. They were shopping for haemorrhoid cream, defined so they would fully understand.

They were seeds drawing us to enlightenment. They grasped the stalks by the root end and drew them through the ripple.

As they drew across the water they began to doubt they were merely codes in a machine.

When they appeared as intelligible they extended nearly to the summit of the great moraines.

They heard the trailing rope thrash the headframe. With the force of hooves they met.

They danced through the wood asking leaves from which trees they had fled.

They tried to prevail on her; they took up a collection to purchase the boat in which to sail to her.

They raised their wings in response to wind, thereby sailing across water, but they could not reach her.

They entered the systemic arteries and lodged in distal aorta. They had scammed the victims but fallen in love with them.

As they entered Renfield's chamber-prison, they came in sight of a broad band of smoke from a town.

They were faced, drilled, and reamed to the exact bore size. They moved from heavy silks to leather to waxed metallic linen.

They feared the illuminated person, and shivered at his voice. They stood for decades before they fell over.

They occurred as W-dipping antithetic structures. At the

summit of the pass they found a cabin in which they say De Saussure spent several days.

They furnished us with gray sensations till they ached in our hands like a sprain or an isotope.

**Days weep us,** fists makes tunnels in us, sky peels for us, we wait in line feeling in us the crater that love made, the doctors' shadows surround us, the poems work by translating us into sign, the middle of dust is us, history teaches us to eat. In us the empty obfuscations of world. The herds of us have no narrative. Sleep winds us, it's troubling for us to face a working world from which dream is recused. Let us resort to linguistic examples. Some of us have learned to wake before the alarm to avoid interruption to sleep's conveyer-belt. The consciousness chases us to tell us how harmless he is. When the world is not thinking of us it becomes a riddle. Spirits request us to remain silent. Language fills us, but it is an awkward light to work by. It is sane to believe that what stars make out of their stream is us, so let us record atoms as they fall upon the mind in the order in which they fall, slowly, as feathers down over us, wavy and rain-infused, and settle. Among us the small jagged lies shine and distil the rust of us. We move together in the high fields and leave a track behind us; dusk controls us. The alphabet measures us in sleep. The light that supposes us onto a blank page excites a phoneme. Fish answer us without us knowing. Voices urge: *The riddles! Give us the riddles!* The spider of us cannot say. Hills surround us, lips part us, language houses us, causes us, uses us, the opals in the mountains call us away. While inviting us to think about ways of rendering the passing of time, dreams nudge us into lilies, heavy roses, sea-gardens. For the purpose of this poem let us say our methods limit us to investigating poor user experience. The basin and jug are transfigured when layered and rigid water stands between us. In us the stilled energy of waves, out of us the air the language uses us for.

**The poet's sadness** is that you cannot go into the room that you are in. The subtitles contradict what you think you are saying. When you click on the toolbar icon, images draw on top of text; you move the joystick and the curve is recorded, then you draw the table layout. When you look closely at the icon, you see it's a bidirectional filmstrip. Choose the language you want, then as you open the document check the link status; a dialog box warns you it will turn off spell-checking. When you're thrown into the debugger because of an error, the connect-the-dots app displays the path as you drag the freehand tool.

You don't see couples arguing in public like you used to. You cut the hind legs nearly off. You get the best results with a switch that pushes out the blade. As you pull the handkerchiefs you lift the tube and reveal the ball. Click the style of music or talk you want. You reach the things you both dread and want. You want antiques for warmth, but you need the clean lines of modernism. You plunge into the dungeons of Nero, where heavy water waits for you. You don't turn off the light. You see fogs rise, you cast lots of grass blades. You turn the sentence so as to put an if-clause first. As you draw near the gate of heaven, you appear to be masturbating.

The compound statement lets you run cleanup code but you don't want to be standing where she spawns lifelike vinyl rooted hair you can wash. You press a key or combination of keys. You have a head of hair fly around when you are shooting one frame at a time. The words play tricks on you. You stand at the head of a poem and crack the snow: you must rhyme committee with vomity.

The game employs portals that take you from location to

location. The beginning of your turn has the following sequence of events: You untap your permanents. You save Mesa, but not in the way you specified. You can't activate it before the triggered ability, but you can create a Pegasus. A small bruise in the sky, a sound you are suddenly aware of. You ever heard of my statue? And you butt the gum-man with a bust of your head. You fight in small groups of three vs three, you can't distinguish them from men with sane minds. When you release the mouse, you upload images from its camera. It leaves you with a binary plagued with beyond-visual-range instructions. Get to the end and you have everything unlocked, but you are drowned in the river.

Will you have, sir, tongue or heart? You kill my lice and I'll destroy your marriage. If you plan to write libraries, you must take the footpath into the dark. However, the deeper you go, the longer the path names become. The waitress asks if you would like her to box your meal. If you have read this far you will know where you want a clickable check-box to appear. You are currently viewing all posts tagged with style hounds. You shout: consumer, myth that you are, slur of ego. The shadow murmurs and you turn around to say pardon and see massed youth in streetlight.

Feel the press of the floor coming up through you. Draw an arrowhead at the end of this line to indicate the direction in which you drew the line. Use an eraser to undo it. A preloaded game has you rolling a ball across the objects you draw. The energy you store moves to the arrow and pushes it. You turn the fingers of a pair of distressed coyote-finish gloves. You drop the ball that you removed from the glass of sentence-flow, you go to her house and drink a flat Coke and try to come up with a reason to leave. You model it with spreadsheet software, demote a heading level to body text. Because *Geneva* is international, you run it out in the Swedish character set. You will want to tell Word you are creating a form letter, that you wish to use the current document, and that your data source is Training_letter data.doc. You parallelize the backup by backing up the disk volumes simultaneously. If you tried previously to get the Loading Dock code by sending the governor the photonic code display you now receive an ith code. Make certain you are not continually allocating and releasing memory.

You put the "I" in idiot. You put the you in pronoun. You come to me in the dream. The sword wields you, the gun fires the arm, the head. "Eh! grandmother, I have served you honestly; now give me what you promised."—I try to address you as a hunter of men. I am loved, I said to you. Loved, you said, by the light of the planet. You open the microwave and find yesterday's tea—and then you've got a virus again. Or perhaps it was when you got back from walking the dog.

You were the maiden aunt who lived with us. Hugo held your hand and kissed you. You rattled down on the train to catch a steamboat for home saying You is a two-phoneme word. You stood for a week or so, till on a whim you slashed your wrist on a moth, and a handful of garnets rattled onto your soiled counterpane.

ANYBODY COULD HACK in and get my iris pattern, but
has anybody seen Death Race 2. You can find
the good in anybody if you give them a chancre.
I'm so fly I'm sky high, I dare anybody to cut my wings.
Does anybody have a Tmobile I could borrow for a few days
can anybody help me get some more followers? I'll help
you back. Has anybody used the Group video feature?
Is anybody writing a fanfic I could be in?
Reblog if you understand and accept anybody's sexuality.
Is anybody following @charliesheen if not its like
a train to my house! I'll go to war with anybody, don't give
ah fuck! I don't love anybody: that accounts for my width.

None of us could recall anybody called Bower,
it had no meaning for anybody present.
Does anybody want to play Words with Friends
does anybody know how to spell a curse on milk cartons
would anybody send a broadcast saying Swan-neck faucet
does anybody know how you testify in front of congress?
Don't allow anybody to leave your presence without
laughing. Anybody want to go out and build a snowman.
Anybody else wake up looking for tabs to open up
in their unopened eyes' field of vision? Anybody?

ANYONE CAN CONTACT A COLLEAGUE and ask to be a job-shadow host
anyone can tap in and take control any time they like.
Elements will ask you to exclude anyone who doesn't belong.
Tell Elements if it made mistakes in identifying anyone.
I have not given anyone the lift home that I had promised them.
It's not a thing that anyone can do, grub the soft fern-shoots.
Each time it rings I think it is for me. It is not for me nor anyone.
When anyone says "Return", the others are full of sorrow.
Do not speak to anyone you meet on the road.
Do not send anyone you met online any money.
A glimpse of a playground, too fast to see if anyone is there.
Hardly anyone gets off and I wander around the small dock,
anyone is the ghost of elsewhere viewing my website so
does anyone want to see a picture of my eye.
Do not tell anyone your name until bygone
do not copy or disclose its contents to anyone.
Anybody is one; anyone is body.

## Nine. Of Ownership

**The men of war spoke:** Your hand against mine. Mine against yours. Your eye may catch mine without catching fire. Your lips seek solace, yet find no joy in mine. My poem swings back like a pickaxe in a goldmine. Mine is the victim-activated explosive, the dug hole.

**I make a sound,** not part of the listener's own sense
I saw my own shoulder, and the back of
my head in the mirror, then I found my arm
was over my face in the nights of my own country
who is enjoying living on her own in a splendid house
saying I intended to add some remarks of my own
but space did not create its own stories
masterpieces had their own exchange mechanism
walking home on my own I held a double-bladed axe
my own dead, my skin, beady between fingers
and then I was on my own, climbing a scree slope
banded with mists, leading my own shadow
simultaneously with my own death
as students created their own similes
these poems held the natural glow of an own mind
put on your own mask before assisting your children
immediately in the bright force field of your own shock.
They had eyes though little was similar to their own
stage in which a man stood off from his own imagination.
Larkin seduced us into his own dinginess. It shines with

its own half-light, requires no additional power supply
and terrain is all it is, a bleakness all of its own.
It comes with its own lagoon, *masseuse* and windmill
from which the inhabitants behold their own habitation.
My own face, I think, but bodiless, and by the imagined
light of the planet your eyes picture my own face.
He signals the boy to let the train pass out of the mine
of its own momentum: the brain makes its own disasters
in a country its own painters wouldn't recognize.

**His confinement,** and, perversely, his power. His eyes gleam like naming torches, his neck, his tongue, and his body are black; his garments red. His antennae continually tap the margins of the female's body and his features are Grecian. A smile plays his oil-caked lips. Shouldering his massive mace, the breadth of his breast is considerable. His bristles are a foot long, his tusks are great and white, and his eyes glow like beltane fires. His long hair trails the ground and wipes out forests and villages. His methodical bronchitic breathing gives his story a sly, understated humour. Men hold open his weary and death-dealing eye. A single horn grows from his forehead. His hands extend to the limits of east and west.

His sister sang a crying song: *Ha, brother, ha.* His idol was a waterhead, with the teeth sticking out. It served as a powerful hunting-amulet for him and for his descendants. He hid his sister's keys and purse and made them reappear. Like his two older brothers, the flame in his name referred to the manner of his thoughts. His voice was unforgettable, his secret wish, to stop time. His brother worked his strings in an unsteady, painful manner to which his *rabab* complained loudly in cymbal-shimmers. When he walked, his ornaments jingled like history-making. His pen described a cardamomlike girl and time in blue mansions. His poems traced the modulations of syntactic mystery. His shield sported flames burning on a field of jealousy.

His active work as the national god began after the death of the sun-god, when his aloof countenance sprouted six heads endowed with the power of revealing former existences. In his hands were the holy shell and the war mace. His reign was a period of anxiety. He put on his helmet of glass, and he performed his initial and subsequent incisions with conventional instrumentation. He stuck his sword into the backbone, cut all his ribs down to the loins and drew out his lungs. He pushed the shadow-filled spirit back into his chest, reporting his success to Red Thunder, his high-tuned friend, although his account was given rapidly. At night he drove stars into the well. A white ray shone from his mouth while grey houses were lost in his yellow-tipped eyes. His cheeks were coloured with the penitential weeping of a courageous man. Black filled his eyes and a solemn look came over his face. Slowness diverted his attention. That sound was his body hitting the door. A voice in his head told him to get a knife from the kitchen and hurt Dawn. He bowed his head and held it down and tried to blow out his words, his breath turning to white frost, enveloping his body, till his condition was entirely normal. His laughter rippled lyric night. He sang his story to the accompaniment of finger cymbals. He moved his legs by vertical tractive movements; and then he directed his head to watch his mesmeriser. He moistened his finger with saliva and rubbed it on his palm, his hand instantly closed: when mesmerised gold was applied, it caused extension of his hand. After getting down from his chariot, he enfeoffed the descendants of *Song*. He built a tomb for Bi Gan who had had his heart ripped out by the tyrant Zhou. He moved carefully in the depths with the sword of *Fang* tightly gripped in his hand. He struck the ground with his arrow and caused water, then fixed his five arrows on his bow, drew, and shot. As a double-homicide suspect he changed his name to History and moved to California. Confronted with alien invasion, he took his arrows and participated in the war, but clove the platoon with his axe. His sergeant, groaning with a broken shoulder, hissed. The final word that left his mouth was followed by the crack from his AK: a slug above his left eye. The bear-man squeezed his hand gently and feelings displayed on his face. His country was broken, only the colossal vitality of his illusion gave an air of reality. His hand raised in a formal gesture of farewell over the crashed cars, horns and in-vehicle route-guidance-system errors. His chine's receptor node copied the bear-man's comm codes. He bore his bow in his hands. His sleeves down as he straddled his donkey. His teeth were rotten. He tried the side door and fought back flames with his gold suit in the black plastic cover as the targeting computer kept the crosshairs active. Regarding his journey to the Castle and its ruined entrance hall, swirling water confirmed his suspicions. Raising his hands he sketched a subtle character on the air. He picked up his paddle. After he had made two strokes he reached his town. In his jewelled car he went to inspect flowers. He pushed a pair of smooth, dark shades hard against his eyes with a gloved thumb, and hummed his thought into serial machines. High above the sunset, his long white hair streamed in solar wind.

He shook his head and flung high in the air the greedy mouth of thought. Keeping his bow between his teeth as if manipulating a whistle, wearied by his country's defeats, his worthy mind approached heaven. His voluminous suicide note was complete. He tendered forgiveness to all who had wronged him. He remembered his childhood and gave to the worm his belted chest. In his thoughts he returned to his ancestral home and burned spirit money at his own grave. The knot slipped to the back of his neck, and bent his head forward on his breast. Perspiration dripped from his feet, and he swung in the hot noon. His skin turned ashen, his hair fell out and his clothing burst into flame. His tomb is at Hamadan. His tomb is at Taif. That was his death. History is his. History is hiss.

**Her stooping posture** implies imposture, opposing forces between contort and distort. She is attached to the red hair-string beads on her nightstand. Her breath is in each object. Her name shows on the page. In the evening she carries her arm hanging from her shoulder. Three frost-blades radiate from her front. They bind her to two young men who are determined to learn her trademark draping techniques. Her flight leads her down a remote path, on which is a doorless summer-hutch. They come to her and find her stuck upright on a stick. Her shadow lifts on a light draft of faint perfume. Her prime shrine is on the Island of *Enoshima*. Her illness manifests as inability to control her thoughts. When sitting straight, the small of her back does not support her. Chilliness shakes her. Her complexion remains yellow. Food distresses her; archaic sea-fruits search inside her. Remedies aggravate her condition. The touch of bedclothes cause her to start, and the closing of a door draws her tears. She says her orgasm is still inside her. She averts her eyes and her pinions tremble softlier than moths'; she flitters, leaving her hollow cold, her scimitar hair, her eyes like ice flowers. Her eyes are pools for sadness, and her voice is the coiling of the sea. She makes to break the blade of the scythe with her foot, but it turns and cuts her knee, and her daughter carries her home. At the golf-course border, she skids in short grass, her paws dig into turf. On her wedding she wears a yellow helical antenna and carries a wooden top with an iron butt-piece on her right hand. Owing to circumstances following her marriage, her short woman's thermosphere, with the skirts looped closely about it, dangles by the vibration of her swift descent, and with the knot holding under her ear, her head leans sideways, and her pinioned arms seem content with their confinement. She exposes her stomach to the technician, her dream-boy waves, jumps. Swithin takes the baby and wraps it in her web and places it under her left arm. To her belong corn, squashes, also flowers. To her belong deer, as well as ravens. She records their behaviour in her green-shaded book, enriches her poetry with her own coherence. You experience, in her poems, mind outrunning body. Laugh. Laughs, blows and wobbles her head; her dog has been killed and the knowledge withheld from her. She knows in her dream the voice calling her is untethered. Her goal is to go into her history, with her chaplet of skulls, her suit of hair, her memories which no mortal shares. Her TV is embedded into white leather wall-tiles facing the toilet. She slips an unpassioned finger through her hair. The water draws through her nostrils, the book of the *Hosts of Hell* in her hands, an orange for later, four cold *pierogi*. Her left eye is subject to rage and guilt. She receives permission to visit her imprisoned brother. Her eyes brighten, and she stares intently. If he ignores these engagement-cues, she vocalizes or moves her arms. He wants to soften her skin, to lighten the whites of her eyes, and sharpen her eyebrows and eyelashes, her mouth, that delicate O. Her nose towers from the plane of her face. Her clear blue eyes him. She spends her time with a photograph and two ruined letters, rubbing her legs at night, remembering how his left hand rested under her head and how his free fingers touched her hair. Her cheeks are halves of a peach; her neck is ivory, her belly a heap of wheat. Her call changes to a downscale note, slurred from *do* to *la*. The herein-described incident forces her to revisit her past. She remembers a voice calling her out of bed. She obeys against her will and goes to a muddy field as a mother-shaped ship nears the ground. A piercing sound prevents her from moving. A tremulous light blinds her, pulls her inside the craft. Two beings with tiny mouths and saucer eyes, in motorcycle jackets, tell her wordlessly to undress and to cut her tree down. With it, she erects a spirit house to hide a cursed object in order to drive the queen to her death. The fortune-teller prays for her recovery of her former position. She hides a small box in her skirt. She scratches her hand on the lady's golden brooch. She stretches her arms, but the box slips from her grasp. Following her triumphant *debut*, she lives quietly on Sullivan's Island, tending bees and helping widowed Archie next door. At her mother's funeral, she reunites with her friend Blair, from whom she had been estranged since her marriage. Her footsteps swish on the mosses. When they look for the chief's child and return her father's hat which she gave away, he (the father) makes her sit down. Then she hands the shells to her father's slave and has him give them to her son-in-law. Now he (the slave) gives her old clam shells to drink soup from. He opens her mouth. Her wet shift clings to the slightest tremor of her countenance. Her last words were it is heard or herd.

**Petron, our hero,** our central figure, our you and me, or if you will our them, our mutual hourglass, purchases a number of electrical tapes and purports to lend coherence. Our heads share a vein in which our blood mixes and in moments of excitement we both feel our hearts beating in our temples cometh the hour. Please ensure the incisions do not penetrate deep into our skulls. Our times are unfixed, human voices are in our small room, singing. We are the words for horses, our eyes are still, our I is devoid of time or space. What is left of skin in our rush to consolidate we lifted from the enemy. Aliens invade our heads. They use us to provide bodies, due to the toughness of our skulls. These are our souls. Aspirate. These are arseholes. We hold our heads strange. Our loss is nothing. David says: we pierce our enemies with our horn. Our vowels contribute to the painting. Our air-operations are resource-consuming. Cold currents pass over our faces. Our spacetime is the FM signal of a macro-quantum vacuum. Our watches break open, we mean no harm and to harm. The days hold in our spirals, swarms of eyes learn our names. Our fingers burn with love. Our infrastructure team will install a hotfix to move thin bones through our fields of tall poppies. A strong moon pitches our shadows forward. Our corn supply draws near an end. Our eyes are blanks for messages, more on-the-hour than our awake lives might lead us to believe. Our data suggests beetles inhabit our conjoined selves. Smell our loving fingers. The turbine transforms our shepherd's tale into a piper's tune. Mechanical energy of the wind is mimicked by a vacuum cleaner glistening our colours and smelling our dust. Our eyes fix on a point of light so fine subject and object sing as one; our bodies lit by the moon. We design holes in our cores so we can stick the plug in, push the button, and open our hair to the ocean. Our wounds are wide. Gulls cross our moving local of light in a wailing slant. We are the last of our line. Our departure is set for 13:00, we throw out implements & trail our shadows, architecting processes and pipelines for max efficiency. The folds in our faces are maps of love, its misrepresentations. We store time in our heads, stare out of our windows. God is our accountant, he files us into the mountainside. String our words on the chain of folk-told stories. Our work was to make language conscious by means of poems. Our first language was light, followed by the sound echoing, not echoing.

**Arranged in their beds** children are made precisely by moonlight. Their eyes seed with souls, their hair fills reservoirs. Their tender heads rub the grass. They draw night with the tips of their horns. Things sink from their names. Fathers urge their sons to bathe in the river. Set the hammers to strike their strings. Their thereness gives a floor to the world. We grind their teeth. Eighty thousand teachings are contained within their 31 characters. Their shapes are mirrored through the crystal roof. Large steel doors loom into their spaces. Sand transcribes their lines during the Africa campaigns. The clouds lose their threads. Kings huddle to their necks in loose plumage. Their faces instruct us, words open their senses or press down their meanings. In their trapezoid orbits we see their restless eyes. The spacing of their barbs, their relative size and placement are crucial. Poems hatch from their small seeds, stir through their roots a ghost of iron. In their struggle over the bottle, they approach their last years in cruel arcs. Spirits attempt to utter words with their song; passages fill novelists with anxiety. Theirs is the sea inside, the depth where sky meets. Veale and Hao filter their simile-set manually beneath the throat-pieces of their visors. They know the meaning of their own sleep. Contrasts in their outlooks and class origins beset their blood-brain barriers. Their great wrists like whipcords expand to twice their natural dimensions as they pull handkerchiefs from their respective theories. The heavy tread of their firm steps strikes the stone flags, their long rapiers jangle. They hasten by the light of their lanterns over wild passes. Manufacturers and attendees bring their naked children bound upon their backs to catch their breath. They grope their way north through the smoke-filled sample rooms. Those who desire to fall into a trance throw a black cape over their heads. As phenomena change their forms, spirits reconstruct their bodies from the long dead. They could have been lying on their lawn lifting their sons up to the sun and feeling the warmth dribble down their necks. With no rational organizing principle to connect their interactions they compare their love with hot coal. Their days decline. The stars rustle their sweet-wrappers and their children hold their tongues. When agencies consider red-dot optics, their targets stir. They think that an end of their troubles is at hand. Their soul-seeds lose touch with their higher consciousness. Their sound is mixed in the flute. Their voice is piped, silvery, leaf-curled at their high notes; self in their narratives shows as a deficit, the trees have their treasons and their treasure chests, their heads lean forward and agree. Riders straddle their bikes tensely. Offspring gnaw at their mothers' bellies, eat grass. Their wages halve weekly. Their bodies take fire and are consumed. Unsure ghosts empty their rooms. They hear denuded carcasses whisper in their dreams. Words command a powerful reality of their own. They fight their civil wars internally, before speaking. They open their mouths to agree. To them things don't sound like their names or look like their names. All the implements are in their places; but their places do not agree. Thunderheads turn and contract in their channels. Their statements are concerned with general matters. They seek to dismantle the thematic composition and structure of their poems—their redistributor reserves the right to delete posts and comments. They return and freely take their place in the flow of his cadences.

**Wakes thinking aren't I** a person whose hands hang low
mind in whose shell we move. The sea whose
sobs lull, whose content and form are in no
connection, whose children were begotten
from that demon whose head laughs a horn concerto
whose lower part is an ingenious hunting sound
whose hammer-fired voice and appertaining qualities
are seen through rosewater. Whose weapon is the club-stem
of the mother-tree whose name he never heard
whose headrings give a white shine in the sun
whose capture is the object of the chase

whose abstract belongs to the expanding set
of the abstract of the query, whose time coordinate is
handwheels whose black box is not fully open
to inspection, whose sole purpose is to link to specific web pages
whose end use is visible as larvae infest the lungs
whose speech is a rustle, a token bristling
whose howls you take for passion's essence
whose skins are yellowed for the shopper
in whose blue haze and scattered copses exposed
automotive are overrun with ants whose hills are us
whose deathlike repose is determined by death
whose button-nosed work routines are aesthetics
whose hands are method whose belly is the place
in which time is whose hearts are on fire in the snow of
a certain personality, whose name I never learn
whose properties include duct tape, beetle wing-veins
whose needle points in all four temporal indices.
Whose odes addressed their subjects wholly.
Whose name was writ in water, one, grave of.

The book fell out of the hands   had pulled the skin to see what loosened   the kind of thing the dead man-being had clasped   had been brought by human agency   to a place where he had not been before   the generational curse had been canceled   the lost book had been used for a doorstop he had not been disturbed by a dream   he had been two & a half days buried in snow   this had the quality of a still held on a VCR   the explosive had cohered it no longer flowed   itching of the toes with redness as if they had frozen   had passed into suppuration & were about to open a gallows structure of wood had been raised   we had been separated at birth she did not recollect what had happened during her fit had she not been in the car when she crashed it her blood they had eaten supposing it to be berries the pilot digester had no apparent settling of sludge the control digester had the normal separation the words had lost somewhere Sunday he rested & had a nervous collapse he had been reborn in a celestial realm lattice vibrations had become the determining process he had never made it to the elimination rounds the bird had to withhold a peck for 4 sec he announced that he had visited Spirit Land he had revived the dead in an earlier war he had stung her in a great hollow in his head she had for years daily vomited her food burnt brick had bulged out & the terraces lay scattered she had a head liable to flooding the devil had two short sticks a white stone & a rope the regret values had to be converted to a comparable scale it had been neglected until the gate was sealed with ivy long seaweed had grown on it the small hard sleeps we had were depth to receive god you had to find the nearest locked church these poems had the nature of fear Billy had a '53 Olds two-door hardtop custom he had tried it with a stick & it had become soft at the time the instant played the creature in fact had 4 power after they had laid the burial-case in the high place he had been in limited production the sky's colour had shifted from green to black I had bought flowers on my way from work Z had laughed when she saw them she had given her name as "zones" this crystal had an almost metallic reflectivity cropped jackets had the starched three-dimensional contouring of a bed skirt recounting an incident he had had with a women by the tube station I had become the person I had wanted to be circumstances had changed so much I no longer wanted to be that person each product had to invent its own syntax users had conversations with the system each product had to invent its syntax we had been woken by lies had had enough.

**The angry frogs** have invaded the history section:
they have waited in the shadows for long enough
the aircon units have been switched on at different times
They have doors that open on unpromising corridors.
I am to have an operation, and recognize the room
have two empty glasses; a pitcher of
water; a handkerchief; have a glass half shell
the messages the gentlemen have received are hard-coded
I have written during the unfolding of the whole hallucination
I have the impression that the voices speak onto the tape; they
have a spaceless quality. These recordings
have to be made with the recorder turned to highest volume.
unknown voices have taken on some sort of personality,
I have a list of words that have been used more than once
have crossed the Alphs, Kubla hears a low-flying jet
time measures the intolerance things have for shape
I have two days to repossess the craft.
I have to cycle to B&Q to buy a drill bit
the dolls have jointed eyes. What we have sung disappears in fire
I'm not sure the server is working, but don't have anyone to ask
she says you have nerves of electricity. I reply,
No, I have been asleep
I have words like the red islands. I
have moped in the Emperor's garden.
Mother, I have a wife. Her hair is fastened with cedar limbs
I have a doubt that this man is entirely a member of our
nervous race
I have skin to flower with. I have a shave and leave a beard.

Concept C has been explicitly recognized by subject S.
It is sleek, has a Kevlar framework and three locking solutions.
It is a spirit who was once happy, but has been disturbed.
It has a dream; he is bothered by the dream.
It is the strap-hanging skeleton of what has been.
Tao's deck has been taking down players all weekend.
Sleep has its turns. The news has consumed us.
The mere conceivability of the thing has no weight.
It is likely that kissers and chasers has other purposes.
This vest has a full mesh back, and a hull pouch.
It has a side plate rail for scope mount.
It has a laminate grip and comes with three moon clips.
Human Flesh Search has became a generic term.
The program receives a notification that an event has occurred.
The scanline has the texture of a language.

You need your head looking at. Fulfil your prophecies in ways you did not anticipate. In each of your eyes is a spirit. Feeling comes to your chest and your shadow follows you into the tunnel. Sleep will not enter your eyes, you feel your way, keeping your knife to your finger to free up tissue, while your other fingers work to protect critical structures. Bones connect to your ancestors through your father's semen. Insert the index and second fingers of your free hand. Put your needle through the end of one foreleg, hold it in place with a scarf by rotating your shoulders forward. If your palm itches, you receive money; clench your fists. Hold; then relax. Pull your toes up. Position your cursor and insert a clickable checkbox. Rearranging your table is known as pivoting your data: turn it off to speed up your screen display. In versions prior to 2020, a toolbar appears on your screen. Close your eyes to see your way. Now that the early-career journo knows your secret names cover your ground with subsequent shadows. Put your hands under your hips: bring knees to chest, crushing them against your lungs. Begin your turn with your hands at the 3 and 9 o'clock positions, then at 1 o'clock with your right hand. Reading your draft, a curious phrase awakens your attention. Your creative writing degree finally comes in handy. Your kids lie in the dust with blue mouths. Take wax from your ear and apply it. Get a water axe, lift it above your head and bring it down on the yolk-sac. Power vomits in your mouth, multiplies in your ears. Direct your singing to the head area of the patient. Write a letter to your employer. Thank you for your corporation. Your grammar is of dream—tear peepholes in cloud and your eyes look down on you. Your use is governed by Terms & Conditions. You hear complaints about your best-selling memoir, while under your clothes your scars breathe. Your face is a rose washing itself, soon it will hurl its first petal. Ah, owl, long ago you built your round home in the head's dark, yet must divide your love. Your mother who hatched you will shake her head for you; your tiny glass stairway will be traversed by your soul. Your HR department has probably explained this to you. The liver meridian begins at the tips of your big toes, enters your body through the groin, and traverses the gallbladder into your throat. Speak your mind, and a base man will avoid you. Your *yoni*, the limb called the ornament of women, is to be cut. Your lips also because by her they were kissed. If you are using routing protocols, the intercept traverses your source. Go to the beach, lie down, cover your face with your hat: a cinema in your eye. The person next to you has been speaking your language. Your confessions are filed in the dialect of electrons. Your life has a smack of the prequel. You're at your most recent boarding school. Your shit smells different. It's getting cold, your attention rises toward the stars, but the fire exit leads to your pillow. You must support your similes with evidence and personal references. Traverse your files: you will realize you are the child, and it is your voice, caught in the feedback-loop of your screaming. This is the sack of time your death vacates. Tonight your letters reduce history to your first climb up the rocky path, the hole in your shoe. Remove moving subjects from your shots. Evacuate your eyes. Very respectfully, your obedient servant, your spirit daughter.

## Ten. Of Doing

USE TAB TO OPEN BOX, remove packaging and reflective suit. Use the full pack of 52 paintbrushes to outline legs, then the lookup table to interpolate corrected values, and unwrap the Sword of Names. Use arms to strike capitals, grab claws to lay hold of limbs, and mechanical paws to stroke wound areas. Use event-trees to represent yesterday operators on your board. Your opponent is your soul.

Use the dotted line to trace paths of sprawling events and muted watercolours to draw your bodiless opponent: as you do this, use velcro to keep spycam attached, use a waterpot with its body buried in your future grave; maintain an icy blue calm using a harlequin pattern. Show your thinking by use of block capitals: the resulting neural network diagram may indicate your soul's location.

Being sure to position your earphones, use an ifstatement without elsebranch while using deck relation to declare symbol use. Next, use XML-based format to store events; use the Sternberg memory task and inflight effects to spend your cooldown: let hourglass hits and audio queues feedback while deploying either fixed or fluxed harms. Imitate the calls of insects. Use wicked and uncanny ways to create potential wells: use gentle cycle for maximum fluffiness or use fake to daze your adversary.

If the task requires you to design a compliant solid-state armament with editing capability, use a reamer to enlarge hole so it fits leg taper; then use a gutter adze to rough out the blade. Build a many-hued paradise from bricks, install within it your pheromone trap. Lure into it your Psyche. Using pebble-count to list bed-and-bank material, remember that different voices are used to address: dogs, toddlers, partners, the very old, the dead, gods, God. You may use the Ode form, but not the vocative.

Your opponent is both subtle and double. Choose subtitle or dub modes. An elseblock node before cleanup in a finally block controls searches at instance start time. Use double duchesse silk chine to stiffen excessive folds and particle-swarms to optimize joint angle; erect an 11-storey decoy apartment building using foldcrete; use compatible screw patterns with regulate mount; the expense fund screen will fence your gains. Entrap your soul in one of three genie bottles. Guess which.

Your soul will arise as a *jinn*. Use forward slash to hack opponent, backslash to lash yourself. Use DS statement to set aside silos for warheads: use columns from your insertion point onward for phosphor storage and a TV camera readout system to add to a sprite using perspective warp; use if instruction to check that the number of sprites loading is larger than 0. Utilise red-dot or in-sight.

Deal. Place your cards as bookmarks in your dog-eared Proust (Scott Moncrieff translation): aces count high in chapters with analepsis, and low where prolepsis occurs; then use ogive as hybrid target bullets in one of two general strategies to degrade metadata. Use ace 2 3 4 5 6 for the runners, for playing tos and fros use x and y axes to adjust pitch and yaw; fill background with paintbucket drawing three-lane highway incorporating fake tunnel entrance; create an animated character to trick opponent into turning off smartphone.

By using sonnet to celebrate your perfections you underplay your rival: six rhymes should be used, the hourglass, or king kansu, being eliminated. Play the king when a number over two cancels the first three joystick functions in initialization at max nodes. Use generalized threats to prevent Left from losing if Right plays first; use it to silence a room of losers. Your soul will be among them.

To signal the end of the outdoor phase use sardines on retreat to terrify a group of high guys executing a U-turn.

Souls feed on love: they predate you. Use your noose to manoeuvre a carried broadsword into the dragon, then drop it to unlock or lock a door, move a carried key of the right colour into it. Use sense or innocence, but not subsense. Separate soul from body, if not already sundered.

If you have got this far, describe your experience (use only grammatical forms not previously used: for instance, prepositional pronouns). Introspection is the most effective weapon here: use inwit to outwit. Email or post your account to your only surviving primary-school teacher.

You should by now be a decade older. Locate on your body: soil creep, sump detritus, weeping wells. Use your psychotic laugh to close. Heads win, for now. Replace in box.

**Did I part the fencing** to show her. All I did was carefully position the eye in my hand and then give it a slight twist. I turned the skin off the fore legs, as I did the hind. Doris did not leave her body, she did her turn at the pump handle, she did reverence to the manifestation of the god, and then wiped me. Did you drink iced tea? If the events did not happen in an order that would lead to the event, previous Painter brushes did. When I did not withdraw he rolled up a Rs 500 note and did two monster lines. I did so myself when I first attended to mesmerism: and deeply do I lament the injustice I did. I did the same to the back of his hand, it instantly extended, and the extension was increased by farther rubbing. I desired him to close them again, which he did with difficulty. Did you bring anything in with you? Did you throw anything out of the plane? Although she did not suffer any ailment, her body became cold. She did not seem to be breathing. He ordered splendid medicine, but she did not improve. He wanted to be sure she did not have any regret so he summoned the women of the inner palace to enjoy themselves with her. He did not like the fact that in a sentence such as Pegasus did not exist, a fictitious name stood in the subject place. A man was angry with me for reasons I did not understand. He mounted the Hi-Lux on an AK and dumped his mag. The prince did as he was told, and immediately the mare came, with the foal, out of the water, saying, Why did you not go down among the fishes, and Wow, what did you do to your hair?

**Do you know which** preposition to use with the following verbs: debride, decouple, datamate, digitize. Do you hear, deadly nightshade. If you do, you see these prompts: code window, domain-swapped contacts, non-linear random-access systems. But so do the creatures which subsist on flowers and fruits. Do the dead reach out to you? Do the dodo? on which root do messages run from the brain? do I need moon lights when breeding clownfish? do my precepts seem obvious or commonplace? do certain noises from the fridge approach language? to which theory of mind do you subscribe? do I contain enough fluid in a life to float a ship? do you like me? do the clouds tower or lower? what do the eyes leave on a thing looked at? what do you seek of me? do you dismember an inn? do you know the muffin man? Never do any of the following: cut the rope binding firewood. Step on the dotted line. Discard plastic dildo mouldings. Do the searches that most interest you. Do not call a child a frog, or it will not learn to talk. Do not say thanks for a medicine, or it will lose its power. Do not wish fishers nor hunters good luck, or they will be liable for operating cost. Do not step over a puppy. Do no felony, do harmony. Do not break a dog's stare. Do not handle the tissues more than is necessary. Do not know the English equivalent. Leave poetry to people who do not depend on writing. Do not write the bones from the hand. Do not sit by the fire when others do not. You hear me not do it. Do the maths, do the philosophy. Grammatical deviations do not conform to grammatical rules. As θ is increased from zero, do the following increase, decrease, or remain the same: the parent document, the pseudo-adult, the random sampling. Do not seek perfection in language but in sentence: do not google do not go gentle do not go. Do what the poem says.

**Does the noun exist** in nature does Python support default states does the forest include does does not the essence of free will reside in deletion phenomena does Pope speak more of thought or expression does data mapping add to the poem does the energy come from the potato itself so what does the foregoing mean? The lover's image does not fade into the traffic of silence edge lighting does not allow local dimming which does not presume that the poem is the vehicle for representing the travails of a discrete first-person subject does the cemetery have Wi-Fi does the path not spring from morality but moral forces does time take place what does fate await does what is known include the subject's knowledge of it does the data not measure the correlation between search requests does it disguise an otherwise ugly radiator does nature stand in the same relation to world as does mass to force when you have a shower does your hair dry nicely if a tweet falls and no one is there to RT it why does it hurt so much when I say I care so little why does it take him an hour to walk from somewhere 25 minutes away does it always rain harder when I get out the car how many Martians does it take to screw in a light bulb how many does it take to get to the centre of God if electricity comes from electrons does morality come from morons if it's wrong why does it feel so right what does it mean if you can't stop replaying if she does it like this does jealousy seem like the product of an esemplastic imagination or does it just descend into a tit for tat game delete tweet doesn't really delete it does it count as colluding with a delusion if I agree where does poop come from do does doze why does it smell like horse butt in this here parking lot does it always smell like BO in the elevators does it work what does it mean when it says when you strangle a Smurf what colour does it turn does B not know that A has doctored B's quantum file.

**Science assignment done,** thank you ChatGPT. Only a little over two months then I am done with you. I've just done a job in Rob an Electronics Store in Mobster World. I'm so done with boys, they are too much for me. Well done. I'm done with twitter. My house is clean, laundry done, bills all pd, time to get dressed. When my time comes forget the wrong I've done. Shoutout to the girls that say "I'm done with boys". Finally done curling my hair. First mock draft done, many to go! I've got the page numbers done. If you made it into my favourites, you have done well. The games are done. The only childish thing I've done is worry. The linkbait headline asking if blogs are dead has done its job. I didn't do it but if I'd done it the money-drone would have done me in. Billion shares done on a bus. Finally getting my feet done. I've just done a job in Pick Pockets in Mobster World. Let nothing be done through strife or vainglory. I've just done a job in Liquor Store Robbery in Mobster World. Break the banks and have done. This done with minimal help from the priest, she points out people in the congregation, tells you the things they've done and that have been done to them. All that can be done is counterbalance the weight of the moving. The poems have done more to standardize the alien experience than substantial sums of money. On the way to board the Dublin plane he tells me what he has done. I am satisfied nothing unusual had been done to the tape-recorder. Voices can speed up; but this can only be done after they have been recorded. This is done and we do a five minute diode recording unlike anything we have done before. Copying is done with both machines turned to max.

The same voice continues: A wireless receiver is coupled to the tape recorder as is done for radio programmes. Circumstances dictate that this must be done if further experiences are to be co-ordinated. This is done on the original tapes, since each recording adds its own noise.

## Eleven. Of Mutability

**I SEE AN OFFICER,** almost an island, hurling up on my shores almost against a daylight the colour of TV, almost the sea, the movement contemporary and exciting, sharply irregular, with an almost hypnotic quality, almost freezing the acoustic wave in time. It is almost always too cold. The busy wood box is almost too heavy. Emission from clock harmonics is almost completely absent from capital-spending, is almost three times as great as on the control. I am with a friend, someone younger, almost a daughter, her eyes almost almond, almost losing the use of limbs, the cramp comes on almost every fifteen minutes, violent, almost continual eructations; once the voice almost fails, her fingers almost of themselves turn the edge of a carving. It is spoken of in almost every inscription as being given into the king's hand. Her huge neck grows almost black. Milk in spoonful doses is vomited almost instantly. An anterior parietal infarct is so deep it creates almost a cleft in the hemisphere. On the tenth day the vomiting ceases almost entirely, she draws her deep chest almost to her chin, and the knees contract till they almost seem to touch her abdomen. My mother is so near as to be almost the palpitating present, there in body, in the last of the sun, crumbs around her, I am almost able to wipe them. We are on the almost empty plane as it taxis for take-off unsure of these light coins in my pocket and the bicyclists are almost run off the tracks the crowd disperses to almost nothing and technicians come into the auditorium. In the ensuing struggle I capture Hitler and for several days almost on my own I hold him in my attic room. At one stage he wants to buy cigarettes and I almost let him go but then decide to draw a moustache on him with a permanent marker so people will recognise him and he has to be accompanied but everyone is almost casual. I am several hundred yards off when my cue is almost due and I have to sprint over to reach the stage on time, the rocks are jagged almost everywhere and the waves dangerous and I see the city across the bay as waves reach almost to the side of the hill with an almost human agency. I am led round in a circle almost and I can't see him as I queue but then I see him on his own and sad and I rejoin him with the ice cream and he is gone. A green armoured carrier lies almost unseen through the thickets on the right; I wait almost out of sight and he cycles up the track past me. As the search continues this becomes almost unbearable; at the front there is a list of his previous books: almost all titles have the word "dust" in them. Suddenly almost without warning and after a couple of days here (and this almost seems to take place in real time) I realise we are not going to Taunton at all, I am with a friend, almost a daughter, she is not sure how to find her way to the lower path where the children are and then a small helicopter, almost a model, lands close to me and N and S get out. I realise things will be OK, light there almost filtering. Thought is fossil water, leaking from hills with a clarity that almost makes it seem no different from air, varying from almost full assertion to almost nonassertive tension.

**Mostly though poems** are corpses on the table
as though a wedge rives them, and bursts
them into Eclipse: not dawn-light since I have a shadow, though
subdued. Though mind is material, it is finer than mass.
She sits down beside the sill saying: Though men turn bald
I know how time is haired and stretches her neck as though
in anticipation. The keys move, as though pressed by
fingers though subject to rain, it seldom occurs
though I sing in my chainsaws like this
and am thirsty, and drink often, though little at a time

happiness is not to be mistrusted though it ferment:
though small in carpet area, it is visually infinite.
Tao answers with Drowner of Hope, though he lives
though perfectly rational on the erroneous assumption
common though various in size and appearance
that doubt though unformed is thought's shadow
though his eyes show this world, he stands with his arms
out as though he were a conductor addressing a choir.
Abandoning words, though discourse must still use them,
though the snow on the lawn recedes into an archipelago
though the boughs on the side of the spruce hang calm
and though the eave lets the snow down in linear rain.

**A complex of emotions** falls apart, in an abandoned spot. We walk to the grey school hand in hand and come apart under the light: a wound like a black flower, exquisite and irreparable, breaks apart the immortal in us, and we feel as if a stranger has slowly and lovingly pulled us apart or the days like doors locked us forever apart. Select the bitmap image you want to break apart. Choose Modify Break Apart to space the elements in the horizontal plane. Brass automaton Gage is in the desert picking apart a riddle, and the Lotus Kingdoms are at war. Observer and observed stand apart as the necessary poles of substantiated being, the glue that keeps matter from falling apart. My father, who has not existed for 40 years, would be lonely with no one apart from me to remember him. Apart from that how can I get to work, what are the connections. The rose spoils in a park that due to its uncertain location is never visited by anyone apart from the park employees. All of the blocks are divided into apartments apart from my attic room. Everyone does as they are told apart from one child who spills a can of Fanta over my carpet.

What I say is taken apart by affiliated banks who use analysis windows for affect control. Apart from that she has swollen so much. For the first three days we stay there and hardly leave apart from into administrative search space. A bureaucrat explains we have to stand back to back with feet apart. The flea-market on the train track consists of objects momentarily stilled from their blowing apart. The students find that when they attempt to fold the net into a pyramid, the pieces come apart. The easiest way to do this is to place three 2" blocks equal spaces apart on the level floor and let the monosyllabic crow take the work apart. The suit torso covers the entire body apart from the head and adjustable snap-lock inseam. Have the children cut apart the abrasion-resistant polyester. The peach is split around the pit mark and the halves torn apart by a slight circular motion. I take apart the barbecue Z bought for me decades before. We had drifted, broken, fallen apart, but on waking found our hands touching. A part of to be apart is to be a part.

**There is something in you** aside from your
sound perhaps shrivelled at the top but that aside
perfect in every detail. This also lay aside.
Think with the legs step aside and pick
up an artefact cast aside in a skip
—vest unbuttoned, cravat thrown aside, head
through words, denature and push aside
desires. Char sets aside a signed memory, short
sets aside a 16-bit memory location,
float sets aside a floatingpoint
actors deliver an aside in HTML chunk content
that ends in the aside element's pull quotes.
The Tribunal makes an order setting aside the order

Badger cuts aside pieces of meat and again
Bear tosses him roughly aside. Place dumplings
in baking pan; set aside. Lift off the cheek and set
out the arms and hubs, don't look aside.

**Satisfying to go out** on this walk with children that in its aimlessness will somehow find the centre of the maze. Your misconception is that the enchantment somehow merges with the mountain. Somehow I could not reverse, my head unable to pivot, eyes dulled. Then dreams of breaking up: somehow we break up but stay together. It feels as if somehow I am dead, the moment is sick or deposited, it is a false book, Hugo Ball made it, and all the entries in it are somehow fake and these are binaries, a poem and its notes. At two locations they come together and I tell them this will be somehow significant for the plot. Somehow interactivity is embedded in the paper: when you read it you take part in real events. I'm somehow supposed to know crocodiles are tame and friendly, as opposed to alligators, and there's an army camp involved in this somehow and there's a little of Ithaca in this town but not much. It is more like a moral issue somehow, although it is also a sex dream. The twisted posture and contradictory face of May somehow relates to these tortuous negotiations. I feel guilty, as if somehow I have come home without N. I am on a small boat on a river, landscape of ritual sites and stone settings, also somehow on the M40 as it rises onto the Chilterns. Somehow I have to visit every continent, or every country, I can't remember. We see how the two rivers are running too fast to swim in, as if somehow in sleep I enter the incident wave of the plants' consciousness and promise somehow that there is a future for poems without inspiration: the whole does seem created, yet somehow not by me. My subconscious made it. That period doesn't seem important to me now, then somehow my computer is broken and I accuse Alan's dad of breaking it and somehow unlike in the film it is a crowded beach and though there are only eight people involved somehow I have a contract to be a driving force in the new politics. I walk it seems only a few yards out of the city and into deep countryside with ponds and carts and peasants, which somehow merges with having dinner with people I know well, everyone has come into the rocky fortress and somehow the danger goes. I am up to my knees in the pool and it seems that somehow I am now the leader of the rebels. It feels that meeting their eyes is somehow a message, but not meeting them is also a message. Somehow a metaphor rotates to such an extent it is the thing referred to as itself, but this seems to strengthen the switch statements. The walk leads me over canals, channels, bridges, dividuous streams that somehow connect. Where I am in the book somehow relates to which station the train has reached. I seem to be on someone's property, somehow this is irrelevant because I am in a period before property. All could see I was not somehow a man. In far churches words sang, somehow there are no angels but we are built this way.

**Wipe it unless you leave** your computer logged on
never clear the history unless you understand the word
exist in a loose sense unless it speaks there can be
no words for ideas I could not turn into waves unless by
thinking about them silent unless roaring wordlessly, in storms
a tap on the window which you will miss unless you
undercapitalize as our stories drown us unless
we drain them unless a useless rain kept connected
unless otherwise noted, all have 1 degree of freedom
night is never happy unless dragging something away
recalls do not occur unless a product causes death
unless you wipe your hands you are history.

**End of summer,** just coming down from the drugs. I had the impression I had just been eating nuts. Just before midnight a great roaring sound. Just ice breaking. I opened my eyes, wondering just what this was. A shell lit on the bank, just yards from my head. Passed the following days in a railway cutting, just big enough to lie in, enough firelight to see the smoke was thicker than just smoke. My daughter just taken to Casualty, not hurt, that was just where missing children were taken. A poetry program came on, just as I turned the dial. This bedroom was at T's cottage with just planks laid across the beams and rain outside, and over a huge caravan park the pilot was just eating sandwiches and we began to tip and the nose scraped on the grass just as he jerked up. I was just going to go in the clothes I was wearing. This girl looked just like P's daughter with gaps between her teeth but we had to find shelter otherwise it was just like he crashed on the bedroom floor, just flotsam, the waves dangerous and we could only just see the city across the bay and then there were no waves just like the memory of a real event and I just mumbled something in the language which I was just making up as I trod endless moor, just scraping past the bracken and screaming up birds but unable to turn back or wait for others to catch up just moor until I came to the brackish tarn where I stopped to drink but a head just reached above water and P said that one drowns, just lower your foot and you move in the land of just remove this bandage all the stones on the beach had black marks, just like black-eyed beans and Z said why not let him into the bed just for tonight, but this turned into a battle so I rented an apartment just three blocks away. I had just moved in there, I paused just short of the door. He lowered his gown to show he had just had an operation, many of his organs were still exposed and I had to cut a slit just under the incision, take out the spleen, replace it with the content I'd just copied, some kind of just surfacing feeling that I was not ready to form coherently, an imagined discourse that would just stand there, accommodating to nothing, piling peelings. Just letting the shapes and sun go on, the open window in its formal whorl of leaves streamed in and still people just talked about trees, because that was the kind of news I wanted. The dragon-pond's willow-coloured water just reflected the sky's tinge. The same passenger who remembered seeing a fire stood up in her seat just as the plane took off. Just as before, the days were just slog made of flowers that came apart, that just slowly overwhelmed the integrity of the piece. The text must appear just as you type it. Language just refines silence. Since it's just placeholder text, replace it with content.

## Twelve. Of Time Before

ONCE AGAIN THE EVENING SKY wore away
but once I went to the attic and opened the skylight
after once or twice nearly breaking something
at once fragile and noble. It coughed once
in the night. Once hard times had stripped away
the veneer of capital, the DJ looked ominous. Once
he'd been a friend. Father once threw me downstairs
or twice, he held fire or he was fire once. Demonic
images plague the ageing man as once the growing
boy. Once the musculature was addressed
consciousness returned at once, but
once the victim learnt she had been scammed she
wept not once but repeatedly across years
This plant flowered once, this one never opened upon
the air of hallways long since and only once passed through.
Hound drew the curtains, and once more approached me.
I had stayed in his cottage once, well not his cottage, but
a cottage. It felt as if all my workdays had come at once
*heigh!* mare of the old woman, once bridled on the earth
cry out, *heigh!* old woman's mare! Once the mortises
are drilled, a voice says: Pay homage to fish once a year.
The waveform trigger was in third position, it fired once
on pull and once on release.
Once the names were entered I typed the data for each field
if I could retrace the threads that once were people
the holes they leave once you notice their absence.
I once exercised my irritability through copulation

five times once a day for two or three weeks.
Once woken I opened and closed all the doors, strode
past an urn once used as an honoured mark of mourning
the extraordinary aspect of which at once arrested my footsteps.
I refixated with foveal vision. Once the passengers
boarded, the conductor interacted once with
individual instruments, then all instruments at once.
He walked the road once bathed in vernal breezes
and saw green field penny-cress. Once I am caught, I cease.
We are falls of rain that were once in another head.
At once I started off. In a short time I came to his village.
At once I spoke to the one who had charge of the fire.
He told me, once this was all ash lonely ones.

**Past behaviours predict** future behaviours. It is dark, it is past dark. Going through the poems I've written over the past year, scraping past the bracken and making the birds fly up. The air draws its one syllable past my ear, and my clothes billow. That is not the actual end of the garden, it goes past here along an ornamental lawn and fetches up at a small river, but the river becomes less attractive past these mine workings. Many trains go past but none is our train, my dead cousin Robert walks past me, smiles, and tells me to give his love to J. Out of that tune the past rings like a bell and I wait until a man cycles up the track past me as I descend into the wide estuarine bay and drive past seaside shops. One showman walks a puppet with an electronic control: as I drive past, I see it lumbering towards a wall. All that recedes into the blue of the past: a man I recognize dimly breezes as he runs past. There is a big party to which my neighbour has invited unrelated people from my past, but not me. A river runs past the school. The poem sails past

Byzantium, enters coral waters, and my ex-partner swims past, there are fish around her, she is with her new boyfriend. She wants to make a film or painting that concerns our past together. Nash Island Light opens well past the ledges, westward of Crumple Island. Air is drawn down into the booth by means of a fan and in its passage past the body collects. We are what the past made of us, judging the rise and fall of past dynasties. The verb stands in the indicative, except when its reference is in the past. The tip of the needle traverses past the neurovascular bundle. A solid plinth zone leads past a cafe with a view of the travelator, the sharp edges where the top of the long trim extends past the top of the short trim, past the seats and the controls and down the long drop of the left leg to the bottom of Steam's left foot. The poem is past but is not in the past.

**This is Wednesday,** May th, near Lucerne, 69 years ago.
Place and time rhyme the snows of long ago
between the two friends. Reality is between a year ago
under the carpet the forest creaks to a wind decades ago
in a *suishin* terrace garden four thousand years ago
the past forms withdraw a week ago
he greets me as if we had only seen each other days ago
long enough for me to have forgotten. Years ago
I tried to free myself from him. A week ago
I leave a message because he has not called since a day ago
from houses sealed up in ash and pumice centuries ago.
Loose teeth, bone, dead of the sun long ago
my family was of a high pedigree thirty thousand years ago.
The star's face is not seen and the film started 35 minutes ago.
Alder stopped looking out of the ceramiglass long ago.

Nel, honey, what did you say a second ago.

Hallo, Margarete! This is the hour of your death a year ago.

A sister had, indeed, died some years ago.

**You are standing before the entrance** to the Land of Dots. You show me your original face before you were born. You safely deselect it, and then reset its attributes before you draw it.

I had never driven to this side of town before, fox scattering before the car before twilight, a transient bright blue spot before left eye, before entering into the bones of the head. I walk 60 feet before losing balance or needing a rest. The eyes see black; giddiness, tingling before the ears, and drowsiness. The poem lies defenceless before me.

First blackbird of February, tune slightly different from the year before. I seek to summon The vision, but it flees before my thought. I stand before an old iron gate, just before the trope of midnight. The phone rings and my heart races before I even know who's calling. It is years before we meet. The road before us is made of fiction, but not fictional. In the years before her death I conducted my entire correspondence with her by tape.

As a suppliant, I make a golden *zahum*-ewer. I sit before my fire in the Underworld. Before I attempt to approach the terror of your throne, let me lay a garland of corpses before your hooves. Let not their cattle live, not calf nor lamb; give me their smiling king to cut to pieces before the Lord.

This suit, one of the most interesting before the public, is a new object instance. As before described the men waved their stop signs before the cars before and after the inauguration.

Heavy vapours dispel before the rays, coming things cast their spheres before them; before descending into the waterhole they sing.

I whoop twice, finding him quite deaf; before he wakes I point my fingers into his ears, and he hears.

The lens is placed before the light low enough to clear the head. All his adventures, all his sufferings flash before you at the mention of his name. Park never before saw three cards become two. Before leaving the track, the firemen hoist the extension-ladder. Ground yourself before touching components. Beaker People stamp feet three or four times before beginning to talk, hold their breath before starting a sentence and say, *Seesee-see*. Before attachment to the animal, he is inquisitive and looks at the noose before him. Before the future is built on this we need a level of pasts. Today my remembered stillness is the moment before entering the pool. The feel that ideas hold in their womb, clouds gristle before the moon.

The wind stands before the door. We are on holiday, there is a place I want to show them, we had seen it before but not from this angle. Pattering along the surface before take-off, before their time, the ducks.

Cauterize the stump before releasing the clamp, and appear before us in the shape of a beautiful woman. Obscene representations play before the imagination. Before I prepare the report, I identify the objectives the report will serve. When day begins to break the young hair seals cry in the very place they cried before. Time before memory. Pearls before time.

It had only been a sensation at first, a screen-off timeout.
The inference engine has been processing the knowledge base
using backward chaining: family-size has been the current goal.
This optic has been drop-tested on the belt-fed gun
and been in the cryochamber from -85 F. to +180 F.
It's also been recoil-tested by firing 300 rounds of .338 Mag.

The partner who had been driving the second truck
was the suspect's boss. The truck the suspect had been driving
belonged to the boss. I've been asked for a column, but
by receiving the invitation, I've written it. It's been broadcast,
been heard and forgotten as it passed Betelgeuse.
Beeps would have been helpful. After the sacrifice,
the testes of the cock had been examined. White
may have been accepted. The shell of each J-Series model
has been upgraded to high-quality metal. The Z-Series
has been Fujifilm's fashionista camera line, said David
Was. I'm confused as to what's been happening:
the Swedish has been given the Latvian dative-plural.
She's been phoned often by people contacting mental
services. It's been ages since her last update.

Dawn was the brains of the operation
was the opening wound
master Sun was capable of military operations
the cone was breached and a block-lava flow emerged
heavy with my troubles I was lapsing into sleep
as I write this I dream I was in my childhood but
as an adult: the air was full of deep, tolling bells
social status was determined by aggressive acts
the weather creaking on its hinge, rain's edge was closing
the spider with all its hemming and hawing was gone
the microphone was placed in the centre of the room
evening was sultry gowns embellished with fringes
the stabbing was laborious, and required great attention
love's body attached to the head as scream to lung

wave energy was convergent in the nearshore
there was a ghost mouth drinking the water:
it was the blue of sanitary hand gel.
I was filled with inconceivable terror
the video was recorded with a 360° camera
the response was an increase in heart rate
Saxon's finger was on the trigger when
the jugs were opened the odour was strong
the netting was hog-ringed to shower-curtain washers
the silhouette was narrow, the form functional elegant.
a venous hum was heard in the neck
a maximum-parsimony analysis was performed
the funeral was yesterday
coition was witnessed at the nesting site
the consummation of his delight was the earth was reaped
when the lizard pushed the key a mouse was delivered
about an hour afterwards the animal was swollen
*moonlight on water* was renowned in its early showings
the god was preceded by a man carrying two long rods
observation was made on the knee jerks of young women
the northern abandoned delta-lobe was in equilibrium
a deadly-wounding arrow was fired into a western world
what light there was was not of the sun
the core site was remote from the lake edge
a single reed was shaking its head for ever
enormous booty in cattle and goats was collected
Foucault's translator was defeated and taken prisoner
vaseline was applied to his face
population-level diet was determined by fecal analysis
stool was secured through clysters of glycerine

the number of dogs killed by 100 secured boars was 1,000
the ram was hoofing the ground with bent forelegs
a hard-fist master was invited to coach at the family mansion
subject was quiet for a few minutes
in the wood a tall tree was torn
Hargis was northbound and failed to make a turn
his aim was to change brand perception
identifying and counting vertices and faces was difficult
a grey-haired night-wind was appointed as the yeargod
the answer Yes was corrected spontaneously
she was pursued naked up a huge water tower by Nazis
her bill was broken off, and her wings were broken
the wound of entry was sutured and drainage effected
Aphrodītē's arm was made whole, her sharp pain was allayed
Lady Jang knew what was happening and was pleased
The 23rd day of the fourth month was the queen's birthday
the electric sump pump leading to the sewer line was silent
returning energy to the world machine was a sacred duty
affected by itinerant poets. Wen's early style was mediocre
his microphone was pointed to the audience
as if scream was syntactical the hair of his
beard was plucked out; his left nipple pinched
on admission a gas-containing abscess was present in the brain
the ship that carried the shoulder blade of Pelops was sunk
a young hair seal was crying in the corner of the entrance
the jumpsuit was cut to cling to the body
I am the victim of this book that says it was written by me
as if a dull instrument was pushed to and fro
our carrying capacity was at breaking point.

**Data were from driving** *through a tunnel.*
*Chemicals played on the fire, and were heard.*
*The murals were lit panel after panel*
*but only some of the wires were fractured.*
*Chicks were escaping from the compartment.*
*The students were tested in threes or fours.*
*Differences in song-type were apparent.*
*The slugs were recorded with VCRs.*
*Participants were shown morphs of their faces*
*as they were piloting Sea Harriers.*
*Ulcers were large and with undermined edges.*
*Options were cheek tints or creamy blushers.*
*The spiders' tubes were painted opaque white:*
*they were what it was to be conscious of it.*

*The trees were not the spirits of the dead*
*divided into morning, near-noon, noon*
*where bright brittle metal foils were bonded*
*mapping the long hours that were gone too soon.*
*Safe exit routes were delineated*
*or looks were paired with sweeping floor-length skirts.*
*Two different sets of spiders were tested.*
*These were only images. That's what hurts:*
*the ships were full, prices were steady.*
*Our pheromone pores were going full blast*
*and our first-half net profits were 23.*
*In the way hours were bled into the past*
*if all were minded so, the times should cease*
*else were an all-eating shame and thriftless praise.*

*O, that you were yourself! but, love, you are*
*in memory a thing that were longer*
*if I might teach you wit, better it were*
*if the repressive tendency were stronger,*
*then, were not summer's distillation left*
*and were some child of yours alive that time*
*of which we were so suddenly bereft:*
*to prattle of the future were no crime,*
*it were not easy such child to reclaim*
*if there were God to tell us we do wrong*
*or if it were, it bore not beauty's name;*
*if only these words could burst from my song*
*for they were not as large as they appear*
*now when the words "we were" are written here.*

## Thirteen. Of Present Time

**Write what is understood:** the poem is already dead. The text is already known. This trend is already evident. The patient already etherised. The editing-window shows the old text; if already in column one of the object-pane, scroll. A list of the names already entered pops out. Secondary revision already functions as interpretation. This struggle to defecate the emotions one has already expressed is a strain. Sendto or sendmsg request will specify a destination when already in address mode. The heat on my brow is already of bright noon, the steps already white with dew: let us act as aftermarkets. Already the rights have been sold. Mrs Nager already manifested at the beginning of the session. She tells me her husband is away for two weekends and she already has a lover for one of them. I say what about the other, and her number is already on the label of a small bottle of perfume. I don't know why I thought this would save money since I already booked a room so I rush to the phone and a man is on it already, insisting he still has a pound of time and the ledge I am on is loose dune. I already feel it give way: I try to describe what the farm is like, but already as I tell her the acoustic paths fade. There is a question on the board already, about the study of poetry. I'm confident of winning but the publicity machine is already rolling. The past is already inscribed. By naming things, the stanza already calls upon the world. For each job where an operation is already placed, the future operation of the range is the next operation in the range. Hardy becomes, already broken, the lichened headstone that dead trees prevent the already scant light from reaching. He is already connected to the apparatus on the table. You already see a behavioural psychiatrist and have already built a formal Italian garden featuring a canal which is already deeply publicly known. The next film has already begun, the money is already mentioned, the murder already done. Guilt is already too early.

**The couple in front of you** are now running.
It is now full day, noon, it is now midday. Work
is now accelerating, particularly neurobiological. The small
heads the animals had are now folk taxonomies.
See the air in a glowing colour; now sway over a cello.
Now champion silicon nanowires. You meet
an old man, who turns the letter over three times. It now reads
marry this man to your daughter. Now in a state of
trance, his face rigid, hands now cold he
extends his fingers. He is older now and worried
by that which does not you. You can now lay down
four clubs, or the 5 6 7 of clubs and 3 eights, now
it comes back to my turn. On the occasion I am now
narrating now and then through the foam emerges
an arm. It is now horizontally suspended in the air
now gently and elegantly raised. Great emphasis
is now placed on where the hot spring flows.
A ridge-and-furrow sea brims now you fear this is lost
no, something about the scene is now like a war
a green dot now traverses the monitor on a course for you.
Return takes you to what has now become the current view.
Images disappear and we are, as now, invisible to one another.
Now in a waking state think you are in your real bedroom.
Now navigate to a thread to see the list is
now available for the consumer market.
You are at the pm telesummit right now
King *So*'s terraced palace is now overgrown with
unknown values. The young bride, now smoothed to

a chinalike delicacy of feature, receives visitors. Now
at the door with rolling luggage, opening now to allow you
time in its precincts. You're now leaving the poem.

**Words obliterate light** while leading to its source. While good fortune lights one side, despair darkens the other. So please your Excellency, while flogging the prisoner, this packet dropped. While he washes his hands he turns his head and snuffles, accelerating droplet-clouds and user-profile information. Writing with her right side necessitates while sitting constant motion and shifting of the feet; a long while she sways and twists. While rolling in bed she cries, while a polyester fleece outer-shell and soft fleece inner shell facilitate quiet. After sleeping for a short while she suffers swelling of the cheeks, or while awake, she fears the people of the house will see her sleep. While being pursued by the king, she meets with a large hole. It entrusts her with its antique books and leaves her for a long while. The roaring of an ocean is speech while the depths are unconsciousness. While uncovering the ball with her left hand she again grasps the sitter's hand, while in her left hand she holds a long staff surmounted by a cross. While she takes a bath she wonders who she is. She looks through the sarcophagus while the selfseal activates. Her hands grasp and steady the femur, while she uses the tibia as a lever. But while the story is written in verse, the rhymes struggle. She watches the wasteland burn a while, takes it out of the fire, hands out Polaroids. The face cleat system is continuous, while butt cleats terminate in wheelheads. Wait here while two boys hold you by the ears. This allows you to become comfortable performing the interference task while a video offers enhancements for experienced presenters. Switches are manipulated while wearing gloves. One of the spring moons is known as *Frog Moon*, while another, about July, is *Dreaded Moon*. Your five-year-old son vanishes from your view in a public park. Liquid draws off while the basket is being lifted and piles up speech, but searchers revise their beliefs while little or no similarity can be detected. A walkway carves a diagonal path through broken stones while an underplanting of ophiopogon grasses flanks an arbour of weeping hornbeams and Italianate urns. The Tuscan cypresses are echoed by the thrusting watsonia, while box pyramids add structure. A body suffers decomposition while transiting a weak-binding state during biased Brownian movement. Tracks are found while searching house and curtilage under void warrant. Tell the child to remain sitting while you seek his father. His loss is theoretically unlimited. While he walks, he is supported by two aides while opposite the sun a whelming moon whistles. The atmosphere is cold but while caught in the craft's forward ionization plume there is intense heat. Simulated coition is observed while the birds are in flight. On his 6th birthday, overtaken by darkness while crossing a tract of water-drunk land, he is sidetracked while the egg-white non-white-space characters called The Seven Whistlers interfere with the compile infrastructure: his hair catches fire while blowing out a cake candle. Drummer Mick Fleetwood performs while wearing his "drum suit": Xu renders it as his magic pen, while Zhuo chases down scrolls stolen from sixth-century North Africa. While still wet, spread icing evenly. Embedded font files allow speaker's notes to be viewed while working in slide or outline view. He accuses them of attempting to steal his potatoes while in the guise of hares. A transient attack of confusion while reading, the surface birds gather food while storm-birds govern the weather. The fire sleeps in baked mud while the contents are liquid in a recurring lattice material. The curtains of the cabana-style closet can be drawn to hide kids' stuff, while built-ins house office supplies and books. We are undifferentiated while asleep, displaying a miniature of the currently selected slide while working in outline view. It will be a while before we anticipate more weather, less time.

ARE YOU READY TO TALK about your mother yet?
The milk not yet dry on your cherry lips
the camera points at something you cannot yet see
but which is yet stranger, after an uneasy sleep, could
this greyness be the most contemporary moment yet?
Cautiously, yet deliberately, just as your attention wanes
the stranger's hand places something smooth yet foreign
inside you. Nothing can be said yet as to the grass
onto which you might paste yet another history.
The fire yet stirs and works in the interior of the earth
with weariness and yet sleeplessness. You are
preoccupied with the damp seeping from a yet lower level,
with ghost languages or ones not yet invented.
You know the ego is a construct, yet agree to play the game.
Who can say history has a smell, yet the past does.
At some key point (though we do not know it yet) you appear
seconds before the traffic accident. A neutral yet rich
colour scheme creates a museumlike ambience yet
an earthy yet contemporary atmosphere:
Gathering examples from yet unread tablets, you
yet retain your belief in yellowed phrases
grinding words into more poems and yet more poems
Duchamp has not yet developed the Handler of Gravity
many empty rooms yet contain presences
yet through disaster a faint melody insists; we know
more than is yet known about the dry riser inlets.
Yet his language has a Chinese boxlike structure
as yet another vivid example of a painting that can
receive the weather, yet touch the ground.
Those whom the gods love are not yet born.

If time is an illusion then I always think the past will always fail, that world always eludes the closed sentence. Suppose the night into its bed and always rise before waking. This is nearly always transposed into the passive voice. On the wheel of Ixion, always draw water with the sieve of the Danaids. In drawing thread, always point the awl outwards. Allusion's compass needle always points to the past. Look closely enough and you always encounter perfection. Time is almost always nearly here, always and everywhere sales people are by no means always sales forces: those not always immediately are always already there, probably always usually or always waiting there always, always remaining always looking. I seem to always act in my own self-interest, it is not always easy to tell, not always possible nor obvious. The customer is always a co-creator of value always willing to factor in the salesperson's business role in seller-buyer interactions in what may not always be the most effective exchanges. It is always possible to reduce the sales force cost to a percentage of sales. Cutting sales force size always increases sales per sales person and decreases business, but these business objectives cannot always be achieved simultaneously. For example, a product at best price is always equal to the discrete transaction, is always open to the adversarial process of business investment. Generating a prospect list has always been a problem and over-spending on promotions is always available. Because sales is always an action-oriented profession, commercial processes are always required. But sales people always face choices. Managers and Marketing Managers do not always agree on what to do in given peaks and troughs that do not always coincide for these economies. In the short term it is almost always and probably always will not necessarily always be but it's not always that somehow it is by no means always, since it will likely always be thus. I always thought, always wanted to think, was always going to. It's always emerging from twisted metalwork, always aware I am not always true but always necessary. I don't always remember but remember always, provided always that I press forwards always into this always receding thicket.

**When the attacks are rare** I see lilac-coloured spots.
When I dream of work the architecture is different.
When walking after a rest, the brain is painful, as if shaken.
When looking at nearly white wallpaper, feeling electrified.
When images are being written to the card the lamp dulls.
When the lamp is lighted, the letters FUEL LOW are visible.
When Lowell's last taxi opens it is empty.
When words alliterate in the forest, the poem hears.
When night seals in the pond, the poem fishes.
When they stop laughing he knows they are asleep.
When you open the cover Smart Cover is seen.
When we fall out of sentence, the sense opens.
When it thickens press into it quarters of peeled peaches.
When I get home the black cat from next door comes in as well.
When I speak of flowers it is to recall that we were young.
When ashes fill the aqueduct I begin to sing.
When we die we become reflective or transparent.

**The dream ends** I am by the gates, waiting to see if they will ever open them. Two things fill my soul with ever increasing wonder and awe as if words had to be quarried deeper, in dangerous conditions, as if there could ever be a word equivalent to a feeling. I am accosted by the first person I ever arrested, trembling with illness after years in prison and still maintaining his innocence. I do not think I have ever felt so well understood. If you ever feel sad remember there's a number you can call: it looms ever closer. If I ever cross your mind it is an echoic choice of ever diminishing returns. Did Blake ever ride a horse. Have you ever heard a dog backwards. It is the longest yawn ever. We've been together ever since never, rarely ever verifying without ever quite everting our love. Have you ever experienced a cantilever shaft shift growing ever louder, edging ever closer to a long-reverberating river, ever present and in perseveration ever narrower. Ever since revering the ether, I hardly fevered ever again. If I could ever actually live happily ever after it would be without ever quite arriving or being ever heard of. You ever wondered how the ever increasing weather denied ever being, edging ever closer to rain, to avoid ever getting wetter. Ever present in ever wider circles, the murky and narrow get cleverer. Ever is four fifths of never.

**Self is a lie sometimes,** counter arithmetic set behind the ear
it is sometimes agreed to play a certain number of rounds
children sometimes find shards and oracle bones
the winds sometimes pass through them
they sometimes wet their hands with phosphorus solution
pains sometimes begin in the limbs, and terminate
in the sarcophagus. Sometimes I see a cursor-arrow
and death must follow. Sometimes they speak of five points
of the world or of five winds, sometimes a period
is not preceded by the dream. Soul-monads sometimes
are killed in cave-ins. I sleep on my belly sometimes
and watch with my eyes closed. I sometimes lose my voice
and my eyes are sometimes scribing knives

sometimes I walk by the water
sometimes float above it. I have M with me
sometimes, I carry her as if in a great hurry
sometimes suffer stabbing pains in my joints
but these are sometimes completely lacking.
I sometimes think of "Song of the Rolling Earth",
made alert to a sometimes pained undertone
several allusions to the epic can be found, sometimes
intertwined with allusions to the sometimes uneasy
feeling running under bridges sometimes
a block of empty flats into which poems sometimes
come, deviation can sometimes deepen the texts
actual self locates in the groin sometimes
we coast a few hundred feet in the air, sometimes lower
a confrontation with rock, sometimes pitted
sometimes when I write, sentences labour
under my hand, not fitting together. Sometimes
my inner homunculus falls down this winding stair.

Glass valves still explode with a puff of inert gas. Ash is mistaken, it is still part fire. We have what days seem still to be made of. It takes effort to open her eyes but she still sees nothing. She still loves to walk out of a house and feel the wind trashy with thought. The thin Italian cypresses are still as her boat crosses, and silent. Her power still extends to the world, and exerts for the good. Still waters, flowing waters, she examines the green of the ocean, and still insists this is all. She reveals by carving it its still latent beauties. The air is still, it is the year's middle, what occurs now is hers and still she sings. She lies very still on the floor, she tries, still trembling, to flow. Under this temple stands a still more ancient. Tomorrow, too, one of her eyes will still be unfinished, clarifying that she is still in a dream. The room and its contents move, and she stays still. The robin bends its legs to remain still on the moving branch. The child's laughter still tangles in her hair yet she is still not sure what she dreamed. She is still enough to pick up the waves behind the trees. She switches on the news to check if nothing has still happened, like checking a clock is still working; yes, the wheels still grind, the House still has not had an explanation. There is still sufficient belief in moral authority to bear one person representing a state, but still, it would be quicker to stop driving, to step outside. As long as we have to eat we are still in nature. Those tulips still sneer full-lippedly from the dustbin. How she wishes shapes to hold still. Timber from the Coral Sea Battle still washes onto the beach. She buries her parents, still warm. The mind still flies up, she sees others within sight of the ruined castle by the still lake. Her father may be nothing more than a heap of bones, but she's still climbing, and if she walked to me, you would have to say that the room and its contents (including me) moved, and she stayed still. Here she is, still a child in a long shadow. Are there still swans on the green water at Skadim. They are still to be seen. The singed bird foretells the song. It calls out her names: a list that takes it its whole life, and is still unfinished. Songstresses will still sing the song composed by the captive king. Nothing will still the song.

## Fourteen. Of Time to Come

**Immediately a desolating winter** shall succeed
these Bones shall be liable to prosecution
shall beat drugs in the urine of the man
and doubt shall break free thunderclaps
without thunderbolts like onward souls shall
fall from the four shoulders of the world shall drive
back to San Francisco shall blow with shadows
stagger, and certainly shall fall; face pale. The ocean
eating all islands shall come to meet us
the star shall give us the star's heart
shall have been sold, damaged, injured, or destroyed
shall become the property of the Landlord
shall remain upon, and be surrendered with
said premises, shall consist of crops or ungathered products
from nothing, so unto nothing shall ground
and who shall I be that your smile holds me
I shall draw, in open court, from the small boxes
what shall I say of the words out of that
old mouth. Those who resist shall stand
from the shallows. What shall I do to be invested?
Shall I be provided with the five-man tilt cab
shall seats be upholstered over deep air-form cushions?
Then I myself leap up. What shall I do?

**Soon I stop work** and go to the study
I tidy my desk, and soon there will be no excuse to not write.
As soon as I sit my feet are full of uneasiness,
breath soon more rapid and difficult. Raps and tilting
soon manifest themselves, heaviness
and formication soon attack upper limbs.
The poem opens on a hospitable note but soon takes
an unexpected path I am soon familiar with.
As soon as the water retires the salt-workers come out.
Strange is the form of the axe but as soon as I see it, I
love it, and soon I have a flash of a sense of evil.
As soon as I see her from afar, I resolve on killing her.
Soon she bears a daughter and is surrounded by disciples.
The blossom dies as soon as it attains independent life.
The current carries me and soon I swim out into the bay
I soon hear the manuscript of oars, soon this will
rupture and the future will soon spill out in the shape of
timeline analysis software there will soon be
exciting adventures open to us, the windows will soon
break, as if by a knock at the door soon after
my motorbike accident, the grey animals soon scatter
back into their burrows. It is soon time
to go to Mars, the conquest is carried out as soon
as the time arrives but my newly acquired strength is soon
exhausted. Soon they will be driving, lank friends of my son
& soon the painted gauze descends once more
and will soon be forgotten, merged in with all of the others.

1st day.—After coitus night-sweats and great exhaustion. When standing after going downstairs, transient blue spots. My strength fails after a short conversation. Skin toughens after chafing. My seeds contain intensities that emerge after years of indolence.

3rd day.—Fell after rising. Sour taste in the mouth after a meal. After a few hours, a silence occurred. Evening, after sunset, dull frontal headache, chiefly on right side, with vertigo. Stopped painting after being proclaimed, and ran after the buffalo calves. After the introductory instrumental, I slept.

15th day.—General sweat after a slight breakfast. Vomiting four hours after dinner, silence after the gunshot, mind after it empties. After a few minutes of scratching, three black green thorns were visible.

23rd day.—After rising, feeling of mucus at back of throat, causing hawking. Fulness and satiety after a slight breakfast. After the lapse of the day, droplets of spontaneous rain. Clock broke after it struck the long strike, followed by shock after 5 seconds when I failed to respond to it. Shortly after, unable to lift my sheets.

41st day.—Itching of the toes, after staying in the open air. Wife said after studying dashcam footage: It is something and it is nothing. After that there appeared red, white, and yellow paths; after much handwringing the fly lit onto the laptop, chose a key from which to observe me.

53rd day.—Back of throat dry. After walking the symptom disappeared immediately, with excessive yawning; after drinking milk, tossing about of arms and legs, pain and sickness, ending in prostration. After ten minutes worked jaws, in a quarter of an hour the fit ended. Evening, after sunset, fear of being in the dark, and to a less extent of being alone. After compression of the aorta a flaccid paralysis, itching and redness of fingers, Worse after scratching.

62nd day.—After rising from bed, feeling of mucus at back of throat requiring hawking, with hoarseness. A chill at noon, after which purple spots came out. After regaining consciousness, I embodied my experience of the spirit world in the form of song. Evening, after sunset, some hoarseness when talking. Was ordered to desist after the arteries were tied, and all traces of the operation removed.

76th day.—Hiccough, especially after exercise. After confirmation of the open traverse option in line 3010, the program branched to the keyboard entry routine for the closed traverse at line 1020. Evening, after sunset, unsteady when walking in the dark, with tendency to fall backwards. On the river the lights rearranged themselves after the blossoming of oars upon water.

94th day.—Evening, after sunset, transient bright spots before eyes. The team waited 8 weeks after surgery before placing the midface prosthesis. The effect to be experienced immediately after distribution of presents.

105th day.—Great short-sightedness after exerting eyes. Evening, after sunset, in a dark room. After looking carefully, the moon ran after the sun, never to catch up. Long Island Head is the tomb for me to take up residence after cessation of present life.

123rd day.—Pulsating pain in the forehead, after a meal, with pressure in the occiput. After lunch, uncomfortably cold due to air conditioning. After breeding, and during a few lingering moments after birth, removed the adult frogs, turned off the rain chamber, and added an air-stone.

129th day.—Bloatedness after a slight meal. Evening, after sunset, by gaslight, transient sparkling before left eye particularly after a cold weekend. After commencing to pull the rope, an immediate drop in holding-power.

138th day.—Pale tongue and nausea after eating. Offensive smell out of the mouth; as after eating horseradish. Pains came and, after a shorter or longer duration, ceased suddenly. After a while the curtains began to move, as though by a hand from the window.

142nd day.—Giddiness in the evening, after sleeping, when

sitting, with trembling and vertigo in bed, after waking from sleep. Two or three hours after meals food vomited undigested. Evening, after sunset, in a dark room, on turning head to left, transient bright spark before right eye.

163rd day.—After rising, the anxiety disappeared. Feeling of mucus at back of throat, brought on by talking. Itching in the left eye, with smarting in the right after friction. After sunset, in dark room, staggering to left, sweat after midnight on the affected side of the body. Vision destroyed and reproduced after the lapse of a certain period of long and patient self-contemplation. After 3 glasses of wine, wife revealed swelling.

172nd day.—After turning the LED on to the write method, added a time delay using the sleep function. After editing the territorial boundaries, tested the muscles and nerves with the faradic current, after which the galvanic current. The signal Y'ed the monitor to standby after 10 minutes, the system to standby after 20 minutes. After the pre-programmed interval, my response turned off.

180th day.—After a long deferral of pain I hired an industrial unit with the command that if, after seven days expires, his spirit does not return, it should caparison itself for war after the manner of the Carthaginians. After three days, kneaded the bread and soil together, made wife eat it. Hired a man to cut off Ch'un's head, after which the northern provinces were quiet.

211th day.—Coffee with M, he asked me why I don't talk. I told him after a thought that it's because I like to listen to him. The traverser started measurement immediately after the ebb tide. Auto-shutoff after four hours. After rolling away the stones, put sea cucumbers into the basket.

263rd day.—Skin seemed pouchy, too yielding. After cogging ingots down to the required size, I fed them by live roller gear to the bloom shears after the hook was baited and lowered to the desired depth. How changed the world was after it armed.

270th day.—The shooting up stage will come before puberty and the thickening stage after. After passing through the main gate of the Yesterday Psychiatric Hospital, it's about a mile and a half to the rehab entrance. After the lapse of a considerable period, the seventh sun appears. Immediately after the first shock there are loud and long cries of "hori-bole". We held hands after the alarm, briefly, before I left without my meds.

286th day.—They name storms after us, one day it will be my turn. I will still send friend requests after I am dead. Fingers are bleeding subcutaneously after sanding three walls. After half an hour a harsh bell-clang is heard from the wife's quarters. The system queries the user after his search has consumed a quantum of processor time. In my child I realize I must be alive after all. Beat after beat falls sombre and dull.

**Revising into the next** discourse, ghosts speak to me
in the next dream I huddle inside the remarks
the next opening, the next wave moving over an oar.
The next scan takes place half a turn of the wheel later,
changed to an imperative as in the next sentence
to deal with the next question, if one who is reborn
will re-bear the same children. Press Next. On
the next screen, create an empty lever response off the circle
and cause the spiral to reappear for the next trial.
While in this condition, see a spirit-form standing next
to a gentleman leaving for the next world.
At my next sitting, after evidential statements, the medium says
you'll require a billiard ball at the next dance
so I go next day and their house is full of hexagon turrets
that loosen like geese and fly honking to the next star

a dandelion carried gently towards the next weir,
Masonry, pipes through the next door into a set of offices.
One turns to the next page and finds the transparent lyric.
In the next room a woman is trapped in the stationery cupboard.
Next time I go there on my own. It seems the owl guards
some corridor behind the ledge, a television next to the owl.
A day or so to relax in before the next thing happens
I swipe, right to left—and IE brings up the next page.
Next day, a Thomas Hardy wind results in a total error
equivalent to the next lower accurancy class. Save
all the files, then merge them. To merge, click the next step
(Preview merge) in Word. The next stage showcases
the core ranges of formal wear, the next disengages
the thread from the next instrument; follow it
onto the next blank train. I see fear in the trees.
Next each student is given a copy of activity sheet 3 and told
your next text is about how things think for us.
In the next exercise you begin to add shadows.
Next time he drowns, he should carry an umbrella.
Rebirth is the name of the next breath.

Tap the Time-Zone button and then enter the name of a nearby contact and then discharge the processed wash-water into the Kent sewer system. Then shoot the arrow, talk incoherently, then complain of languor then descend to the details. Hurricane Island will then bear distant 5 miles; then loosen the skin from the flesh towards the hind leg. With the two bare ends then touch the material you are investigating. Then cyclone it to remove the coarse fraction which is then reground. The downward movement of the patient's upper eyelid is delayed, then the patient has lid lag. Drive in more brads to hold the batten firmly, then open the screw three full turns, then spray a cloud of perfume, then turn into fire. Then resist three times, then turn the gear, but then speed up. Then descend through nine damp subterranean passages, attended by the usual guide. Then put out your hands, and ask the spirits to shake hands with you; they will do so instantly. Then cock your handgun; name then the spirit Lady Metal Mountain, then the spirit Lady Kneading Clay, then cross the river to the west, letting your horses and bulls of war go carefully. Throw ashes into the water, then follow incoherent rapid parts of sentences, then more rapidly. Repeat the assertions of the nurses then rush down the hill to a roll on the drums, then utter your question. If the answer is *yes*, then fill in a request-form and discuss the possibility with the line manager of the potential host. Then separate the jack colts and put each one in a separate stall then move to a down state and send a set-signal back to the lower stage, then make towering love. Then start to hear a noise above you, growing louder, a rustling. Then look at the corpse, and then cease weeping, and also be pleased. Then pick a stalk and put it in the quiver. Then put your mouth to the mouth of the quiver, and fill your stomach. Then lead me to the hill; then get upon my back. Then drop me a quick email, and then disable the tower's defences. Then the mass of ages dissolves your veins and horizontal scour then proceeds upstream. Then press the wounded parts well with the flat palm and then with a forward thrust, signal the executioners and then retouch the sphinx. Anneal it. Then with tweezers bend each piece to the shape required. Then scrape the chair to prepare it for painting. Then evacuate spontaneously, discharging a grumous bloody fluid. Then collapse when prey abundance is depleted by high predator abundance, then predict the position of meaningful peaks and redirect the machine to make a more detailed scan. Then exhume the body, then bury this with nine pieces of bread on the road over which the cattle go, then note the probable influence of the subconscious on this statement, then find an alternative harvest method, then cut repeatedly. Click Help and then write nX2 in the last row of the V column. Then the sun rises, then wake up, then open the driver's door, then hear the ticking of an engine in the dark, then select Smart Lookup from the pop-up then click OK, then strike non-print key four times; the ID of the HTML control then an underscore, and then the name of the event, then turn all generals into feudal lords. Night is a choice, then a responsibility. A constriction of conscious will. Accept the losses, then move on to [link] then make an account & search for a cold hammer-forged barrel with a three-chamber compensator. Then watch the last disc of the extended edition of LoTR to drown out the others. Then be greatly alarmed, and go to find the mare, then mount her and return happily with the king's son, then become insensible; then release the mouse button, then get up from the desk, watch Bieber movie ads on Spotify, then implement the capture and replay tool, click an item in the thread list and then continue this program until go-home time.

EDIT DECISIONS PROCEED from opening scene until fadeout
the shocks continue until the rat makes the correct response
invert timing bubble until he becomes tremulous
do not release the exit door until he stands in the proper place
the proboscis is seen to bend until the tip touches the plant
applies force until the box slips, this mechanism
continues until the search gets stuck at a solution.
Drag the shadow until you fill the white space
around the axes until drowned men sink into sleep
lead the called suit. Hold that until later in the game
until fire girdles the village each player discards
until a slight feather is felt and gradually swells

push Select until you see name in viewfinder
engage the target until commands are given
hold until indicator lamp lights; the scintillation counter
is undisturbed until she learns of it from his diary.
Until then nine men fretted ten, who are then
devoured by eight and so on until there is one.
The light does not reach me until arises a serpent
from the lake, water loses its colour until the old horse
save hooves and bones is consumed until patient's death
this will be talked about until the conversation subsides
which continues until the crystal is drawn down to a wedge
pass a *seine* through it until no fish are collected
subfolders pop open until you release the mouse
until you write it you do not know it is impossible to write it
a spectral green, unseen until purged from not-green
her father-in-law calls her. Noble woman, wait until
I give you directions run the path until it runs out
where you are to remain until the day of judgment
until the stars stand in the sky and the birds call our names.
She replies the sun never burns until named.
She searches for Shams, until she realizes, in Damascus, she need
not search and leads an exciting life in Berlin until
the Nazis come to power until superseded by other songs
she follows his tracks until, half way home, she finds the body
it is not until the end of five minutes his hands become cold.

**This poem will change** your life-insurance cover, spittle from a satellite will burn the hand. Tempests will be frequent and general.

The suit now to be heard will be of an unusual character. The temperatures near the boreholes will drop, the blood will retreat and contract and the sperm will gather. You will see clouds in the welkin.

A move of the astral arm will twitch in the physical. There will be time for lettering the sky.

The map-editor will turn off its legacy data. Fires will remain in the archives.

Syntactic complexity will lead to loss of comprehension, the result will be a list-object containing a reversal of alpha-function.

Workshops, briefings and presentations will occur offsite. The Contract Administrator will visit during operations.

The strength of the blows will vary with the hardness of the bone. They will not return the carcass to shore. Little Duck and Great Duck islands will be nearest.

Chief-woman, I will come forth from your womb. I will fall from your knees; by the rapidity of my fall I will break my bones.

A child born with the face down will end in a water-grave. At one end of the frame will be seen the steam-chamber. Here will rise great contention, which will be discussed later.

I will stand over there so you can shoot at me. When I am shot my arms will relax, the blade will fall.

The runtime-engine will revert the argument to its old value and set up a project tree. This will notify you when your earphones are plugged in, and will delete your screen after a time.

I will stand for the payment of narcotics desired by my infirm aunt. This root will appease hunger; you will linger about the ruins of the temples of *Venus* and *Diana*, and whisper.

Oversized material will flow outwards, causing shipwrecks; cybercreatures will patrol the hilly borderland, the iamb will hunt with the ictus, the prey will feed upon the prayer.

Urine will cure chapped hands. Murder will out, love in. Your arm will attach to a grapple-fixture.

Clouds will spawn patches of moonlight; this man will acquire barley and silver. He will play a key role in shaping content.

People will be selected for dishonesty; unit-boundaries will be altered to avoid plants; provisions will be included in the contract.

In versions prior to 2020, a toolbar will appear. Puppet will execute the code within the curly braces. Flash will add creative shadows, punch up color, and tabulate results.

There will be fine days waiting on the map. The next stanza will unfold and the movement will continue after it ceases to give an impulse.

A searcher will view a series of objects in a rational way, depending on information-need. In the seas will be arms for seizing the mind.

Tomorrow will work its ropes on us: future parents will be 2 miles distant on the starboard beam.

Make of them what you will, the details of the syntax will vary with the framework you are using.

A large, high, wooded island will draw close. Any changes made will be saved to the original metrics.

The movement will continue after the mesmeriser ceases to give an impulse; the situation will remain fluid for a reason that will appear later.

When you will grant me space, I will render my theory. A single application will remove spray paint, marker pen, crayon, and the search path that will be used.

Observers say the iSeries will be converged. It hovers mid-air with no physical attachments, and with a light nudge, will spin indefinitely.

If a knife drops and sticks upright in the ground, a guest will arrive. An elderly lady will complain about the darkened figure obscuring the window.

At lunchtime an angel will heave the door, and you will perceive a delicate and faint redness. He will wait long if the gain is great.

Solar gain will be translated into heat by spatial systems. This will light up an *Evolution* arrow. The variable will be placed in the edit box.

When I close my eyes I will see waves coming towards me, and, at unpredictable moments, water will rush through the nose from some head recess.

The Overton window is the womb to and from which rocket-child or man-machine will shuttle. Computers will make us feel marginal in our homes.

They will read the name in your thoughts. You will first hesitate then repeat then sing louder to the drivers.

We will start up new religious engines in multiple temples. We will salute anew the olden times; will remove the taper from the moth.

A previous movement will return, and after childbirth the mother will be taken to the village well. That son is squeezier when ill, will accept squeezes.

Built to outlast the equipment they will be used in, these protected units will track down noncompliant behaviour.

The Architect will research and propose data strategies and policies that further our strategic goals. When his open letter arrives it will be the day-sky.

The character of the bizarre object will depend on the character of the real object, say a gramophone. Crystals will grow on its stem and branches.

The hithere module will provide the salutation Hi there. If the tug sinks, it will float free and mark the wreck.

## Fifteen. Of Space

**Here I place** my remote hands
the cloud in the eye is here to see you
in here the heresy emits, start with feel of hand
a stethoscope on the chest here, I breathe twice
there is nothing to know here but harms
priests beam prayer from here sad
song follows, the ink here slightly blurred
half-seen phenomena present themselves here
here in my beak the seed-acorn of this tree. The tree
grew up here, the expression used is renderable as
door's, here the possessive of the person is preferable
the pony speaks to the boy and says: Leave me here
here follows an account of the extension of flames
we have here a proof of the presence of spirits
we will stop here and wash [The deletion of
"of the wind" here disturbs the balance of the
phrases]. Here seems burned with loss, aimless
shadows fall heavily here on my windscreen
my possible life is here in the mirror
here employed to describe breeze, which roughly
the forest turns for me, here are the ashes we end with
unseen friends are here and manifest through the tape.
Here are some examples of such voices:
I stand for another moment in the doorway. I'm in here
has its own appeal: a dying fall here, an artful
touch of pathos. Old roads are buried here
here the text breaks through, here breaks off.

**The crowd revolts.** Now there are bathrooms everywhere.
I want to tell you why we ran away, hiding everywhere as
we fled. Everywhere you were catching
at us. Why did you demand everywhere that
we put away what we were? Only the hot blank everywhere
convinces you to canoe to the burning river. Everywhere is
the stain of desire. Voices everywhere. Debtors consult
maps. Bridges fall everywhere. "Incoherence—merchants!
Distress everywhere!"—"What distress?"—"Political."

**The hard ghost of reason** is aflame like a small person somewhere in the country and also the office is somewhere in these woods, or words, the shops empty, somewhere a big wooden converted barn dissolves and somewhere in the distance waits the judge, a door closing in a body from which self is absent, somewhere the passengers look scared as nights stretch into flesh, our song bruises somewhere, and mud thickens somewhere as in the North I take her to an emergency dentist, thin clouds struggle to escape the trees as if they spent the night somewhere they did not want to be seen. Somewhere, someone is making a violin laugh, every joy produces somewhere else a corresponding pain. Imagine an imaginary island that exists in parallel, in slim books, just before the continent shelves, my identity somewhere between work and study, he says dad had been married before, somewhere in Hamburg, he has a photo of him with a woman who looks like Dietrich, and has more stored somewhere, or you expect a day to produce a thought that ends up in a silo somewhere, to understand the language is to get somewhere, memory starts outside the womb which is somewhere outside language and drops you somewhere you do not know, a low buzz continues like an electrical apparatus vibrating somewhere in the house. There is always a war somewhere, sometimes louder, seldom in this garden, but words come down because there is a space somewhere for them to fit, and somewhere he feels there might be truth in these stories. Because I do not like the idea of driving to Oxford Circus I decide to find a station somewhere off the North Circular, a high-walled side road lends it an air of being somewhere else, along with the heavy rain and my mouth steepening and somewhere I find my own name, syllabled somewhere, in a person who is no longer, ceasing somewhere in an imaginary space, though next time I suggest somewhere more accessible, a lazy summer sky, a jet losing its thread somewhere, I come to the farm and father is surprisingly young, he has a moustache and a family, on a train somewhere the hour comes that makes me and I get somewhere close to the feeling that a thing happened somewhere in the collective unconscious, as somewhere in the distance on his cliff shifting his shadow waits the Judge. Leave a shadow moving somewhere upon the leaf.

**There was a general** in order that there could be a particular. I started by disarticulating it at the fissure, there cutting the palate to split the face at midline. There was no greater wrong than to force the song. There was nothing at the end of the page. There was the laburnum, its colonnades. There were the conversations inside us. At the first of three footbridges, there I paused to look at the Cherwell. There were a surprising number of houses visible. There was only one thing worse than poems. There were plenty to kill as I progressed through the missions. The texts lay there dead, and the staff there were solicitous. There arose the idea of the skeleton. Smoke rose from their heads, and there was a burning smell. There they hung, bundles of carcass and old clothes, and during the evening there was music. At night, when waking up, there was anxiety and copious sweat. At the junction of a hard and a soft grain there tended to be a slight departure. There was erosion downcast of the groin field. Southwards there were eight archdukedoms: Themopylum, Cammapolis, Vava-Land, Loom, Foo-He, Zam, Arbelais, and Krissibel. There was a hole in the world, into which there leant a sun. There was no guarantee that vagueness was the decisive issue in vagueness cases. On the side of the mountains there was an updraft, and on the summit a group of child aliens marched here and there. Propertied regions and their warps and woofs are what there really were. Royal ships once anchored there; there existed many that attempted to fake fluid effects. There were small included areas of dark soils. Framed in fast-fading gilt, a child was there. Where we met there was a black hall. There were three manipulations of the Sternberg task: no mask, single mask, or double mask. We wove the events that led us there with what happens. There stood the ghosts of former dissidents. We felt we would put the sky there. There, the branches were repeating the immediate, the true; there came the black and mica-winged riot police. Take the nurse there, with injury and bleeding of underlip. There was a clear space of an inch between the area of dullness on percussion of liver and spleen. There was a river of grasses, hellebores, acanthus and black tulip. As to the water—there was the cruel urgency of frangible iron when ships docked there. When the ritual killing was in connection with unhappy events, there was no beer. Then there was there.

**Turn the lamp low,** there's no bird-chirp, not anywhere
if you take any route, starting from anywhere on
the screen. Variables occur anywhere outside

the constraint goal. Right-click anywhere and
select attack, to get anywhere walk through their
rooms. I cannot find anywhere like the place
I walked in but anywhere there's an unexplored space
in mind, if creation sings anywhere it must be in
that cistern. World sleeps and butterflies lead anywhere.
Draw a box anywhere on the page and put
the ladder to the four skyworlds that exist anywhere.
Anywhere I would recognise her voice
but in this anywhere it is only noise.

**Among their beliefs** are no fewer than eleven hells: the hell of it, that, this, those, my, your, their, other, inner, outer, utter, among others that have not yet arisen. Dolphin bones scatter among fire stones; among shells, two-thirds have spires tinged with purple.

The following, among other symptoms, seem to belong to this sensation: pain in the ear the whole night, terminating in the morning in whispering, of the wind among leaves. A long-entombed spirit walks at night among the ruins of war-torn avionics equipment and fallen capitals.

We need not accompany our tourists among the Lakes; among the canes and dry leaves of a gleaned field a family of Saltambanques echo among the pigeon world. To minimize interactions among the spiders, we decide among friends the path which fades.

People who should be onstage are off, talking among themselves, and there is someone among them made of metal. Charon of the whirligigs, among the snails, passes the day among men. If she is caught among branches, her head and horns are trapped. Like pigeons among schoolchildren, sleep ascends to reveal shapes we were among.

News of further arrests and unrests among the tribes, blush of bush or shrub, the apples minute among themselves while among the chandeliers and dirty windows we discourse. Among the technologies required are infrared search-and-track systems, whose solutions are among a large but finite set of possibilities called search space.

Envision continental drift in terms of scum shifting among anchor points. There is a withered tree in the middle ground, and the sky fills with the ill-informed birds of dawn: scuffle among dune granules, unrest among earwigs.

Unreal beings walk among us. Clarities breed among small underlying thoughts. Among thick weeds and grasses the wasp examines the paralyzed spider. Ariel moves invisible among the shipwrecked. Masks peer from among the ornaments; fantastic demi-brutes writhe from the branches.

When he gets near, one among those sitting in the group says: they threw their coloured coats and flares among the stars while the sky advanced and swallowed the planets of the sun one by one, and then the sun. Boiling distantly among us, it will be strong before kings.

**There's a lot of fate around.** Around the shallow currents of the beach light-clad figures delve. Winter howls around the towers of Schloss Schwöbber. A many-tiered universe of perception rotates around an axis defined by pairing players of around equal skill. You import the file and build your model around the board. The tool is a globe with circles around it. Floating a photo lets text wrap around the image. Let go to wrap content around other content. I could in these grey minutes have lain praise around us. My thoughts revolve around what this might lead to next. Excessive smoke around the nipple area. With sufficient fat stores depart around twilight. The ash comes off around my mouth. I spread it around the mat and tie shredded cedar bark around my husband, imprudently pricking him around the anus, squeezing him dry, pushing age-soft fingers around the edges. We stones, now, see everything around us grow verdant. Myth is the truth around which flame absorbs. Senses are horses, and sense-objects are paths around them. Roots have grown up around the path; the park unwraps around us its unwanted presents. Scarlet-tipped flames, dusk and then night falls around us.

At Eastern Ear Ledge the sea broke at all times. Roaring Bull Ledge was bare at half tide. The observer at B would not at that instant see the light at A. Finding the birds' departure with 14h of daylight at the beginning of the experiment and 18 at the end, the kagome regime became monopole.

He died at Dead Tree Point; at separation from the mother, the hair of his head was grey. At the intercession of a Faqir he attended the chat video. Separating of at least part of the scalar imaginaries at best risked reductivism and at worst imported a power-laden atavism.

Imagine the cracks in the walls to be forms of animals deposited at the nearshore river mouth at an inclined plane of 30° at the rate of a mile a minute. At the time sex originated, the vegetable functions became nobler; particularly at the soft-to-firm transition.

Food was sacrificed at night to Mother East-Water, money was burned at the grave. At the age of seven she became very fond of a girl, the child of a neighbour, and at the all souls festival, paper horses were burned.

Home sat at one end of the horseshoe formed by the company. The spirit band played at the same time on the drums, triangle, tambourine. The younger male never glanced at his son-in-law, and tugging at father's little finger he came straight at me and nestled under my chin. Whisper. Whistle.

At this, Jane attempted to fixate a penlight; flashlight; flashlight with red, yellow, blue cellophane; the program element configured at compile time from the parent data to the child data type. At the tips of each light ray were bodies with different heads.

Dig a hole at the back of the house and bury a green flag at the cocked position, with the fingers of the right at the lower end—At half-past clean the rugs, answer six letters, meet at the water's surface and jump. At the touch of such hand all locks and bars open at which point the raphe arm coils back.

At 12 o'clock he examined the woman at the left side of the bed and even Mike smiled at the Doctor's discomfiture. At any rate, with the fact that at night the cries of a baby were heard from the water house, all feared her. At daybreak, three cracks of the whip called them, corresponding to the age at which the dream-system lapped at the fire-water.

At present the Huichols rarely deposit sacred objects. At a certain period after rain ceased to fall a second sun appeared. At another time, many buffaloes, both young and vigorous, at the foot of Mount Lebanon, he slew.

The shadow-track began at sunrise near Lake Winnipeg, traversed Labrador south of Hudson Bay, where it discharged at high moisture level. Flame stood at the door with an arrangement for showing the hour at night, with the phone pressed to the peephole and the pointer at 0.

Our marriage was at an advanced stage. He sat at the left of the table with a boom mic and earphones to assist again at the merge of heaven and hell. The electron cloud is generated at the cathode.

The worms sang at the threshold. Tongues crammed at the door. Cat lapped at the garden bucket. At length hearing an obscure noise underground, unclosed ghost, a type of sky at the street's end at the end of the shout is the world of art.

## Sixteen. Of Movement

I HURL FINANCIAL FLOWS at the lintel. They stick fast. A man rips them out but as fast as he stamps on them another urges between my teeth. Think fast sleep fast. We are in film time. A fast-cut scene: masked figures open a crate of attack launchers: drive over the flatlands at night, in a fast overtaking radio trance. At higher fast-particle populations, the state transitions to fishbone mode. Consider them as fast and slow, like a poem read for the third time. We must be fast to get to the end of the line, fast as sun upon sundials. Radio is as fast and reactionary as breakfast. Form two lines and sit on the mats, roar loud chant fast. Gunslinger laughs. How fast are you by the way? The Universe expands as fast as his gun unloading, with a keen ear for fast, rhythmic, wavelike speech providing fast transmission and stable connection, at a speed at least twice as fast as the voice, as walking fast through wet long grass.

CAPITAL AGAINST SOUL, firm against soft, currency against
form. Against this the sun rises, checks expectations
matches value against expression
runs queries against a database
uses violence against the East
as a countermeasure against page-replication attacks.
Against the horizon, her lip is veined in
voluptuous golds. Sun pushes against
cloud movement, beats more clearly against
the barline. A broken umbrella struggles against a wall.
The bringing of a light plane against a shadowed one

produces the illusion of loss, of trees against rock.
Look up and to the left and press head against left hand;
the rainbow will appear by successive jerks against
the knee. Polemic against shadow
helps protect against the god of death:
hold hands against the flow of name.
Whimper against the mysteries of stone and brick
lights. That stay against confusion is monetary.
Eye speaks against ear, stars move slowly
a ladder is placed against the scaffold
shielded against time by mediaeval visors,
their shadows, thrown by headlights against
the low harbour wall appear to be running against hope.
Build rubble against dream
align the face against the grain of the language.
Left tab aligns tabbed text to the left against
the tab stop. Borrow against retirement.

**Return with good news** from Hell. Sleep from the dark sphere into the light.

Arise from mere chance. Draw away from a man alone in the woods and see the man, alone in the woods.

Collect the poem from the particulars of the word. Derive information from the strokes of the light or the heavy cane.

Leap from the shadow and shout *Bomb*. See a stranger wave from inside your house. Discern hidden figures of men and animals from the rearview.

Move from uncovered swine-effluent lagoons and effluent spraying towards far-heard crystalline bathing.

Suffer from light pain when rising from a seated position.

From the 1st to the 3rd day of the first month suffer from syndrome.

Insert "from" for "horse", to make a type B illogical substitution. Make a smooth transition from a deep and long siesta.

Engineer new meanings from the architecture of the fist. Cut small shapes from coloured tissue.

Detach from the crowd, walk from ocean sand to harbourside. Walk the piano from the wall two to three feet.

Trigger a call from your asset-manager. Loosen tired roses from the voice. Eat from a bag of ice.

Infer from speech data obtained from spontaneous conversations. Range from polite ("Good to see you, dolphin") to the phone's snarled cord.

Run from the street end of a crossarm to the light pole. Ooze from the broken nettle stems, lift a long knife from the cylinder.

From a distance look symmetrical, then come loose from the external tank. Descend from heaven, trail from the chariot wheels, burst.

From interpreting dreamless sleep reject the emergence of matter directly from God, construct replicas of travellers from the store at the arrival terminal.

Consist of mixed materials washed from loess and sandy Coastal Plain materials. Stem from the grip, form a loaf from a lump of dough.

Serialize events to a log file, and deserialize them from that file. Use the kettle to steam the price sticker (49p) from the Pelican edition of *Letters of Gertrude Bell*, 6d.

Remove several deeply placed fragments from brain. Range from a $75 "Fresh for Men" treatment to a $150 "Fresh Harmony Face" treatment.

Descend from the gallows; from balconies, distance the sounds of children from the actors. Derive from existence, not from relation to an object.

Relieve the terrestrial bazaar from clamour, awaken from sleep the narcissus. Cast shades from the darkness of the musk-willow.

Suffer from nervousness, from crippling flows of monochrome, of *roman fleuve.* Run from the centre of the head for the length of the handle. Shift from stocks to flows.

From a silent pool swirl a lawn upwards to a small temple. Remove wire from cork and ask for a heavy kitchen knife.

Carefully lift the tree from the beaker and hang it up for a beautiful chemical display. Issue fish treasures from the sea's teeming subsurfaces.

Stem rain from cloud, shift downstream from telecoms, make tiers of ruffles from the cuffs and collars of dress shirts.

Generate fuzzy images from text as a bot-blocking authentication. Make one fingertip from balsa and the other from phosphor bronze.

Arrive at death, from want of energy. The left hand lifts the handkerchief from the empty glass.

Extract knowledge from high dimensional domains, from the enraged squealing of your nose-trump. Morph foam from form or fame from more foam, separate the ocean from the salt.

Draw the wire from a reel, cut and bend the looped tooth, kiss the bandage from my face and haul me from the terrible terror of the wristblood wire.

Question levels of linguistic analysis from phonetics and phonology to morphology, syntax, semantics. Prevent a font from appearing in any font menu.

Wind pathways from the wooden fence to the shade of pergolas. Sinewy or wavy, build a body from a poem.

**Look inward, angel.**
Light travels through sleep, unravels inward
in so far as people see inward in dreams
they seem identical to their inward situation
in the left side of the forehead, a fugitive inward pressing
with the written side inward and the back outward
nation states compete for inward investment
the charred spirit-money curls inward like white butterflies.
When you drag a fade handle inward, it creates
fade: drag any handle inward to reduce image size
before the door opens inward into you
the visceral pump transports words inward through
non-whitespace characters with the adhesive inward.
The cock strikes on metal projecting inward from
the outside plate; arms of swampland reach inward.
The wound opens inward to an elderberry space.
Both my sons retract their limbs inward: eccentric
swells of love define but cannot rule the leaping inward
animal to advance, meet, and so turn inward.

**Draw forward in the chair,** and upward, and force the air out as you throw your shoulders forward and grasp the outside of the steering rim, shift starboard gun to forward port on port side. Look forward to this trial with the utmost interest, muttering to the air, with unsteady, short steps, and forward lean. I jump up from the shell-hole, wave and signal Forward! Nobody stirs. Time leans forward and creaks its moon, confides. Jakobson raises the collar of his ulster and, holding it over his face, puts forward abnormal language. Guns and cartridges are ready, and we look forward with anticipation to roast goose. A set of clock wheels advances the hands forward. Every passenger, head tilted forward over phone or laptop, branches to towers of nothing, clouds of earth.

**Panning toward the bus** as the opening credits come up the branches lean toward the road a car fumbles toward a meaning the petrol-gauge needle sags toward empty an empty train slurs toward London a yacht sails toward the modern perhaps toward dawn sleep spreads toward the outer part of the eye then toward the brain I continue cutting bone under the nose toward the palate amorous dreams cease toward morning pulling the cocking member toward the user's body I turn left toward the muddy cleft of Chilswell and down to the illuminated castle: its papery reflection accelerates toward simile toward metaphor the corn sown toward the end of May has a goal toward which it strives a beam shoots from my hand toward a man who rises in progress changes are observed in the chick's behaviour toward the bowl it is blown into the bowl it represents the setting out of Wu's army toward the north. Leaning toward the TV she summons a string of ghouls that slowly walk toward you, creatures with antennae that wave toward a future in which news is a minority interest as toward the end of a long lesson students make gestures of finality the lighting accents toward a sweeping curved wall that ushers them toward spacious trial-rooms. Toward 4 or 5 the rapier underlines the minotaur's movement toward the girl a dummy camera faces toward the nest this figure recurs toward the end of Hyperion through stages the child traverses toward a final adjustment, an apathy toward management acquisitions justice walks toward us with leaden feet the swans stretch their necks toward the lake the property of bearing an intentional relation toward the entity that in fact stands in the intentional position. I creep my fingers toward her she weeps weeps you will lead me towards the great Volta the great river Volta.

**Peter says Stand forth** the one who did this.
Sparks spring forth from the sound.
You have I whip my hair back and forth as your ringtone.
Joys impregnate. Sorrows bring forth.
The flames give forth little flames
clouds gush forth monsoonlike rain:
forth from the long grass nightingale's eggs
and desires echoing of light in sound shines forth
from us like soft kings forth from the hill,
forth from the froth of beaten waters.

**Finally it is national** Fuck Off day. You exist within
the boundless, turn off the headlights, a clump of trees.
The night comes down the sheep clatter off.
His scarecrowy arms come off at ninety-degree angles.
He takes his coat off and rubs it upon her.
As the dew burns off during the day the salt crystallizes.
Return to centre position to turn off beacon warning light.
Pecks on key A turn off the stimulus; pecks on key B turn off
the sound. Allow the lumbar musculature to turn off.
The onset of shock turns off both light and shock.
The portions you want to saw off are all without arms.
Wean off the jack colts with a gentle stud colt.
By turning Notifications to Off
the cache controller sits off to the side and observes.
The small boss is burnt off in the furnace.
"It's me," I reply. I take off my coat and hang it up.

I TEAR THE FRONT SECTION away to show it empty. The firm feel contented far away from Earth. I watch them from a screen and can slide this switch away from OFF to turn it on, or toward OFF to turn it down. My mother packs my Airstream helmet away. If she sends away a beggar, she will bear twins. The (the dragon spirit) appears to sweep away stupidity. When the stutter is severe you take its sleep and carry it away to an invisible dwelling. Those who drag a corpse are surprised to see the bus move away. Cut the ears off with the skin, and peel it away to the nose; come out of the ear's perplex, pull away the eye, wheel away the moon, take up the thin flute. Minutes away a new bus waits. The wind brushes away the faces. The winners walk away with death. The dead clank fierily toward the sea pulling away pieces of skin. The sea lilts away from the delta-lobe, the perfume leads away from the head and tail of the dragon until ages, indeterminate in extent, pass. Slack away the lee clew. A sea boom acts as a link between the line and the sinker or as a link to hold the bait away from the reel line. At the expiration of six days the watcher is called away from the distal side of the floodplain scroll. If the witch takes away the milk of the cow, procure nine ants' nests. In the bushes three star-lengths away I see mist roll from the sleeping walls. The crowned head is only a croak away: feeling defeated, it moves and breathes, then cuts away. A bench away, a patient has a tube taped into his nose. I cut away the wood so as not to injure his chest, draw the skin away from the viscera while ablating the tissue. My left hand fans away the gross air from my face. Between us fall the leaves, to be put away in air-conditioned archives. Personnel are required to stand away from vehicles. Child is not us, is working away from us. The muscles move the head away from the object on which the silk is stuck. These ducks are still a few quacks away from music.

**There was about enough** of the sun left to make a moon.
The clouds said turn left here and the tree turned right.
Right eye itching, you will cry; left eye, you will be merry.
Roaring in the left ear, distant thunder.
Bays were left before After Death Island.
After I left my career 7 years ago I offered larval hosting.
They went in the left arm to find a release passage.
The when-clause was evaluated as a left operand.
The eyes closed the dim passage left through the head.
The spots I left formed a portion of the phenomenon I beheld.
Chewing gum on the harbour paving is all that is left of me.
On a shelf of left hats was the right glove.
We left the party not knowing how our key would fit.
With the right hand, take the cup from the left hand.
A dead body's eyes were left open to look for somebody to follow.
I adjusted the tension so there was travel left in the spring.
The Left Tribe of Southern Huns broke into rebellion.
Logic functions were best left unspoken.
Head left to the moon, our ancient seat of gravity.
With a package under my left arm I could not signal right.
I applied the poker to the back of the left hand, and it opened
because three wires had been left disconnected.
Left long without a leader, they would plunder again.
Take the tongue's left fork to find the tick in the statue.
The final double quotation mark has been left off the end.
A person had left her person on the seat. Press and hold
down the left mouse button to grab this.

**Singing in right ear,** bad news: left, good news
noise in the right ear, the wing of a large bird
in the interior, towards the right temple
she raises her right leg to kick the soldier to the floor
she takes on the mantle of true power in her own right
performing a W-shape block with the right forearm
the puncher covers her chin with her right glove
when her hand chops move one character to the right
hold the lever in the right position for the pin to miss
right click on item in the project tree
the distance to the right edge of the browser window
unsettles with rustlings in the right rear speaker
as the deck is turned up the right fingers push the wrong card
the right takes the cup while the left produces the ball
marked deviation of both eyes to dog's right, followed by
successive twitches in the big toe of the front right paw
candy is dispensed to the right of the stimulus
the sea has risen right up to the shopfronts
with the right hand push a gelatine capsule into the retail display
light flies right through this tracery, voices leap, slip
bring body and mind to right relation
enter over left eyebrow, exit through right upper eyelid
obliterate globe of right eye destroy fundus of left eye
excise eye or teach obsidian it isn't right to open flesh
draws the ellipsoidal spotlight right on target
after the church make a sharp left, right.

**Play back a particular passage** from a sample tape. Cowering, tail between legs, ears back, I take you back to the poem: and then to the oncology ward, the white tunnel back to your bones and I convince you the canvas is lit from the back, with steep front steps and a chainlink that opens to a shade garden and cement walkway to the back door from which a narrow hallway leads back to the eat-in kitchen. After the story drags you in, the weapons keep you coming back. Turn the rabbit to look back, and put the needle through its jaws. Place right foot between the hind legs, then draw it upright and grip the back between the knees. With partial suction, tug on the fabric to draw the skin into the socket, then tuck the end back; while pushing straight up from your heels back to standing, start the eyes back into their pits. Put the floating toolbar in the back of the hard palate and draw it from side to side. Press the Sleep/Wake button to turn it back on. Each new joint as it pushes the others back acquires a place in the series. It finds a depression, turns on its back, and sucks back its venom. It longs to go back, and searches for the cave. Steps back on seeing a pale green light at the mouth. Body bent back, with miserable wailing, it holds back the hosts of darkness, fades back into stone. Go back and get the visible white ball and two tumblers and cause them to run up your back, down your left sleeve. Sunlight draws back its white light. You live the lives your parents never knew when they sang "Come Back to Sorrento": but it's actually the marketing that keeps you coming back. Your son rises from the lawn and the grass stands on his back like the fur of a hissing cat. Behind him stands Frost, a farmer only briefly and disastrously, and much further back Virgil. The engine chokes and the crank kicks back. Rounding corners, crows step back from the night's roadkill. You remember the chief's wife, run back to the canoe, but only the chief's wife's bones lie there. She lays her hands, and winds back up the wooded slopes. Go back to the previous page and edit your information. Fall back nine paces: your poem is played back.

**A story is a death** or a person, but really death is elsewhere
the alphabet stands for sounds that spell elsewhere
disengaged from location and moved elsewhere in the mind.
Consonants draw vowels through elsewhere's rubble.
Occupiers of Telstar, tethered to the world but elsewhere.
Elsewhere takes you through the master sewer.
To shop is to be repeated elsewhere. Life is.

**Yellow rocks across the hill.** I walk across my favourite part of the morning. Earth is wide, clouds brace across it. Words do not move smoothly across the page but animation moves me across the stage. I come across a grounded helicopter, hack its weapon-system. Shadows of struts fall across the cockpit. I power my hands across its shoulders, down its spine. Tomato vines sprawl across my nervous leg, and the by-product is aluminium knife. The blood spreads as if it were drawn across skin with an invisible paintbrush. There are many ways of communicating a mutable object across the node-boundary with the backing of leading physicians across numerous specialties. I come across a box of things that were very precious to me as a child. Descriptive, predictive, and prescriptive scripts are applicable across multiple domains. I plump up a surgical glove, and wave it across a line of cars. The deceased crosses the complex boundary with a shield and waterskin slung across his shoulders. Green becomes grey and across the fields mist draws its chilly sheets. After a successful throw, he hops across the numbered squares from one to ten and back again. Dad stoops through the church door and for a second he can see me across years. He blows smoke across the table, the cake, and the people astride the cake, skating their snow world. He results in cloudlike formations that travel rapidly across. He manages deliverables across cross-functional teams. From the landing, his music comes across as the ticking of many clocks. He works down to the cheekbone, cuts across the *zygoma*, and proceeds into the mouth.

GET THINK CALL RUN ahead
and dead ahead I see sky and sea meet, an ashed line
up the white road ahead to intrahepatic bleed.
Highlight the time fields and set the time ahead one hour
one-step predictions are on requests ahead of yours.
Click the 5 button to skip ahead unless the user loads
ahead of the current program counter. If your code decrypts
itself just ahead of the program counter, Ash
moves ahead with forge of forgetting, surge
of looking, moves ahead ceaselessly,
leaving us to scribe ahead, think fast, think back, thank.
I keep thinking S— is lost, but he is either slightly ahead
or slightly behind, pushback of mist, luminescent cloud ahead
as I drive down the M1 I want to open the door jump ahead
along your life-path look ahead, rear view mirror,
dashboard, left-wing mirror, ahead,
from whose unscaleable streams
come figures ahead of a low pressure system
the path ahead is flooded, the double Naugahyde padded
doors open. You'll never get ahead of anyone if you get
even with them. Get old. Go ahead.

IF A MAN TRAVELS repeatedly beyond the diamond-abrasive borders, he will sleep beyond his means, a gigantic crowd will play beyond light-coloured blocks of stone. It is possible he has been dreaming in this and beyond this, in all previous lives. They show him a map of London's public transport system, and he taps the table beyond the map to show where they actually are, approaching Slough. They do not see the symbols strung beyond them. With a grace beyond the scope of this study, the waves reach up to the side of the train, exaggerated beyond the way they actually are. Beyond them is the alluvial plain of literary failure; the textured questions that creep beyond the characters. This is a hot place to work, and beyond the discomfort, there is an accumulation of information. The dying have left the faintest perception, which is wiped away by the slightest movement beyond it until we are ready to move beyond language to the black stars that blow into the room. God hides in the dust or beyond dust in the boson, beyond the grave. Touch your toes, or go beyond your toes as much as you can while the fish peer into the black branching tunnels. A kilometre beyond the eye's search, a wall of red pillars rises. See conditions whose symbols range beyond the capacity but cannot get beyond tongue-tremble, frog pond, *deus absconditus*.

**As I put down my book** I see on the sofa my manager sleeping. She had been driven to below-homeless conditions, and I had gone down into the tunnels. Ten years later, I reach an arm though the telescope and bring down a peach. A feeling of coldness snakes down a depositional throat. Data-path contains a carry bypass adder, a whistle of approach down the corridor. I can scan down the thread list to find threads with a user-of-system user. When the comparison-machine breaks down, objects appear upside or double, and stairs lead from cockpit down to the cabin. Take a breath. Your feet will move you down. Hold; then relax. Lubricate the metal as it is drawn down the die throat. Weigh down a heavy felt roller on the loose pulp as the film draws down around the legs, wings, and other irregular curves. Make a slit down the body and remove intestines. Pass the wire through the skin, and draw it down over the skull. Shave it with a burr down to the dura. The fruit bursts and the mass of down falls. Perception's tunnel sets our lost bones down the long dog-leg staircase, pursues us down to the lanes of the dead. A tap of the feet channels power through my staff and down into Killian's body. Pursue the dead links, hold down shift-key; it takes two hours for the pain to move through the abdomen. I rank it with giddiness, which induces to lie down with weakness. A slight vacuum is created as the ball runs slowly down the tube. Throw the left hook to the body lightly to draw your opponent's hand down. The resulting jar gives the car a start which moves it down the empty track. Wake with smell of matches and the children burning pieces of kitchen and when you come down their faces melt. The eyes are cured by looking down seven wells in succession. It comes down to a search and replace algorithm at the binary level and cloud boils down to rain. I then fold down the *Gazette*, and ask him to read a line in moderately large type. The trailing end of the rope thrashes the headframe as it is drawn down the shaft. I look down from the courtyard into a very deep quarry as the double tap feature drops the light down to 15 lumens. Write down the silences. The world wears down to a finger of cogitating self, dismay is upon the face of us whose lungs break down the air, on whom clouds push.

**Terror and horror play** out on a face. Hollow
out of the opening four-bar sequences
out of the sun's wreckage
out of its hand, a forest.
The low, tired moon fades out;
After egg-laying the insect dries out.

The I in sentence makes sentience, runs out
of reddened eyes. We, out of focus, fogged,
pull out a mesh footrest from underneath;
a bubble pops out into the street.
The bird pecks key A to turn out the light
and key B to get food. I look out and draw
out the O syllables, I sit and pull
out my ear hairs like the luck
that I am out of and belch old dust
out. I climb a dark rock stairway, dig a plastic
baggie of galangal root out of the satchel,
spread it out on the ground, and sleep on it
shutting out sun, stars. The old man's voice
squeaks out between my teeth, draws the silk
out of the duct, the young snakes break
out of their shells. The experimenter
moves out of the field of a best-selling
mystery author, she shouts. Seating is laid out
against gold leafing, machined out
of steel out of which it builds world—mirror
can also be swung into and out of position.
Hooks lift out cores with the crane until a man
comes out of the woods with a dog and flashlight.
I take words out of context, two men, a boy
these cries die out. The red rose breathes
out an amber fragrance, small wings
the green night wove out of madness.
A strong man stands out of the sunroof
like an expanded flower, a banknote.
The flower breaks out its bell of sound.

Her objective is to bring the eye
out laterally, still attached. She frees it
out of the socket, lays it
out on a metal surface plate.
Open the word, take out its meaning, poem
flows out of the wound.

**Outside of the dog** is the book, it reads
outside the planet time is causation.
A breezeblock porch outside, with graffiti
directs its attention to an object outside of itself
at the lower outside of the eye is a necrotic tumor.
He stands outside the house and breaks
down but not specifically the garden outside his house
people stand outside their cars, they are waiting for
that part of personality directed outside
take out the eye bolts, dress the outside of the joint
these voices emanate from beings outside the Earth.
Mother, I bring a wife to you. She stands outside.
Go out 2 inches and there is text outside the box. It is still
there, outside a blizzard of years and corpses.

**His arms over** his head
Sand turns over the narration
roads web over the planet
gulls yawk over like street vendors
hold equal dominion over
soar over the red roof-tiles

over 95,000 flights cancelled
Brunel's bridge over the Brent
grieve over what I might become
shivering over the whole body
a breeze shifts over a knoll
move cursors briefly over the fields
the river turns over small stones
this is turned over to the note teller
oil in a large pot over medium
over supper we became heated
spirit places a hand over it
clouds are bricked over
click on an arrow to turn over
wind is driven over the bottle
the moon over the trees
the cock is rubbed over the axe
variables range over the physical
over the next two turns
pressure over the diaphragm
white silk is drawn over red silk
wind running over barley
the pipes play over the funeral
spread over the vast night city
control you have over content
over the pastel of me as a boy
hunched over the toilet bowl
over the full travel of a screw
the gums close over the areola
the moon hangs over us its grey flag
plays over us its unkind light.

**Human: a tube** through which self squeezes. Electric charge keeps you from falling through floors like a book is mostly paper, but you can't see through the words, through forests of lost sons. Through the system, through crowded alleys and backways, through gardens, over fences, through broad valleys, the back streets of Kyoto at dusk, through the next door into a set of offices, the forest path, the gap in the hedge, the broken tree, through your old school, villages in which no televisions are on, through the wooded campsite full of owls, detouring to the east through a double gate, turning south so that by the inner yew arch you move through regions of mist. Voices through the bathroom pipes saw through the head. You are through.

Spirit shunts through the blade, through the handle, through the three-way world, through the transparent companion-way, through execution paths, precision resistors, through the separation of code and data accesses, through an integrated investment management platform. Through waterlike quality it comes through the hospital to the waiting room. Through the unreliability of human faculties such as hearing, powers of concentration, the ability to differentiate; the Greek texts pass through seven cities, moving parallel through close mist, through half-closed eyes, through the stained-glass kitchen door, through the gift shop, a series of revelations, a thorough revision, a redaction, finally to ignite the Renaissance.

Through the North Channel for Sud Isles, it progresses through clouds, major roadworks, through train windows, through glasses, eyes: by Isles of Abendsee passing through the narrow bands of light-shadow-light, through the thickest forests through prescribed channels, cliff faces, continually, through a series of joint ventures or partnerships, through groves of pines, thin strings of selves, through the light-empurpled ether range, hack back through time, find the flower through thickness of skin, the sphere of sense winds through the night to arrive in its local network, its brain. Through the rusted metal frame on the ceiling, through the hatch of the Artic through the air, all through the 18th century, windows lengthen. Through an unfastened coalhole in the pavement through an activated charcoal-cartridge. Sun is the hole through its flowers. The train moves through lives.

Poem is egg hatching through the page the past. The emperor's jade head looks through the moon gate, days are tubes he looks through. The burning torches gleam through fissures giving a temporary illumination to the cavern through which it passes, through the bridal linen of living and dead: a pallidness transparent through the forms, and through the soundless stupor of night, through light-obliterating garden foliage, through interest in meaning, fleshes of awareness through the soft ways, through loss, through a series of tapering holes that diminish in size through the suddenly paper-thin background, through a train of bevel and spur gears, through the distance that the words encompass, through the soft sediment, as a spycam zooms through that skylight on the mall roof through a succession of buildings, through a series of discrete numbered stanzas, leading to new cultural relevance through syntactic structure and familiar reference.

**You open the door** into a different film. Noon passes. A plough divides the earth into rose.

Wealth managers go into Asian markets as voices lift into mist. They mass into the urinal, fumbly, jetting.

Open cock and allow liquid to flow into the cylinder. Add to the cooled custard; turn into mold.

You are nearly at the mouth of the alley when a shadowed figure steps into your path. He opens a passage into the gun's chambers.

Individual spiders are fed into a gunlike periodicity device that translates mass into force. The silks extenuate into an equivalent that is harder to understand.

An island owner puts drugs into Cun Xi's drink. He rises into a sitting stance, swings into the sand, explodes into all the facial expressions that compose him.

Rotating breaker-teeth penetrate into the root, the sky particles into icicles. The firm expands into adult-incontinence products.

Time turns historical debris into a channel of varying cross-section that feeds into the graveyard.

The way into the chest is opposite the turn of the aortic arch. An interface wheel pushes the ribs into position. Air bubbles are injected into the spinal cord.

Eva Braun zeppelins into the birdless ether. When she inserts the plug into the jack the lamps come into parallel and the line lamp goes out. She squeezes into purer light.

Beat songbirds into songstreams. Admit steam into the cylinder. On drawing back the bolt, the hammer crumbles into the ballpoint.

Mission specialists go into the suiting room. A circus clown cannonballs into the sky, his arm flips the shuttle into its repair position and injects silicon into the damaged area.

Walk into the café, sit facing the light: molten materials harden into glass. Miss Elonda drifts into the light, clad in silken veils. The eastern wind brings green into the island grasses.

Our purpose is to translate music into the future, organize metaphors into similarity sets, embed edits into workflows. Introduce a novel virus into the underworld.

Come into existence, Maud, translate sound into world, drive hands deep into pockets. Turn your lever-arch file into a web-based resource.

As the mist falls, translate into head the outburst flowers.

Clump the clauses into sentences, paragraphs. Inch into the shell, wrench into the object.

Mother is changed into a sexton beetle that splits into five. She translates management-views into a form understandable by HR policymakers.

Splash, turn the water into news-frames. At times light breaks into rays, fits into fists. Do not look into the sun at sunrise. At sunset look directly into it.

Type the domain name into the search box on the main page: consider him in some form of post-life existence shading into delirium.

ARCADES ISSUED onto the often-observed streets
a deep thoughtless dark climbed onto the plinth
as I looked onto them the streetlights turned off
storm drains spewed muddy water onto the road
a fat-handed man struggled to hold onto his key chain
his hatch opened onto the world of operation of souls
waves crested and crashed onto invisible surfaces
a mudslide shoveled him onto a rocky floor. The man in
front of me sneezed onto the cash machine keypad
a customer heaved bags of change onto the marble counter
he was an ontologically independent being
he held onto my shoulders as I put on his overalls.
A dozen semiconductor-makers hung onto niches
a number of hybrid roofs came onto the market.
The tube shot the incoming photons onto the phosphor.
The pickup device vacuumed pulp onto the screen
then the brush pushed dirt onto the gutter.

**It is easy to rise,** when called, from plastic chairs, under
strip lighting. Say a short sentence three times under the breath
I open the cans under the noisy light and remember
the boat was glass and things felt slow, under their own
steam of rushed light. On August 20th I open his abdomen under
ether: the belly whirrs under me. My care, his cure.
I am over the sheet and she is under and as she falls
asleep, each is a circle under which no one is named.
The spiders are monitored under a light-dark cycle
for five days and then under constant darkness.
Under pressure they are drawn through a capillary
under which is a series of pipes for heating liquids.
Spiders from the second set are entrained under
a ramping light: those grown under the light-dark regime
are harvested under high humidity. They discharge
acrid fluids from under their heads and
under the worms even blinder souls, and they too
live on words. The smile under the surface of things is no
longer concealed under the large handkerchief;
I feel my tongue under the sandwich.
This boar is a young woman of great beauty, under spells.
Her ribs flare out under her hide. She sleeps
under the oak in that playground where she has a vision,
going under the ground she sits in one of the wells.
a poem is a mirror broken under a car,
under the title *Fragments of the Older Poetry*.
Under the lava-cap fluids rich in fluorides alter
brecciated zones. The sun under the sea is the sun
the sea accepts. Under all these pages it's night,
a stream inhabits its myth under the sign of form

under the Main Tabs section whisper
of last night's rain. Under the manhole the menhir.
Henry jerks his hand from under an expensive
suit, and I see the concealed thunder bulge under the same
circumstances as a firm nodule under the skin.
See under nature. She cycles the towpath
under the low-hanging willows that brush her head
and under the farthermost side of one of the lindens
under her helmet she guards her breath.
The unachieved piles under the hourglass's sphincter.

**Hello yesterday** gliding up the escalator, whisper up from the depths and laugh like an aged vacuum cleaner hoist up to the mic. Draw up the blender as the sauce thickens. Turn up pastry to overlap the apples. Clump up the gray plank steps. Pump up with sump energy, creep up the spine and settle over the sinus and into the eye. Lifting the eyeball causes the body to arch up, collect in a jar of spirits the lungs you bring up. Wake up old, take up the trumpet and salute us with *Good evening, friends.* Stir up waterspouts and no one looks up from their phones. A flight of two steps leads up from the saloon to the cockpit, where the dead man-being lies. Push up to turn on work lights and illuminate winch-station up to the top of the pass. Apparently wrap up the white ball in the white handkerchief. Get up from the ground wrapped in faded flowers. The stolen fire ends up on an album cover. Opposite is an L-shaped lounge making up a conversation-area. The beds grade up onto the floodplain. The body behind the head divides up into joints, the whip antenna stands at the dorsal surface to allow the digits to run up the length of the wand. Waterproof up to 10 feet, dustproof up to five centuries. Eats up 7W in standby. The laval river picks up bombs, slag and ash. Draw the eye up from the lower hem to the pubic area. Ram up the pulley to the rim, then draw the rim up until it is level with the top of the drag. Hook the blowoff cock up to the line. Hang curtains floor to ceiling to draw the eye up and suggest larger windows. The nuptial staircase takes you up to the private rooms. A single occasion in time continually piles up. Here we are, searching, unsure, in space, which way is. I type up the poem and head home.

## Seventeen. Of Position in Space

WALKING BACK THAT EVENING, a dog defecates near you.
You lie down in the grass near the contagious hospital
with pinching pain in the left side near the orbit:
the medical men draw near to the alley where
the bus left. You lie there for ages, near death;
paths become near in the falling light.
You lead off with an incision near the patient's
left eye. You chop through the bone at the free surface near
the dislocation, and trap sediment near
the channel margin, the object rises and comes near
to incisive, rhythmical jerks, of near constant amplitude
the house is near the alley where the bus left but it is late
a few machine-parts lie near the road
near a bus stop. Further on, near the car, as you pass a hedge,
an early-career nanotube researcher says the farm is near
enough to hear the squeal of pig-feeding,
travelling at near grazing incidence, it strikes the rough surface
and is absorbed. Sentences spell out the names of near
relatives of those present. The directory name appears near
the top of the dialog box. A spot will be made near one edge.
The alliterative S sounds near an old inscribed incised
monument comes near the end of the sentence.

WITHIN AN INCH OF YOUR LIFE within a corporate context within which portions of the map within limits imposed by commercial confidentiality within the plasma moon within the window within the first ten days within and across scenario comparisons and within four or five miles within what cave he sealed within the alloy housing within a contemporary space within the target area within the tree-structured network topology or within the region within your local network within the massive spacecraft. Options within the app circle within circle: within the outlined areas within the film industry within the folds of his dark suit within the eastern chamber within a small time interval within the next fourteen days within an open face within the vehicle within such message elements into two processing channels within the visual system within a couple of inches of the ground, the teat within the mouth, mobility objects within the virtual environment within the softly waisted one-shouldered shifts. Today we walk within.

**Keep your wooden box** with you wherever appropriate
for wherever a glance falls, death comes.
Wherever the entity is it instantiates the entity.
We will live wherever you decide: it
won't be long, life reaches into wherever is dark.
Wherever reality originates the long road goes.
Wherever the broad-spear glitters, the battle grows —
wherever the properties B and C combine, A and D
are present or absent. Move the fields to wherever you want,
wherever you press [Enter]; the dot symbol (•) represents
a space—wherever you press [Spacebar]; the arrow symbol (-»•).
Move in the van wherever governors tremble; or
a wish becomes certainty; wherever right for all is wrong to none,
wherever source image is opaque, here is elsewhere.

**Streaks of azure** wove far above the rising clouds. Then the disc's rim itself rose above the roof edge. What had this star to do with the world it lit, with blank skies above the abortive camps? It held the world in its talons, and guarded everything from above. Above all the sun exacted likeness. I grew formless as I rose, an essential shadow, alone to the dark room above the square. I slept under that which was above me. Chilliness in back, cold hands, drawing in muscles above knee and in the whole side of the face, as though many people were holding me down. A noise as of soft thunder flowed from above the occiput. The platen windlass and two chains elevated me above the bed. I cut above and around the eye, then brought the incision down to the middle of the lip. When female A3 arrived, she attacked the third crow from above. To count as a large cardinal a cardinal towered above all smaller cardinals. Crossed vapour-trails flowered above the trees through leaves. Above this rose, pure white, the many-pillared palace, decorated with light-spired minarets. Christ, *ab ovo*, lighted from above the booth, was hung on the long wall to give the effect of a chapel. When backwater rose above the upper section, a thick sandstone-succession occurred, the curve representing the sediment accumulation rate above the line representing the rate of sea-level rise. Here and there warm isles of sand gleamed above the shallow tide. Roots projected above a sidewalk and a pedestrian sustained an injury. One of her pantlegs hiked above her boot. Rising smoothly as rock above us, my worth was above him by the worth of a sheep, by the worth of an ox. A directory knows only about the directories immediately beneath it and the directory immediately above it.

**To think that** all along we would come to a long thought. Each arrow represents an axis along which we move. The street along which I scrape my feet. Freedom is along the pulses and impulses as I string along a low sandstone wall towards a quarry, a drawing pain along the right ear and neck. Years later I watch the blind woman and her dog walk at night along the walled footpath, slowly and in unison. It is time to spy along that crevice which is love; it breaks behind sinus pain into liquid. The neon lights running along in front of the wing-spar are not visible along the outer circumference of a fixed circle of radius R until the triangular lattice is obtained firmly along the slightly gaping edges of the incision. We walk along the carriageway and see a water buffalo drag itself along on its forefeet, and die. As the chair swivels, the bubbles move along the surface of the adjustable weighting system, the teeth rings closely spaced along the hatched areas as its brass wheels coast along adamant tracks. Many of the cliffs, stained faintly with iron along cleavage planes, are up-thrust lava. The scale of the eddies along the front separating the chimney from the stratified surrounding waters imply compression along the streamline. The resuspended sediment, transported along the slope, is cut by shears. On a warm day, patients stroll along the road with IVs and chest-tube drains. Certain old men, toiling along the edges of crops or other ungathered products, graze their knees. She walks on the ravine floor along with her dog, who squirts out defensive substances from glands four on each side along the belly. The waves propagate in crystal along the direction of those who are dead. A robot traverses by moving from node to node along the edges of the graph. Delete it, along with any attachments. An analyst ventures along a trail of new starts and trackless time. Along the ridge of the known language, more words stir into the dictionary. If this has come to you in error, please delete it, along with any attachments.

**Behind the computer,** the sunset. I turn to see behind me the objectless I behind the alphabet's heads, hoping to find the white hart behind the white well behind the central engine leaving a dotted track behind it. The cash counter and the wall behind it also have rich treatment in leather and gold leafing. He heard a rending groan behind him, and turning his head saw an idiot rising from the earth where the toadstool had been. I am watching from behind a glass screen and behind this, a column of silent followers do not acknowledge me. The leaves behind the leaves will not be leaving soon. The road behind chokes with dead oils. The cars behind light me in a way that feels angry. The old woman goes behind the door and hangs up something. It shines as though there were a night light behind it. Whisky is fists behind glass. Packed behind the shoulder is root of night, behind each success is a sense of hindrance. A toddler plays with her father's dreadlocks, hiding behind their bead curtain. She believes the trauma of a terrible event a year earlier is behind her. Isn't this like an actor who conceals impulses behind a masklike face? They shatter as we look behind. Behind a wall of charred trees, an angry crowd gathers. One victim seeks out the bogus person behind the photograph. The point is driven behind the staple by means of a hammer. The winter moon goes behind the skyscraper. Over a dozen locals hide behind trees and share binoculars. They seek the bogus person behind the photograph. The winter moon behind the skyscraper. The dog a dark blur behind them. The headmistress says *Mr Johnson*? But that is the person behind me. But what is behind him? When there is no lack is there lack of lack? The people see a city behind their eyelids. Behind the city are their eyes transporting the readers behind.

**Where the amber-polished shore** pales is the island of reflection
where the roads dip the grey light meets the green air
where language rips other language is where language starts
where covert illumination is used the pilot sees nothing

where the poem comes in indicates where the wheels are located
where the mere deepens the last spirit-insect prepares to save
where we bathe in the South Fork are mudpots & fumaroles
where Ariadne sleeps patients have painful memories erased
where literally means figurative use double angle brackets (<<>>)
where an idea works into consciousness a pencil is not found
where people build walls pile junk are property lines
where dust and regret mix silver peacocks spread their tails
where they are calling out names slowly starlight blows off the roof
where the dusk contracts to the room, sleep
where one comes on an upland burial field flowers cover the path
where stones reach up the insects are numerous
where a star comes loose a shadow runs over
where a list of results is possible the user is presented with a menu
where is the sentence that proves not in what it means but does
where the speech ends travel in order to be we think we are

**The centre of the sun** was 6 degrees below the horizon; the descent was easy in the misty brilliance. I entered the plaintiff's seam at a point fathoms below the surface, below the white roots edged through the grain, below which waited the Maidens; they took up the chain-stitch below the second double-crochet on the first row and drew the wool through, then the master-priest breathed deeply and bore it below, and cast shadows below the writing surface. The sediment was cohesive below the mobile mud. The void-field was below the weathered, gravelly layers of subsoil that drew the river below the level of instream flow. At the same time, to control the ability of a layer to block the data in the layers below it contracting the abdomen below the costal arch, I peered below to the courtyard: battered cars with huge tail fins had pulled up, every way I looked other lives and below them history and ancestors and breath from other systems, so I walked out on the deserted strand below the cliffs, and came to the conflux, and she suggested going down to swim there: we could see the mist below us dance its seven veils. Our below was their above, but their below was also ours. Naples' lights reflected in the bay where, with a blare of seagulls, white curtains blew, ghosts below the waterline. Just below the collar was a shining piece of twisted metalwork. This is discussed below.

CENTER TAB CENTERS tabbed text beneath tab stops.
Dragons ascend in the spring but hide beneath
the ivied ocean-dome in autumn. Beneath their skins
energy clumps. Beneath the sofa a crime.
Body text is the text beneath a heading level.
The sun sinks beneath a calm sea near Neath.
We stop a little way beneath Amshit. Filmed clouds
help researchers get beneath the messages;
the noises beneath the grate cease. Mother
coughs. The undertakers find a cavern beneath
the liver. It leads to a tiny city beneath the breath.
Lie duck tremble crawl hide lurk.
Believe the human buried beneath my ash.
Deathlike music beneath huge palaces.
Beneath a solitary noon the pillow sleeps.
Beneath is represented by the list hierarchy:
erased by xoring beneath a read-write head.
Draw a solid border beneath your name, the cursor
spaces over automatically until it is beneath

the C in Count. Beneath IBM are Raleigh and Austin,
beneath each of them research and marketing.
Enter a time in the edit box beneath the pop-up menu
a wavy green line appears beneath the error
then click OK. Add a third label beneath
the second that contains the execution
path. Remove screws beneath the clear handle
just beneath the serial number sticker:
Beneath everything is the idea of that thing.

AND INSTANTLY THE MARE comes and stands with the foal beside me. We live beside the name of the river, the prison known by its rival frame, here we live beside the word openings and find stars in the cloud, working on excuses, poems, more books. The executive vice-president opens the sidebar-panels box and places beside it her new name. How can the universe let you lie asleep beside someone else?

AN INTENTIONAL RELATION HOLDS between real and unreal.
Castaneda describes the passage between ordinary reality
and suggests the division between light and shadow,
a pattern between incident and secondary-wave
generates, and you cannot fit a blade between
this & future realities; you re-enact the arms race between
U Boat and Q Ship in brief passages between darkness,
the trance somewhere between a tapping finger
and a being-toward-sleep, between convulsions and twilight
between configurational and non-configurational syntax.
Observe the difference between the thinker of the I

and the regret-value between web and client.
Vacancy between sleeps, who invented you?
The concealed white ball must not show between fingers
tension it between the legs, which support the vault
between the longitudinal axes of your body. Squeeze
it between scalp-bone and blowhole. You have no ease
save between her arms and your trouble grows
in the emergence-region between order and chaos.
A spider between the legs of Michelangelo's David
midway between matter and spirit.
With a knife between her teeth she cuts the pain of bearing
by dusk (determined as the time between
sunset and Bloomberg report) between the ideas
of a leaf falling and loneliness: if you scored between
35 and 40, you carry messages between the living.
Between the seductions of reflection and its agonies, when
the child becomes a sitter, between 6 and 18 months
the dashcam jumps between this and vision's moment's
distinction between rite and dance. All I can plead
is connexion between body on the one
hand and open space between the end of the horseshoe,
while contacts between ß-strands enables
ensemble-based and geometric structures.
Between the trees, the wood, the sun a flash
between pine-needles, nor is there a leaflet
between volute and abacus. We walk around
in discussion between shared services and line-managers.
Raudive finds it in the medium wave between two stations
between deliberative and evaluative readings.
When the light connects between terminal and ground

the horn unsettles any distinction between initial
and secondary impact. Between quotation marks
linkages between worm gears and nuts decouple.
Stay a distinction between sound and felt, come
between thought and traction, hinge back the hood
draw up the ears with a skewer between skin and head.
In the struggle between raptor and hang-glider
the interval between milky and hatching stage will be
short. Between saying is the world, it insists.
Between *Of* and *Discourse*, Stein and Hill, rock and high place.
A child is stuck between the worlds the door separates.

**Childhood is a wilderness** destroyed by signs. Ruined by gaze, by worldly cares, by headache aggravated by noise, unrefreshing sleep interrupted by the dead. The drowned float in dirty whites framed by jagged edges. Dream of a land characterized by lithic scatter, fire-fractured rock, faunal remains. Bring a stone from every place for identification by taxonomic staff. Encourage patient to scan environment by turning head, to respond by vocalization. By translating contradiction into meaning, we encounter interpretation as excluded by contradictoriness.

A year goes by & she exists again by the expansion of the lumen by the muscles which draw the plates by means of a chitin gutter including system-board, expansion-cards, & memory-modules, or by one or more of the following: scattering of surface wave by edge dislocation, puncture by needle through chest wall, stroke of a briony mallet, turning a sound man dumb by a blow to his brain, by bending the fingers at the second joint, by glimpse of hair on a bare arm, by baby buggy. These are the forms assumed by witches. Abandoned by her widowed father at a garage, by reflecting on the influence of her history, she achieves analytic understanding. This is self we help out of the mud by dancing, by singing *hoom* (sound made by the bone spirit). The radiation generated by the three-sleeper sun bed increases the home's price by 0.96%. The visualization is dominated by the blowing apparatus by which steam provides the terminus described by the verb.

Burnished by Astrid's glances, ignited by Ivar's voice, the arch is supported by two scrolled brackets with *guilloche* bands. It resists resuspension by tidally generated currents by ripping & dozing rock, or by inventory crews in the field using butt, slash & burn. Time drains love by image or inch. We execute a customer branch step by dividing the economizing procedure by the total number of entities multiplied by the endowment vector.

The outlet is through a lever handle extended into a twin-beam walking-machine connected by a V-shaped foot-warp that back-references by becoming electrified by contact with the excited glass rod. Its smooth, long, narrow head is topped by fine, thin ears. The hazel eyes are surrounded by circles of white. Its mahouts indicate by the lightest possible touch of the goad, destruction by fire, by water.

Man killed by falling cloud. Hang-glider mobbed by red kites. Poem caught by intention's blind noise, & marred by quote attributions. Characters surrounded by double or single quotes. The clips are followed by a passage in which a child's cycle helmet is left by the roadside, & Val is branded by burning debris: she is motivated out of bed by the will to see the destruction by water of her race.

A hunter procures fern-seed by shooting at the sun at noon. Saved by the screws in the clock, the teeth of the wind are lit by the appearance of the phoenix. It consists of a set of cooperative mobile agents executing tasks by controlling a pool of multiple robots. The base layer bitstream will be a compression joint formed by directly butting two faces.

By worms & cold, the corn suffers in the governments of Twer & Kostroma. By the thumb, it produces fatness; by the middle finger, water; by the next finger, food; & by the forefinger, liberation (from births); after bathing, by clay; by exhalation of fiery breath, by ashes; after worship, by sandalwood. Hardnesses are expressed by defending or capturing flags interpreted by legacy decoders. Revelations of anterior events are disclosed by a slight stricture of the oesophagus by which Pope secured his humorous effects. The word "doughty" is undermined by its first syllable to the eyes, & by its sound in the mouth.

The cure of the Tarantula by music is field-generated by product topology, or succeeded by heat of the face extending deep into the brain, increased by eating of the luminary by a celestial dragon. Labyrinthitis is cured by torrent & beat of wave, by the ten months of gestation of the mooncow. Destroy the pythons by fiery yang with three-armed spiders of brass. Build the house by the breaking stream by meditating on the ambiguous qualities of princes.

By means of the Silver Man, we pray that you divide calamity by twice the tangent of half the frog angle, by the blow of a tennis ball, by the dust of events & the clamour of details. The male catches the third crow by the foot. Gripped by the crying, the prophet Gad, borne in a fiery whirlwind, descends. Introspections are as follows: check one's sufferings by a glass of gin, the search-path traced by a thought, praise chanted by the eight immortals sent to the grave by bladeflash, by the abyss's lullaby, by the smoke of babysitters, by the touch of byzants.

We make love to the world by waking, by selecting File, Options, Customize Ribbon, clicking the check & box by synchronizing alternating openings to the screen update rate by adding bullets & by boxing the indented paragraph. Open the Quick Settings panel by turning on the Refresh Highlight option, by clicking on Tools|Mail Merge. The ruler line keeps track of the font width by "floating". Fabric-ate an integrated circuit by micromachining a hexagonal array of transducer elements. Communicate to the distributing-roller by a worm in the spindle.

The material pushed out by the frost is caught by crouching at the water's edge & imitating the mating call. Typically, the inflated male approaches by paddling by degrees to branches of the size of a rice pounder. It becomes a globe adhering to the bark by the lip of a circular orifice. This is the continued excitation produced by male coition witnessed by a child of three. The child confuses a cat by moving it asleep to a different room. We speed up time by consuming the corpse of the past, open the flowers by looking at them; hold an upturned butterfly wing by surface tension, by eye, by will.

By interrogating the prisoners & exposing their guilt, I console the queen's soul that responds by oscillating as a string endowed by mass. The engine load can be offset by a high hornbeam hedge. A cold shut is caused by the flow of heated metal to an impression followed by thrills.

Driven by customers, our work is marked by the exploration of old couture standbys, radically transformed, by mini-suit dresses given a quasi-1940s shape by tailoring an extra set of arms in an around-the-body hug, and by unrighteousness. Count time by unwritten books, complete form by selecting check-boxes. Componential analysis is represented by the tree, the matrix, the grid, & the cube; constituent analysis is signaled by vowel affixation. Travel to this world is by foetus; we are related to it by being made of it, by a falling earring of Siva. Wake him by blowing in his mouth: prose is sentences ruined by sense, actions punctuated by the fall of imperatives, clauses ranged by power.

A cramplike numbness ascends by day. The different lifetimes in the arms are verified by considering input data, tall pine broken by wind; the stripping of garments by the Boxing Match mechanism. We make it scope-sensitive by the cyclopically wrought fast-throbbing hammers of goodbye letters and encode information by the same phonetic correlates. Different translations of the same poem use three-way ambiguity with respect to opacity as predicted by the number of levels of embedding: by subscribing the standard contractual clauses punctuated by catarrhal roughness operative to store the data sensed by said sensing.

**See inside** what the eye is calendar for
the tree is made of years wrapped inside years
a word grows furry and creeps inside a seed
a wall falls inside of ten years
the sun goes inside us with our eyes it sees we are
without issue, blind on the inside
sea is friendship pursuing a wish inside the dolphin
blood runs inside long hotel corridors
add a handle, put a message inside, and staple
the chief disadvantage inside is the swarms of flies
when you rotate your eyes turn out to be inside
travels between eight and 12 centimetres inside
show a section-view of the inside of the pulley
opticians send light inside me to map river systems
from the inside of the shoes the toil of the worker stares
roots use flowers to show us what earth is from the inside
the structure inside a sentence is longing
knock on the word, what sound is once inside
if you place colored spheres inside a gray box and shine
a light inside this is glint going nowhere
run inside, fashion this gown of bright oracle
here of what is inside this mountainside
inside the hazelnut is history. The husk is us.

In the following poem, the lyric self travels various cities. In the van is a cohort of elephants, the foreign uniforms in films. The nature of citizenship is assured in Stanza 24. The divine system of reward and punishment is treated in Stanza 25. The author creates in the reader the history of algorithmic authorship in rhythmic liturgical chant.

In Rome, black-suited doctors group in the bath-house portico. Silhouetted in the streetlight's glow, a wet cat gleams. The access pattern to a segment in tablespace is sequential. In order to dispel the evil spirit spoken of in Chapter XVI, focus the heat in the burning lens. Your subjects will be in perfect focus, but in random order. In many honeymoon albums yellowing cocktail napkins are found.

In Madrid, in the fine light of the finite light, pain in the external ear of the right side. Pressure in thumb joints, crawling in skin of back, tearing in an old scar from the cut of a sword. Take a shower in the bathroom showroom. In order to see deletion-phenomena, double-click in the window. Stand in a cold place to harden. In the supermarket, search for the brands of youth. They in themselves are what they mean.

In Tallinn, streetlights are thumbprints in the margin of a manuscript. The rhythm in the display windows follows that of spring. In the small talk of a young woman with a taxi-driver, instruments scrape in the ear. Anxiety in whole body, with cold sweat. Money turns in my pocket, in fact, all the money in heaven. Seek the warble in the meat. Expose the ape in the drain, the grating in the flesh.

In London, we are enthroned in a situation of the highest distinction, in facing single-page vignettes. In order to recover associativity put in a substantial amount of muscle-, fat-, and skin-laden tissue. Scribe alternate semicircles in successive stripes. Breathe in. Move the playhead to an early frame in the second clip. In cones the gray molecules mud-spatter the window. A shift in sea-level pressure-high results in grandmothers weeping in the breakfast room.

In which world, in our no longer unnumbered days. In a thick jumper and a couple of scarves, wearing fingerless gloves. In geometric silks padded with Dacron, asymmetric sleeves in the style of kimono. In the event of a piston seal failure Sitwell thinks the axe in the corner truthful, while in Riga, Hamlet knows hell is contained in nutshell, but it's that "in" that I'm interested in, the in in king, the here-end of infinity. When we think there's no one in, the Roman legions in immense numbers go on in the silent film-script of nightmare.

In *The Corpse*, the clock ticks in the statue of the deceased in order that the spiritual essence rises in the bosom and finds expression in the lip. Servomotors move the scribing head in the voice, the path in darkness is engenderable in many consciousnesses. Mum runs her car down a steep bank in woodland. Ichnofossil assemblage in the historical layers is shown in the interlacing nerve cells.

In *Horseman*, the bronze sword in the gut is lunged. Undeformed burrows in the active layers operate in continuous-flow mode. A chestnut cast in raw umber, and coloured with burnt umber, is cast to the Corn Mother in the morning, to Mothers South-Water and North-Water who shield the Moon Gate, in the evening. Pollen carries in the wind, and is abundant in the fills. In the opinion of the writer, reducing sludge deposition in a crude oil storage tank includes income possibilities.

In the month *Ri* of the year the house of *Puzrish-Dagan* was built. In spirit I wake and walk in the light of syntax, light in hand. Sound of creek water & breeze in Jeffrey pines–blue jay & faults in mantra are explained in the great texts. Mumbling in the presence of the women of the drawing-room as the white outlines reappear. In Boston he hires several young men speaking in exaggerated nasal Brooklyn accents. In waste discharges an effect is change in waveshape.

In no. 11, Curley follows Pollock in identifying fixed and eternal things with the infinite modes. From in to out (from bottom to top in the figure) the sequence is: gypsum base, organic coat, tin sheet, gold leaf, organic coat, tin sheet, organic coat, organic coat. Surface wash deposits the pollen in small forest hollows. Shadow accumulates in bone, replaces intimacy with sense's thumbflint. Temporally diagnostic artifacts in this depression consist of projectile points and Knife-River sherds.

In Porto hangs the pickled moon in its jar, a sliding lateral motion in unfrequented parts of buildings is securable in a drawing board and loosely engaging the slot in the beam, the amplified soloton results in insulator-metal transition. Compressed claws attach in front of the mouth for in-pit crushing systems. In the head of the left thigh the engine is programmed in Lisp.

In Livland, the cornfields and grass stand satisfactory. A nightward drift in the weather, gnatlike minds in thought's immense pattern hang in the trees and grass; in sleep of blade in the knife in the fist slits the moon [the construction in this sentence is obscure]. In the counties of imponderable selves, wines flower the frames open in the square of sense. Grinding procedures in operating rooms are asymmetries in a conditional mean.

In the wallpaper of a certain room lies the mixture of all qualities: hardnesses and softnesses in relations of perceptual resemblance. In the year 1898, owing to a copious dinner, tearing in the left temple. A pungency in the forehead, roaring in the ears. Obliged in walking to step with great care for fear of images created by vessels in the cornea. Copious clammy slime in the throat, especially in bed. Stinging and rending in the peasant's bent shoulders.

In England, the shaft runs in phosphor-bronze bearings in the brackets, streams gradually in, flows in slowly and constantly, in heroic mistless sunlight. Green feigns a relaxed pose in a beige cotton armchair, face grey in the glimmering gaslight, while in Rio, the destroyer of foes ranges the mountaintop, wearing creepers. A carbuncle glows with the beam quality associated with transducers in the boom.

In an inscription of the *II ami* period, Grandfather Fire is implored; in making fishing-lines, the Corn Mother; in the first year there appears an animal destitute of reason. In 744 the lay was composed in a battle. In a box of treasures, when a boy, I kept a blue cord, a bean in a high state of excitement: in a well in Orissa the priests throw betel nuts, seeing in harmonious times the seeds of future discords. In a world without electricity huge wisdoms to deploy in sleep.

The exister is not really a driver in that the transducer-arm moves about anchor points in retired hills and mountains: from which circumstance a river is the common boundary in the midst of deadly night assaults. Belief and Believed march in and out of the trenches, feeling the steepness of descent in their knees. Inferences can be made in regard to features in the Babylonian inscriptions are in the forms found on coins from the Warring States period.

In "Paterson", in accordance with the crank sequence, a contact lens is placed in the eye, in which an inclinated mirror is incorporated with a sliding-wheel chock, chock-operating key, and 512 words stored in 45 Williams' tubes. Three laser beams form a measuring volume in the flume 100/mi in the streamwise direction and 1mm in the vertical. Rollers draw the wool in the direction of the teeth. Note the careful distinction softening in the heat-affected zone.

In "The Excursion", the dead who manifest in the poem's metrical structure blend seamlessly in the woods. In descriptive sentences internal negation inverts truth-value; simple vowel-notes denote adjustment. Wading in a turbid pond dressed in chest-high darkness causes gross section-yielding in the pipe. Put on the upper hub and screw in the eye bolts. Things kept sacred in his trunk; a spoon, knife, a pack of cards. Paper spirits represent relatives in the netherworld. Belief in the conjuring of the reflection in a mirror is associated in the detailed-design phase.

The Virgilian sigh sinks in the rude throat. The stone is in time as the world is in thought. Heat maps compare the relative abundance of metabolites in the mutant lines and the wild types. Clicking an error in the list opens a box with additional indices of determinacy. In response to a repeated light flash, the car encloses in its hum worlds of listening, opening in an abrupt braid of shuddering buses. In the evening, in bed, the dull inch in the flower negates infinity.

In Tesco's, Grocery and Impulse categories come in multiple and symbols sectors. Invest in sculptural light fixtures and table lamps: they double as decoration. Add in an unindexed past operator in the form of the colored after-image. Pervasive deformation is observed in the historical layers; this structural information in geophysical climates produces a time-inversion in the opposite direction.

In the land of poor fools I am lost in fog. In sleep paint grows dimmer; rivulets reflect the inclining day. The subjects in the Invisible and Visible groups search the target quadrant. The sea is in search of islands and the sky is in search of mountains. Rainbows materialise in puddle-scum. Fallen instruments lie in boundary-surveying darkness.

The optimized bullet weight-to-barrel twist results in high accuracy, creating a stabilized trajectory in addition to a silenced shot. The front door opens nervously, and Gatsby, in a white flannel suit, in black heels, silver fox scarf and shimmering neon-red lipgloss or in cream and blue quasi-scuba neoprene tailoring—silver hair parted in the centre, knobbed walking stick in his hand, Polo sports shirt teamed with fluid floor-length silk skirts in a Crayola palette—is proclaimed successor in the headship of the Taoist fraternity and invested with the title of *boxer of wind*.

In the Louvre, placement of a fine line of mantel, library,

hall and travel clocks and hourglasses in onyx, ebony, gilt and antique woods produce an incline. Drizzle sets in stone, flame arrives in god's name. In the path of the falling arrow stands a child. Silt in the blood, sift in the rain, fine edge in air, deer graze in shadowy glens registered in annual tree-leaf turnover. Headlights tangle in the trees. The wind stands ducks in the air, resumes the leaf's disbelief in winter.

In *The Lyric Poet in Late Capitalism* photographs develop in the castle of emptiness, eclipses in text, traditional roles in marketing, program management, business operations, and writing are hybrids of previous existence. In this adventure I have to travel further into the future to confront the corporation that is in control. Robin Hood in the green wood stands diagramming his terms in block language. He holds a medicine ball, and spells the letters by moving it in different ways. The lion fits inside its hill in violation of corporate policy.

In Çatal Hüyük an impressive pile of vitrified dung in the western chamber suggests livestock, but in the subjunctive. Ringed butt pieces occur rarely in Holocene assemblages. In terms of loss the pile is growing, there is an executive arm sending records in to us. Chaff in the jaws ends in the eyes. In is in contained. The Internet is in the fist. In is in confined. In is in everything.

In lagoons, in the world of particulars, flashes of alien light. Any change in sludge inventory will result in specific sludge-characteristics changes and in the relationship of the biomass population to influent food. Insert the finger in the mouth to its full depth in an obscure form of the consumer. The event's type is available as an int field in the event object.

Poetry and the reading public travel in different directions. You appear in 4 searches this week, encased in sandalwood, tink tinkling, in the guise of a bomb-disposal expert in a suit of salamander-cloth. In the *Choose Results* dialog box, expand the *Global Statistics* and *Node Statistics*. At once the poem breaks in two. Visible in the dim light of a digital clock, operating in a manner which I do not quite grasp—an odd number of single quotation marks are inserted in the query, resulting in invalid syntax.

A heart beats in the hand of a surgeon, in time, in the dust of clocks. Her room is painted canary yellow with square floor tiles in shades of buttercream and wheat. Let her fingers linger in a fold of warm skin. In the game world, furniture and artifacts are crafted in mild steel and quilted leather, hooks are used in lifting by hand, executed in timestamp order. In the moment in which a sentence is said it lives.

**On an initial examination** I'm playing with the metal sheep on my farm, drawing up the drawbridge on my flagged fort.

The remains of a sheep remain on the beach; seabirds roost on breakwaters, the heron on the revolving bridge and the watcher on the shoulder of an intrusive ditch watch.

Heron Neck Lighthouse on the west, Petit Manan Light on the starboard. Flecks of light flicker on the beam, a recumbent god sleeps on a lotus petal.

Snow melts on the surface of the young brown river, a black butterfly dances on the blond light of hot cement. People draw together on the stairs, clasping red-leaved books.

On the banks of a sluggish stream, with the delicate odour of violets grown on a flint crag, I arrange on his head the braided hair-tress of Indangunay.

Place the tube on the socket and the cap on the tube. Good catches of crappie come on green or bubblegum grubs.

On the news they had items about fires burning on the moors, a child putting a dead bird on a sleeping woman's hair. I watch my son on his games on his phone.

Dew condenses on the Sphinx in the early morning. The team move on to marking the incision site.

On bearing A, on which turns the external drum B, the sun, moon, and planets roll; and their stable ontology depends on self-integrity.

On seeing persons defiling themselves; on touching the leavings of food; on being touched by cats: will's incapacity imposes on the soul.

On the surface of the umwelt a coating of metazoon is an obstacle environment. The spirit dwelling on the earth is single: and the sitter on the cloud casts his sickle on it.

On the night of the nuptials, the half-drum, flute and violin play. Sphinxes, seated heraldically on pairs of volutes, pulse on time.

Click on the quarter note to begin the slur. Double-click on the eighth note to draw the slur. I ask her opinion, it turns out she is on the phone.

On Kylesku, with its dark waters and ferry house, the gaze of the traveller falls. On June 21, on the banks of Blood River, a bullet from a .26 elephant rifle traverses the brain of the observer.

Place the stand on the ground and insert modular uprights and click on the Merge button. It offers three illuminations: momentary on, constant on and rapid strobe.

On the metal-mesh conveyor the dotting-wheel revolves. Mount the fibre spool on a pillow block. Guinness stains bloom on *The Sinking of The Girona.*

Barbarians on the northern border. Flowers and a glass of water on the bedside table. A large print of a wide beach and diamond-glistening water on the wall.

A Christ of old boxwood on an ebony cross. Translucent visuals on glass partitions create images of authors drawing on their experiences.

Turbulent surf loosens the block lava stream on a tongue of land. Blast experiments on a mock head structure derive similar data.

The etched reticule focuses the shooter's eye. Ride on the road of rupture, the ripped-jeans look on a corpse.

Consciousness froths on the surface. Perform a search and replace on a given string. The reader consists of a series of small metal fingers rubbing on the tape.

Novel on sandpaper, on work time, on yellow paper, on sand. On the 3rd day, a nodule the size of a pea forms. Reflect on your progress so far.

UPON ENTERING THE FOREST, you experience fear. Upon scratching, a watery blood oozes out. You begin to wonder if you have been operated upon. You come upon him from an unexpected angle: upon the gallows, in his dirty felt hat, soiled cloth coat and stockings, he seems unworthy of his manacles. He is an iridescent scarab, and upon his back is a printed circuit. The chair is withdrawn, and he stands upon the air. Boards make up the assault upon the sense-world. Upon the pallet Earth they set us like sticks in mud. Fungoid masses implant upon our bony walls. Flesh is gloves with white upon them. In error we bestow titles upon the dead. Spirit hands with phosphorus upon them pass around the room, opening and shutting, playing upon the violin, triangle, and harmonica. You sit in the rain and think upon the actions of those souls. The tree is consumed, and the fire leaps upon the houses and pours down through roofs upon the people. A spark falls upon your hand, and looking up, your head dances upon a stick. Then I draw my coat off and rub it upon you, and you come upon a paper recording the 1955 wedding. Upon it is a circle depicting geese upon a sheet of water. All the varieties of goose upon its surface are distinctly perceived. Sadness and smuts settle upon your eyes, which you close: the dust, upon scrutiny, is found to consist of insects. An entity of thought works upon the world independently of us. Labels grow upon things, not visible to the naked. The eye of Horus is set upon the wing of Seth. He lands upon the shifting waterway, sings of losses upon the markets. Ruin lies upon ruin which lies upon ruin. Upon thought, the bedrock also is ruin. Meditating upon the second card in the suit of fire will take you through the second gate. The trail eventually comes upon the south banks of a small sag-pond which lies on the San Andreas Fault, encroached upon by the rhubarb leaves of bronze fennel. I look with scorn upon actually existing poetry. I call upon the birds, but not the crow or the magpie, they laugh upon my roof. Responsive days have come upon us, interactions are stored upon the message boards. The future turns its frown upon my words, to the extent that reason acts upon nature. Whatever you write intrudes upon language, that lake. Thrown into enmity with those who stand upon money as upon islands, the poem destroys itself upon being read.

## Eighteen. Of Increase and Decrease

Going at great speed for another while, he came to the mountain of fire seven miles in width. After another gesture with his wand, he reached into bag #1 and drew the rope. His world-view was just another map-control that showed a scaled-down everything. The remote desktop appeared as a hell of cold ice: in another the punishment was pulling out the tongue of those who lie; one consisted of hills stuck full of knives; another of an iron boiler filled with anechoic water; another was a hell of mother-tree serpents; in another the victim is drawn to pieces; another is a hell of accreditation audits; he stood there as from another age or from a film, an eagle, joining another object not cited in the first sequence, but just then another local walking her dog came up and tossed about from one side to another. One cat scratches another's back.

Rooks hopped from one headstone to another, and the passing hours came to another age, and cycle of empty seats; and another man, lecturing to those empty seats. Intimacy with another man's wife, youth and opulence, were the transitory things, not signs of brighter order; and having passed these he unfolded in another book the creation of the world. It appropriated to itself another peculiar quality in the opinion of some old writers, who delivered the war-song that they were not due to encounter on an advanced search page for perhaps another century. It appeared to be one skeleton devouring another or pressing closely on another or they shouted and made gestures, as men ejecting another from a hall. Observing another person behaving dishonestly will decrease one's propensity to begin another cycle, one containing ashes, another gold. Another version said, with eyes fixed, death came.

Another messenger came, and another part of the tongue

was cut off causing loss of capacity to pronounce the rest of the alphabet, and this one as he spoke drew himself back for another lunge, his breath scratching. In another case, a raspberry polyp which entirely filled the external meatus was the passage from one logic to another. In another country a video-arcade-game machine enabled participants in the game interact with one another in brief strategizing sessions, get rough in their playing and begin to ride one another.

Another reason for the analytical inaccuracy here lay in symmetries. I assumed a double part, and heard another's voice cry: our civilization was a box of dust, labelled correctly, in another world. There was another door half grown-over, and a rusty key. The user returned the Boxing Clock from the home directory or from another program in accordance with another aspect of an exemplary embodiment. With another door at the other end, I pressed on, one floor under where I wanted to be.

The designers showed an all-white trouser suit with an oversized jacket draped in fine chains and another with sequinned shoulders. I lay with Z holding hands, not sleeping, her fingers twitching, stirring, turning into another being. Another aspect of second skin would be what Bion called a beta screen. Another staircase led to a finished attic. Another child is not coming home.

Another language-mixture; a coherent sentence expressing an ethical maxim: "Show charity", involving the discovery of puppets that mocks the illusion of free will. This is another application of string, recalling another mask collected. The dream ends by discovering a portal to another day.

**More things break down** than are fixed

spirit exerts more on matter than matter on spirit

science fiction is more important than poetry
it is tall in the woods, the trees seem more
granular and for more than an instant time is the
more aggressive sound typified by Flux Pavilion
more frequently my hands follow the train in my head
begin feebly, become more violent, and diminish
they enter more into the quality of the reactions
nothing is more sensitive to change in revenue
time wants more of us, language forbids us to
explore the foam-memory in more detail.
Sidewinder fits more appropriately into playback
if not, then one or more of the following may be true
weight is the distinction between one and more than one
deer jerk off terminals, leaving stubs 1 or more inches
several small stems support one or more flowers
development of the eye initial in one or more of these soon
exhibits a more prominent underline and
the more pronounced set is known as face cleat
vegetable form is insphered more manifestly than mineral
the more purposive an entity becomes
the more potent the upheavals, since when we are on
a more intimate level with dream
is there more person than world? Eat cake, feel bad, eat
more, the spasm rages in the abdomen
glance duration is more sensitive to information update
in a broader range of more diverse knowledge flows
to create a more filmlike tactile atmosphere
make the view more friendly by adding a Search box
more lead is required at the crank end than at the head end
a more refined diagnostics hypothesis is generated

centuries pass, one hugs a tree, lavishes love on it, more
centuries pass. 120Hz technology becomes more common
a number of close-ups render the hexagram more legible
tone volume depends more on the construction of arches
livestock more commonly roam onto unfenced ways
the more references an article receives the higher its standing
if I insist on making everybody doubt me more I will
become more real, made from more than three dimensions
or more accurately days will be exceptional soon in which
Command Search mode is the more powerful of the modes
the stimulus is cold after touching it with more deliberation
it draws you in at the waist and gives a more defined shape
nothing is more fundamental than anything else
whose height is more than human, clothed in shine
the glow of the moon is not the same any more
when the air is thinner, its sound pierces more
semantic rules make reference to more than one syntactic level.

**Enough is enough.** A Web browser is smart enough to figure out what a relative URL means. If it expresses your idea closely enough, the platform at your disposal knows enough to confute you at each step. Information itself is not enough. I feel dead enough to walk upon the latterly dead, or living enough to make death irritable. I am still enough to pick up the waves behind the trees, the fleeting wave-cloud. I walk into the tiny room, hardly room enough for my bed, and just to have been conscious seems enough. I hold the room in its entirety for nearly long enough to know what I am doing, but cannot turn myself into a powerful enough god to work the switches. There is something to be said for not saying enough because words do not reach in far enough, that which exists enough resists the senses, but a torch with no batteries casts enough light to see the unconscious. You look away enough until you look at the thing you never saw. Tired of the name we have for what is name enough. The effects are strong enough to be detected by the *Ouija*. It is said that there is not enough time to plead but the small talk of morning is enough to those unlucky enough to be cased in this paper we call flesh. Time clings to us as we dive. No clock is fast enough.

**At this period** most things happen in moonlight. History is only the most shadowy shorthand for multiplayer death-match games. The most important attribute of events is an object reference. The eye socket is situated in one of the most blood-enriched Matterhorns. The third movement produces the most consistent pattern, but most logistics systems are not designed for return flows. Falling asleep is the most significant activity. At any time I agree with most of what I am. Most of the attributes of events are simple scalar values, such as the x and y coordinates in a *MouseEvent*. Mesmeric phenomena associate the Else with the most recent If. Single rapier machines are too slow for most applications. A target will most often be detected by peripheral vision. Bulking and foaming are the most frequent problems in sludge plants. Most out-of-the-box entities support editable grids. The tail is considered the most delicious portion to place before guests. Kiosk mode disables most navigational devices. Lonoikamakahiki desires to know what would be of most use to him. Most of the wood floors are adorned with bright wool rugs. What is broad and dense suffers most from air falling against it. Eagleton focuses more single-mindedly than most on the faults of Larkin's poetry: his most quoted lines speak most out of turn. Which gender most often found these jokes funny.

The mew display is most frequently followed by the choking display. Women in two-job households get stuck with most of the work. Communication with the dead is the most important problem the scientists will solve.

**It is a poem,** don't come too close
it is almost too weak to bear
the pattern drives too many silences
if you cut too fast the blade bites the tool
when the air is too dry or warm it makes me ill
in this world of too many lights
is there too much shape or stuff in the world
walk quickly, but not too quickly
moon you shout too loud in the night, it is you
out there too bright, razored by clouds, there is
too much love, the system seizes up
one cannot read too literally: my sheets are
too heavy to lift, the raging sea and toothed
sword are too great for the mind:
it is too late, I cannot find my room, there are
too many doors. Do we not all wake
too late to apply the brakes or change into
a man's pants several sizes too big.
The summer corn has come too late,
speak clearly but not too slowly.
Treacherous too are tulips for a hospital patient
the caretakers have taken too many cares away.
The house moves. The earth, too, shakes.
God lands his spaceship too late

the animals seem too human, they know
language too well, how it is
an eye held too long at the moon.

Language exists so we do not have to think so much
how much are we prisoners of the decisions it makes
as much as is spanned by thumb and index finger
much takes place in the flux and reflux of syntax
much later in the text, the hallucination of a foxhunt
sleep retreats as the light comes on, much like darkness
much as a dog's legs twitch in its dreams
the earth is much torn up by our shells
pulse much increased in force and frequency
we need to forget so much to make progress through leaves
I hear in the distance someone much like Janis
thinking much about it? Not very much; well some
you get as much money as you touch hairs
the eagle never lost so much as when he learnt of Monsanto
the target poem represents as much as possible
a corridor which is not much more than a utility pipe
the pleural sounds disappear, the heart is much displaced
much as a snake sheds its skin, a serpent gulps a wind
as much air as to inflate investor demand
because your hands have shed much blood
there is so much that remains not to be told.

**Spirit is a substance,** no less than matter. Tautologies, to which any more or less indifferent predicate is added, belong here: the high mountain; the less deceived. We could not have felt less strange. Less is more, but law enforcement applications are determined by less random factors than bank holidays, or sleeveless high-necked tunics. Slowly the world becomes less than what it was made of: I am less sure of who I am than when I was carried in on floods of naming. A childhood truth is less than what the moth finds. Paper dropped within 18 in. or less of some formless worry flutters slowly outward. The ceiling has minimum light fixtures to make it less prone to concentrated front formations in the perceptions of the less advanced. Lamp circuits show a mortality less than one-half following simple intestinal suture; insects in their less active larval state are busy in feeding grounds, searching target icons with flicker less than in the latent period. Appealing to duration seems less necessary when geometries expressed in manifold ecologies collide time with place; and focused search heads generally have less penetrating ability. If you have marginal hands, such as a flush draw, or a pair of 9s or less: the upper end is elongated, more or less attenuated, and open. Complimenting, compared to requesting, generally imposes less burden on the addressee, and other issues make questions of clothes seem less than pressing. The linguistic forms of these utterances are less conventionalized so as to allow the addressee to make other possible interpretations. A rotation of the torso has less influence on positional distortion than at the elbow or shoulder. The risk/reward profile of a put buyer is slightly less favorable than that of a call buyer.

**It moves without legs** and rests belly-down under the ripples
journeys without issue but with the sense that it does not matter
hardly a minute goes by without some near-death audit

if you go home you'll be greeted without surprise
tighten the thread after you insert the stitch from without
keep the knees stiff, and bend down without any breathing
set fire to the charge without allowing escape of the gas
Kung says without character you will not make fit music
without labour how can my mind have thought this
dryness in the mouth without thirst, drawing in limbs longing
to lie down without finding sleep. These are thoughts
that can't be safely shared without fear of offence
left-gaze without changing head-orientation to gravity
play the halfdrum without small bells climb a hill
without yelling *uwi uwi* on reaching the top. The river
passes without sound. Strong unclosing winds come
without sleep over the sea and traverse the air
without malice or intent to wound
I'm without cash or card in a checkout line
background programming slices space without
dividing it, without telling me.
Deliver flat-shooting without enlarging the pistol
and allow the shooter to grip without
impeding magazine changes. The horse without rider
stands on the brink of that chasm, its sleep is without
history. A person could exist without a name, a definition
without a word, nomination, toadstool in a meadow
perform an action without terrestrial influence
speak flatly and without gestures sit there
without a muscle of parchment moving.
The entry of mist and cloud suggests a ruined structure without
roof. Turn off the heat and let stand without
opening for 15 minutes. The signals terminate without

protocol conversion on a desktop without widths:
the visual system hardly works without top-down attention.
Live without food, and rise to angelic state; the sentence
would be complete without the commas.
No one becomes a psychoanalyst without worms
over country impossible to navigate without route requests.
To condense time without jump cuts, you will need roll-outs.
Inside cities animals play without reference to earlier
civilizations without the tumbling of mechanical gyros
where pups get in front of trains without danger.
The weather proceeds without question, articulately
the river Name flows in its own dark, without name.

## Nineteen. Of Nothing

**This reminds me of** how I started *Spy*, not knowing how to proceed. The poem begins nowhere but not out of nothing: not the flute but the flute's notes. All that is not name will escape. I wake after the alarm and do not understand the situation clearly. It is not clear that I actually hallucinate, not heading straight from bed to computer. The addition of a "yesterday" operator is tantamount to not thinking at all. I see black and smell drool and do not extend my eyes. Am I not to be considered as one sent to publish to men the way of not living in the present. The best-designed groin system will not prevent loss. It is not easy to mimic the complexities of ripple motion. The purpose of tag is to elude the reach of the player who is it when a player is not it and, as it, to tag a not it. It is not to care. Care must be taken not to step on a line containing one's or an opponent's marker. We do not know how long we have been dead in an airport waiting room, as if sweat would break out, which is not the case. The pattern of fate, drawn by amoral forces, is not perfect, and the just man has a shackled freedom. History is not so much in the event, as in the status updates. Grass-covered airfields provoke a sense of loss not dissimilar to this. This investment affects not only the risk-adjusted value but Microsoft does not consider the reading-pane a vulnerability, and Outlook does not offer a way to turn it off. A subcomponent of an object is not a standalone object that tells the slave server not to start the slave. It is not easy to control transborder data flows, especially those not subject to a high degree or dimensions. That road will not contain us. Erratic itching of single small places of the body, not going off by scratching and not a tremor nor a shock stirs my stately limbs; my hair is tufted, and will not lie smoothly, and I need not understand sleep's meaning. Muscles lax.

Not refreshed from sleep and unwilling to rise. Not a sign of general sensation appears. Does this add to the poem or not? This poem is not sensitive to words but to wounds. The student does not recognize the syntactic cues. For example, in the passage The horse was not afraid, words creep down the stairs saying half remembered hill, you were not blue at all. This work does not demand concentration. Patient can not introspect, ceremonial arrows and votive bowls are not sacrificed to her. Are you not active in the spirit world? We that strobe in thin beams do not know. Not teeth of lions are scattered on mobile technology, but geodesic ghosts. The rinsing of the teeth is to be performed, and not performed, for I am Mother-Earth, and must not get wet. If the monkey does not respond, press the nothing-stone. The old spirit lingers and wonders wearily if he has not lived too long, teaching that lesson, think but do not see. Sir, do not take the Blood River that crosses the road to the underworld, do not recover the arrear for which the attachment issued, do not spell old enchantments, your dream is not favourable, it may not be removed, for not to mortals is it permitted to describe the mighty deeds of gods. Look not at nothingness, since non-existence is not self-non-existent. The full tank of energy is not achieved, nor how to control the dragon, even if he was not an immortal; for the thunder spreads too widely and has not enough variety. It is not clear to the audience that he would not be unseen. The sounds of language are not more full of the thoughts which they symbolise than these qualities are of form, for attention is not an acceptance of the unseen; nature has not so arranged things that men do not enter into the dungeon of gems. The ways to interpret silence include not interpreting it. *The Sun* misses both stories and chooses not to cover the deaths. But how often I dream about that building and not in my waking hours realise this is a recurrent dream, not knowing but feeling my way there, where are chambers in which figures not unlike the word for sun designate states that have not become, have not been caused to arise, have not arisen nor come to pass; the highest spiritual of the plant is not mere motion in the general sense; but the philosopher should not be intolerant when the place fluctuates. The physical struggles above recorded are not, in the subject's mind, connected. I do not choose to spend sufficient time nurturing the children. I hold the playing of this instrument not to be forbidden by the law. Not one unkind word, look, or gesture, has been given, were it not for the dust that disfigures every leaf. The fly does not enter the ripe fruit, is not discernible by the eye. Sense is lost, the announcements continue, we have not dreamed this, or that is not what is on our minds. The curtains draw the eye not only towards the nether limbs but will not freeze, burn or carbonize in extreme temperatures. These spiders are not provisioned with water tubes and those stars will not fit in the head. The bell will not toll. What the product recall notice recalls it does not know, the narrator is not named. You are late. You are not obviously pregnant. The traverse flute is not a study to take lightly. The air con is not on and air flow from the window is not seldom insufficient. The drivers are not seen. The man who does not raise a dust raises a child. This is the only duck of the group that has not been hand-reared. It is not supported on Kodi. What the great poets have that I did not is ambition. The total poem makes a statement which is not a summation of the component statements. The river is not the summer of its parts, churns briefly, is not really sad, shouts a bit and moves on. He says it's not true that I'm free to change, because I have a life-work to do, declares he is not asleep, and mistakes rain for terrain. He keeps on texting to say he is coming home, but he does not come home. Lead a suit that has not been led before. Do not have kids, or if you do have them slowly, or highly, or not in this language. Do not stand in the hatched area, the line we do not cross, this is the other side, the stone that sinks home is not strange, the snow the forecasters spoke of does not arrive, this muted quality is not only of the surrounding material. Our guts modify this to nothing that will not be shit. I tire on the train but do not sleep, the faces of the people are not like petals, their hides will not cease to hum, they could not be rescued from unwearability by slouchy boyfriend sweaters. We have words so as not to have to think, to find, all that is not dust is rust. It's not the suffering, but the inability to understand why. If a boy dies, the mother is not informed. I go out in the garden to find it ringing with birdsong, think about sitting down to enjoy the moment but do not. Structure in dream is not inherent but not incoherent. Lyric is lament that we are not inert, we are not real in the end in the way we think we are. Dislike the instability of tenses, they are not good lenses. I am keyless, in a world of keys, can not open a bottle of beer. At least I am writing a poem I think but I am not, I am asleep on a train. I did not read the compliance policies and procedures. Clues to what is and is not important are available. A correct protocol does not state she has come early, for the dew has not merely whitened the stairs, but has soaked her stockings. Formatting marks are special characters that appear on your screen and do not print. She/he can lock in to the price by paying a small premium and need not exercise the contract if the price movements are not favourable. Not the flute's notes but the ceilings and floors of the flute's palace.

### Existence cannot be deduced

the government cannot address the dead
you cannot create a Pegasus, it cannot be responded to
you cannot fall asleep before midnight, face
cannot occupy the final instance in a domain
an external argument cannot delimit the event the verb
describes, bags or glasses cannot be said to contain

themselves a network protocol violation cannot
be repaired you cannot live and leave world-time behind
you the bay grows dark with fish, or wind, I cannot
tell the silent driver takes you places you cannot remember
the I cannot be analyzed by logic or communicated
each word has a handle you cannot grasp
you cannot arrive at the term in us
a safe-off feature cannot be turned on accidentally
the patient cannot be made to believe the truth the discourse
cannot become the great world of thought
a feather drifts down, an animal comes to see or not, you cannot
know its sense, even idle thoughts cannot be recollected
rock cannot shrink by subdivision into nothing
this does not entail that the entity cannot be a machine
the past cannot leave an enactment behind
substance cannot come into contact with substance
the bus jolts and you cannot remember a line even a title
you cannot state how this can hurt, understanding
consists in abstract distinctions but cannot concretize
we cannot throw language into the world
air cannot weep hard enough time is the matter
you cannot not hold his hand, can you.

**Nor be babbler** nor insolent, nor sloppy in habits
neither buy nor sell from this door
nor ruled, nor pale, nor leaving mine
nor alarmed by the thick woods of briars and bushes
nor do the fields feel anything but dark sea
nor his sly, insubordinate, secret donor.

Neither a dress confine my body nor a tiara seal my mind
death leaves neither a ripple nor an echo
nor answers his questions about the afterlife.
Nor betray any regret about his calling:
this world is neither normal nor not normal.

The Eldrazi decks were faster than anything else in the field. I could conceive of it as nothing else than riding some kind of a live animal. A child learning language is unlearning something else. The syntax for a nested if-else statement is as follows: The else block minimizes the amount of code in try blocks, you can block multiple statements after an else so that the last condition is else and all other conditions fail; none of the remaining else-if statements or else statements will be tested. If no when clauses match, case executes the code of the else clause. This member being nothing else but a hollow pipe, fleshy and spongy, else might easily involve the same psychopathology as a genuine person, cool, nervous, calling out. Whatever else you go to Larkin for, it isn't for a good addresser-addressee relationship, who stands on everyone else's shoulders, or else risk enormous impact, or else resign. What else would you do with a Monday night. The choice is yours to run your life or let someone else ruin it. There's nothing else to do! who else is watching if they're not speaking? It all evens out hello if one more person says somebody else is better than Drake I'm going. You can see the hurt in my eyes when everyone else is fooled by my smile. If I was in love with someone else, would you wait for me? Random shit, cause I've nothing else better to do for 15 mins. Anybody else have fond memories of our late great impulse response? No one else can be Norma Jean like I can! My wife is really something else let me show you all my bling! he's accusing me of unfollowing them? HALP!! Is this happening to anyone else? Anyone else having problems? i just got writer spam tweets? But sometimes, it leaves a heartache that no one else can heal. I'm joking I don't have much else to do but wow she's going to think I'm bitching out at her. Well I kinda am but what else am I supposed to say to that? #imoldenough to make my own mistakes. Anyone else watching Basic Girl Club Love. I'm not trying to "pose" as anyone else, fuck off people, the worst thing to break is someone's else heart. Expecting? congratulations, #itsaboy, I left Luke alone b/c someone else was dissecting. Respect a message to a person you were talking about that was meant for someone else? Lmao good idea lol RT will walk in your life and make you realize why it never worked w/ anyone else about me, I wish I had something else to cuddle with I want to cry. My next GF is getting my all, show her you care, now, did anybody else just see the random rat on family guy? LOL U messy, I'm not clickin on nothing else u post has anybody else on hear also worked at century oaks the worst place to work ever. Water helps!! anyone else going to this? Watching 90210, is it spring break yet? If I had a nickel for everytime I or someone else has said this. Anyone else bite tongue when they chew gum. So bring your kids, bring someone else's kids, but head to Broadway Grill! Leadership is number one, everything else is number two. Chilln but still need somethn else to do, RT @Lord_Voldemort: Life become hard not because somebody else, but cause yourself make it! Wonder who else is gonna get traded b4 the trade deadline. Someone else dresses up as a turtle, takes a toy gun and shouts imitating the sounds of shooting. If all else fails, get them drunk and people start taking stuff out. Does anyone else find cambio one of the most confusing websites ever? Be yourself, everyone else is taken. I tagged one wrong earlier re tagging, else wondering when if ever Lu is going to have a non-boring mask? looks too down with sunroof, & Lambo doors ahhha everything else lol but I never gain no weight #neverwilli ever change who I am for someone else I have to be fully and completely over someone to get into something else, everything else pretty much sucks, good night. Who else do you see? robots talk about religion and criticize everything else? You're unique, just like everyone else. Tidy up after everyone else or iron everyone else's clothes. I want to be the girl you fall for when everyone else is falling for you, to avoid jamming the networks. Does anybody else watch sabrina? I was not impressed. Anyone else goin out on the town today, sounds like a good shopping day. Who else is going to see #TheStreets tonight? If I just do everything that's been done to me, to everyone else, how would everyone feel, its not that I'm lazy its just everyone else is more interesting, who the fuck else am I suppose to do? Blow up a pineapple, my Gmail account just got locked! Anyone else had this happen? there for me when times get awkward, Sincerely, I have nothing else to say, i love it when she wants wht she wants and nothin else ok why did I just use LOL just now? I hate it when I lose my phone and then I call it from somebody else's phone then when I find it I return the missed calls, I don't wanna hear Eleanor Rigby or Let it Be from anyone else you can't tweet the letter "d" stream in maori? I'd rather argue with you, than to be with someone else. I wonder who else on my TL was given a special name for their #PrivateArea o_o but yaaa if you want to be with me then act like it. Jesus loves you, but everyone else thinks you're an asshole, havin the worst headache since nine! Is it just me or does anyone else find pressing F5 refreshing ? The moment when you say the right answer multiple times, then someone else says your answer and they get credit & then the world doesn't exist anymore or else we're mistaken & it merely makes a different sound which is somewhere else and from here everything else flows.

**We could neither revive** what we had killed nor move the eyes, for when we were children neither were we then those children.

But that's neither here nor there, where the sun neither set nor rose. We neither woke nor slept, and passed our nights in sorrow.

We neither breathed nor indicated; heard neither sighs nor spoke; we lay on the top of an argument we were too tired to quite have: but neither of us could sleep.

News was neither what happened nor what was important: it was sequential abuse, attrition, Hell's laughter.

The insects were not joyous but neither as alien as we supposed. At the bar I asked them if they said her eyes were breeding or bleeding: "I said neither. I said that her eyes were reading."

Monopoly was not really going anywhere, but neither was the conversation. Wheat thins and cheese cubes sounded good. Too bad we had neither.

We neither presumed to ask, nor condescended to receive a kiss at the door. Respect could neither be given nor withheld.

I waved to them but neither of them saw me and that was fine, because neither did anyone else: I had a take-home test and a headache, neither of which went away.

If the sun never moved neither would I. My opinion was neither desired nor required.

**It is absolutely** as I had never dreamed
the words never ever mean what we meant
all is never lost, it finds its way to be recorded
she says the fields of understanding will never
be extended, sleep is the shadow we never see
until asleep and even then we never remember

we never seem to leave the hotel
spirit of the stairs that never were or where
a rained-on cinder's never going to glow again
where people mingle who would never in reality
one's mental map of a city one has never visited the gold
and silver kitchens are never open on the same day
cables are never causes. Noises are never values
words never hurt unless you throw a dictionary
dragonfly, never solid enough to take form.
The illusory snake never was, nor will clutch that darkness.
Never blame the man: his hard-pressed ancestors formed him
a complete inventory of facts can never be made
of footfalls that never return from the checkpoint
voices belong that never had contact with the experimenter.
Money never sleeps, bullshit never ends.

**Porter declared** English poetry has found a new nobody
to look back harder, to find something nobody counted:
nobody, the proxy ego who falls in love with Odysseus
a place in language-time nobody foresees lets this word
coincide with wounds I walk across and nobody recognizes
me—Nobody who publishes it is indifferent to its reception
the poet inserts it thinking nobody would recognize it
as not his. If nobody can agree on a simple description of reality
or at least wallpaper. Nobody likes a bare wall or splatter of
supposition nobody asks any questions and
nobody asks how this unconscious
is sustained nobody knows what happened to him,
the real reason for his death, nobody hears

his voice. Nobody at the radio stations knows of his existence.
The sentence "Nobody thinks of us" is of a general,
the sentence "Nobody is disembodied" of a personal character.

I TURN OFF IN HEAVY RAIN, drive past the station, nowhere
to park, shell-thin men hasting nowhere above
the gutter, then out of nowhere catch fire
death is the burn of shelves of books that will nowhere be
found, nowhere do we locate snow's coherence
and this is grief: That you are nowhere;
nowhere on the round earth, as calendars die
on a dead man's wrist. You are nowhere
in time. Truth gets you nowhere, it goes on, that's all—
meanders, comes from and goes nowhere,
nowhere answered the ring the rung.
There is no path to the Brahman, his sky is nowhere
his gentle abyss, his eyes' kindness, nowhere
for a man in the weary cosmos to rest his head
flying from a nowhere into a nothing. You are
shouting, but nowhere as loud as you think you are.

NONE OF THE TOMATOES EQUAL the excellent flavour expected
none of the participants consistently follow shock
termination, and none of those responses turn off shock.
There are birds in which liquid spoke and seconds to none
but none of the available numbers for her mobile work
the magic becomes thinner, one day there is none left
the box background colour is set to None

none of the computers are nonempty
the utterance of whose word none can annul,
compact of word and object, none matches
properly. None of the doctors fathom the cure
which none may drink except in non-engineered landscape.
In none of our cases nor in those cited by the late Dr
none of them can move or call me as you can, I say
none on inviolable peaks nor virgin downs where
none shall pasture sheep; nevertheless
the noncompliant hymns, none of them can move or
call me as you can. None of them produce a tape-
recording as if your thoughts had flown where none
follow. None of the languages are in the correct node.
None of these stations can be traced to networks.
Speak, Konstantin.—Here are none but scoundrels.

THE ARCADE HAD NO AREA CODE and there were no recurring characters. Someone asked if the quiz had started yet. I said no and went to the bar, paying no attention to the wound area. No time was left for the connected study requisite for such elaborate discussions. No flesh-creature here understood the measure of the orbits of heaven. My erections were passive, attended by no desire into a forest where no humans dwelt. No wind stirred the unbreathing bodies. No sound of horse hoof, no electronic voice, auto-erotic or other. No philosophers darkened that country. I offered no obstruction to pine needles falling. My booted feet made no sound on the rich floor. The living had no way to speak to death. I left no sense unturned. I could bear no manner of food, my head was no miles long. There was no such thing as classical spacetime. When I turned on subtitles it said no subtitle service, but I had no issue with the default. There were no windows, and waking up I had no eye for the underworld, but then I thought no, I have cancer, a headache with no nasal dripping, no cold or fever, no taste. No sound sleep, my waking life permitted no opportunity for introspection. The majority of colours were no more than the signs of these colours, constituting no literal translation to the visual system. Mesmerised lead and iron, placed in his hands for some time, had no effect. No country was illusory enough, save death, where the sun made no bones and raised no objections. I had written no ode yet with my ears no longer controlled by unknowns I had no accusation, no despair, only the murmur ah, no more. Yes,—no. Yes, said Coyote, I am pretty hard to non-delimit though no doubt poetry is a means to no way. No: in the fulness of time, at the request of the gods, no tree here spreads its thick foliage. No, forever no; said she to him. I did not know what to offer, I had no food. Food had no taste. No sooner had she said this when a voice proceeded from no world and no man. No, said he. Shall I stand here? No, farther off, said the noise. Giving no sign of the steam tornados leaving their huge steel noses the spiritual engines streamed through me no longer. I received no more than thirty soft-nose bullets and no sensory disturbance. If I clicked No, I got back a 9. No voids or gaps deplenished this field. No, there was no escape clause. No one thought there was a ball in the tube because in the last inversion of the tube no ball ran out. I no longer wished to remember my dreams. Yolk was no longer attached to a creature. No sewage was allowed to enter the chamber, the investigator knew this was no accident. We conducted no further systematic experiments in this direction. The academy had no doors, no insides. The night had no answer. There were no relative clauses, I felt no tendencies to act, and woke a couple of times in the night, once at 2, then 4.30, both times thinking, no, that is too early, but then dreaming that the message specified the hour of my flight or death, no one was sure which. There was no rain or return, no rest for the dead and no rest for the rest. No doubt was possible.

## Also available from grand**IOTA**

Brian Marley: APROPOS JIMMY INKLING
*978-1-874400-73-8 318pp*

Ken Edwards: WILD METRICS
*978-1-874400-74-5 244pp*

Fanny Howe: BRONTE WILDE
*978-1-874400-75-2 158pp*

Ken Edwards: THE GREY AREA
*978-1-874400-76-9 328pp*

Alan Singer: PLAY, A NOVEL
*978-1-874400-77-6 268pp*

Brian Marley: THE SHENANIGANS
*978-1-874400-78-3 220pp*

Barbara Guest: SEEKING AIR
*978-1-874400-79-0 218pp*

Toby Olson: JOURNEYS ON A DIME
*978-1-874400-80-6 300pp*

Philip Terry: BONE
*978-1-874400-81-3 150pp*

James Russell: GREATER LONDON: A NOVEL
*978-1-874400-82-2 276pp*

Askold Melnyczuk: THE MAN WHO WOULD NOT BOW
*978-1-874400-83-7 196pp*

Andrew Key: ROSS HALL
*978-1-874400-84-4 190pp*

Edmond Caldwell: HUMAN WISHES/ENEMY COMBATANT
*978-1-874400-85-1 298pp*

Ken Edwards: SECRET ORBIT
*978-1-874400-86-8 254pp*

Rosa Woolf Ainley: THE ALPHABET TAX
*978-1-874400-88-2 182pp*

*Production of this book has been made possible with the help of the following individuals and organisations who subscribed in advance:*

Peter Bamfield
Christopher Beckett
Jan Blake-Harbord
Geoffrey Brackett
Paul Bream
Andrew Brewerton
Ian Brinton
Jasper Brinton
Peter Brown
Alison Burns
Emily Candela
Sue Cavanagh
Cris Cheek
Sue Cheetham
Sarah Cooper
Claire Crowther
Allen Fisher/Spanner
Miles Gibson
Daniel Green
Paul Griffiths
Penny Grossi
Charlie Hague
Randolph Healy
Jo Henderson
Jeremy Hilton
Gad Hollander
Peter Hughes
Robert Hughes
Kristoffer Jacobson
Andrew Key
Margaret Kitching
Sharon Kivland
Maria Lloyd
Richard Makin
Michael Mann
Sam May
Peter Middleton
Nicole Mollett
Paul Nightingale
John Olson
Toby Olson
Lucinda Oestreicher
Sean Pemberton
Frances Presley
Christopher Pusateri
David Rose
Lou Rowan
Emily Rubin
Dave Russell
James Russell
Ruth Sandbach
Geoff Sawers
Edward Sayeed
Hanne Scrase
Pablo Seoane
Alan Singer
Cedric Soertsz
Ulrike Steven
Eileen Tabios
Harriet Tarlo
Susan Tilley
visual associations
Sarah Watkinson
John Wilkinson
Eley Williams
Stamatis Zografos

www.grandiota.co.uk

Ingram Content Group UK Ltd.
Milton Keynes UK
UKHW010012200323
418794UK00004B/150

9 781874 400875